THE INTERNATIONAL PSYCHO-ANALYTICAL LIBRARY

No. 37

The International Psycho-Analytical Library
No. 37, edited by Ernest Jones, M.D.

SIGMUND FREUD

COLLECTED PAPERS

VOLUME 5

EDITED BY

JAMES STRACHEY

New York   Basic Books, Inc.   Publishers

FIRST AMERICAN EDITION 1959

Published by Basic Books, Inc.
by arrangement with
The Hogarth Press Ltd and
The Institute of Psycho-Analysis, London

First printing, 1959
Second printing, 1959
Third printing, 1960

LIBRARY OF CONGRESS CATALOG CARD NUMBER 59-8642
MANUFACTURED IN THE UNITED STATES OF AMERICA

COLLECTED PAPERS

VOLUME V

MISCELLANEOUS PAPERS, 1888–1938

EDITORIAL NOTE

THE bulk of the contents of this Fifth Volume of Freud's *Collected Papers* is made up of his shorter writings published since the issue of the Fourth Volume in 1925. The opportunity has, however, been taken of including a number of earlier papers which, for various reasons, were omitted from the first four volumes of this series. Finally, a selection has also been included of his very scanty posthumous works, which were published in German under the title of *Schriften aus dem Nachlass* in 1941.

About a dozen of the papers included in this volume (Nos. II A, B and C, III, IV, V, VIII B, IX, XIV, XXIX and XXXIII) now appear for the first time in English. Of the remainder, the majority were first published in English in the *International Journal of Psycho-Analysis*, while a few have been collected from other sources. All of these have been revised and in a number of instances (Nos. VI, VIII A, C and D, XIX, XXII and XXV) fresh translations have been made for the present volume.

The whole of the material has been arranged, with one or two small exceptions, in chronological order. Details of the origin of each paper will be found in a footnote at its beginning, and a complete list of references appears at the end of the whole book. As in the earlier volumes in the series, the translator's name is appended to each paper. Editorial additions are indicated by square brackets.

The editor's thanks are due to Miss Anna Freud for reading through the greater part of the volume ; and to Dr. Martin James and Mr. Masud Khan for help in preparing the index.

J. S.

CONTENTS OF VOLUME V

I

HYPNOTISM AND SUGGESTION[1]

(1888)

THIS book has already received warm commenda-
tion from Professor Forel of Zurich, and it is to
be hoped that its readers will discover in it all
the qualities which have led the translator to present
it in German. They will find that the work of Dr. Bernheim of Nancy provides an admirable introduction to
the study of hypnotism (a subject which can no longer
be neglected by physicians), that it is in many respects
stimulating and indeed enlightening, and that it is well
calculated to destroy the belief that the problem of
hypnosis is still surrounded. as Meynert asserts, by a
halo of absurdity.

The achievement of Bernheim (and of his colleagues
at Nancy who are working along the same lines) consists
precisely in having stripped the manifestations of hypnotism of their strangeness by linking them up with

---

[1] [This work, to which the title has been added by the present translator, is Freud's preface to his translation of Bernheim's *De la suggestion
et de ses applications à la thérapeutique* (1886; second ed. 1887). The
German original has never been reprinted and was not included in
Freud's *Gesammelte Schriften*. In his *Autobiographical Study* (1925*a*),
Freud relates how he spent some months in Paris in 1885–86 studying
under Charcot and then returned to Vienna to set up as a specialist in
nervous diseases. He goes on to describe his awakening interest in
hypnotism and suggestion and how in the summer of 1889 he visited
Bernheim at Nancy. 'I had many stimulating conversations with him',
he writes, 'and undertook to translate into German his two works upon
suggestion and its therapeutic effects.' There is some mistake here, for
in fact, as will be seen, his preface to his translation of the first of Bernheim's books is dated a year earlier than this, in August, 1888. The book
bore the title *Die Suggestion und ihre Heilwirkung* and was published in
Vienna by Deuticke. The date 1888 also appears on the title-page, but
the work was evidently issued in parts, for a postscript by the translator
apologizing for some delay in the publication of its second half is dated
January, 1889. However this may be, the preface belongs to the period
during which Freud's interest was passing over from physiology to
psychology, and it may perhaps claim to be his earliest published writing
in the field of psychology. Translation, reprinted from *Int. J. Psycho-
Anal.*, **27** (1946), 59, by James Strachey.]

familiar phenomena of normal psychological life and of sleep. The principal value of this book seems to me to lie in the evidence it gives of the relations between hypnotic phenomena and the ordinary processes of waking and sleeping, and in its bringing to light the psychological laws that apply to both classes of events. In this way the problem of hypnosis is carried over completely into the sphere of psychology, and 'suggestion' is established as the nucleus of hypnotism and the key to its understanding. Moreover in the last chapters the importance of suggestion is traced in fields other than that of hypnosis. In the second part of the book evidence is offered that the use of hypnotic suggestion provides the physician with a powerful therapeutic method, which seems indeed to be the most suitable for combating certain nervous disorders and the most appropriate to their mechanism. This lends the volume a quite unusual practical importance. And its insistence upon the fact that both hypnosis and hypnotic suggestion can be applied, not only to hysterical and to seriously neuropathic patients, but also to the majority of healthy persons, is calculated to extend the interest of physicians in this therapeutic method beyond the narrow circle of neuropathologists.

The subject of hypnotism has had a most unfavourable reception among the leaders of the German medical profession (apart from such few exceptions as Krafft-Ebing, Forel, etc.). Yet, in spite of this, one may venture to express a wish that German physicians may turn their attention to this problem and to this therapeutic procedure, since it remains true that in scientific matters it is always experience, and never authority without experience, that gives the final verdict, whether in favour or against. Indeed, the objections which we have hitherto heard in Germany against the study and use of hypnosis deserve attention only on account of the names of their authors, and Professor Forel has had little trouble in refuting a whole crowd of those objections in a short essay.

Some ten years ago the prevalent view in Germany was still one which doubted the reality of hypnotic phenomena and sought to explain the accounts given of them as due to a combination of credulity on the part of the observers and of simulation on the part of the subjects of the experiments. This position is to-day no longer tenable, thanks to the works of Heidenhain and Charcot, to name only the greatest of those who have testified to their belief in the reality of hypnotism. Even the most violent opponents of hypnotism have become aware of this, and consequently their writings, though they still betray a clear inclination to deny the reality of hypnosis, also include attempts at explaining it and thus in fact recognize the existence of these phenomena.

Another line of argument hostile to hypnosis rejects it as being dangerous to the mental health of the subject and labels it as 'an experimentally produced psychosis'. Evidence that hypnosis leads to injurious results in a few cases would be no more decisive against its general usefulness than, for instance, the occurrence of isolated instances of death under chloroform narcosis forbids the use of chloroform for the purposes of surgical anaes-thesia. It is a very remarkable fact, however, that this analogy cannot be carried any further. The largest number of accidents in chloroform narcosis are experi-enced by the surgeons who carry out the largest number of operations. But the majority of reports of the injurious effects of hypnosis are derived from observers who have worked very little with hypnosis or not at all, whereas all those research workers who have had a large amount of hypnotic experience are united in their belief in the harmlessness of the procedure. In order, there-fore, to avoid any injurious effects in hypnosis, all that is probably necessary is to carry out the procedure with care, with a sufficiently sure touch and upon correctly selected cases. It must be added that there is little to be gained by calling suggestions 'compulsive ideas' and hypnosis 'an experimental psychosis'. It seems likely, indeed, that more light will be thrown on compulsive ideas by comparing them with suggestions than the other way round. And anyone who is scared by the abusive term 'psychosis' may well ask himself whether our natural sleep has any less claim to that description —if, indeed, there is anything at all to be gained from transporting technical names out of their proper spheres. No, hypnotism is in no danger from this quarter. And as soon as a large enough number of doctors are in a position to report observations of the kind that are to be found in the second part of Bernheim's book, it will become an established fact that hypnosis is a harmless condition and that to induce it is a procedure 'worthy' of a physician.

This book also discusses another question, which at the present time divides the supporters of hypnotism into two opposing camps. One party, whose opinions are voiced by Dr. Bernheim in these pages, maintains that all the phenomena of hypnotism have the same origin: they arise, that is, from a suggestion, a conscious idea, which has been introduced into the brain of the hypnotized person by an external influence and has been accepted by him as though it had arisen spontaneously. On this view all hypnotic manifestations would be mental phenomena, effects of suggestions. The other party, on the contrary, insist that some at least of the manifestations of hypnotism are based upon physiological changes, that is, upon displacements of excitability in the nervous system, occurring without those parts of the brain being involved whose activity produces consciousness; they speak, therefore, of the physical or physiological phenomena of hypnosis.

The principal subject of this dispute is 'major hypnotism' ['*grande hypnotisme*']—the phenomena described by Charcot in the case of hypnotized hysterics. Unlike normal hypnotized persons, hysterics are said to exhibit three stages of hypnosis, each of which is distinguished by special physical signs of a most remarkable kind (such as enormous neuro-muscular hyper-excitability, somnambulistic contractures, etc.). It will easily be understood that the conflict of opinion that has just been touched upon must have an important bearing in connection with this region of facts. If the supporters of the suggestion theory are right, all the observations made at the Salpêtrière are worthless; indeed, they become errors in observation. The hypnosis of hysterics would have no characteristics of its own; but every physician would be free to produce any symptomatology that he liked in the patients he hypnotized. We should not learn from the study of major hypnotism what alterations in excitability succeed one another in the nervous system of hysterics in response to certain stimuli; we should merely learn what intentions Charcot suggested (in a manner of which he himself was un-conscious) to the subjects of his experiments—a thing entirely irrelevant to our understanding alike of hyp-nosis and of hysteria.

It is easy to see the further implications of this view and what a convenient explanation it promises of the symptomatology of hysteria in general. If suggestion by the physician has falsified the phenomena of hysterical hypnosis, it is quite possible that it may also have interfered with the observation of the rest of hysterical symptomatology: it may have laid down laws governing hysterical attacks, paralyses, contractures, etc., which are only related to the neurosis by suggestion and which consequently lose their validity as soon as another physician in another place makes an examination of hysterical patients. These inferences follow quite logi-cally, and they have in fact already been drawn. Hückel (1888) expresses his conviction that the first 'transfert' (the transfering of sensibility from a part of the body to the corresponding part on the other side) made by a hysteric was suggested to her on some particular historical occasion and that since then physi-cians have continued constantly producing this pro-fessedly physiological symptom afresh by suggestion.

I am convinced that this view will be most welcome to those who feel an inclination—and it is still the predominant one in Germany to-day— to overlook the fact that hysterical phenomena are governed by laws. Here we should have a splendid example of how neglect of the mental factor of suggestion has misled a great observer into the arti-ficial and false creation of a clinical type as a result of the capriciousness and easy malleability of a neurosis.

Nevertheless there is no difficulty in proving piece by piece the objectivity of the symptomatology of hysteria. Bernheim's criticisms may be fully justified in regard to investigations such as those of Binet and Féré; and in any case those criticisms will give evidence of their importance in the fact that in every future investigation of hysteria and hypnotism the need for excluding the element of suggestion will be more consciously kept in view. But the principal points of the symptomatology of hysteria are safe from the suspicion of having origin-ated from suggestion by a physician. Reports coming from past times and from distant lands, which have been collected by Charcot and his pupils, leave no room for doubt that the peculiarities of hysterical attacks, of hysterogenic zones, of anaesthesias, paralyses and con-tractures, have been manifested at every time and place just as they were at the Salpêtrière when Charcot carried out his memorable investigation of that major neurosis. '*Transfert*' in particular, which seems to lend itself especially well to proving the suggestive origin of hysterical symptoms, is indubitably a genuine process. It comes under observation in uninfluenced cases of hysteria: one frequently comes across patients in whom what is in other respects a typical hemi-anaesthesia stops short at one organ or extremity, and in whom this particular part of the body retains its sensibility on the insensible side whereas the corresponding part on the other side has become anaesthetic. Moreover, '*transfert*' is a phenomenon which is physiologically intelligible.

As has been shown by investigations in Germany and France, it is merely an exaggeration of a relation which is normally present between symmetrical parts of the body: thus, it can be produced in a rudimentary form in healthy persons. Many other hysterical symptoms of sensibility also have their root in normal physiological relations, as has been beautifully demonstrated by the investigations of Urbantschitsch. This is not the proper occasion for carrying out a detailed justification of the symptomatology of hysteria; but we may accept the statement that in essentials it is of a real, objective nature and not falsified by suggestion on the part of the observer. This does not imply any denial that the mechanism of hysterical manifestations is a mental one: but it is not the mechanism of suggestion on the part of the physician.

Once the existence of objective, physiological phenomena in hysteria has been demonstrated, there is no longer any need to abandon the possibility that hysterical 'major' hypnotism may present phenomena which are not derived from suggestion on the part of the investigator. Whether these do in fact occur must be left to a further enquiry with this end in view. Thus it lies with the Salpêtrière school to prove that the three stages of hysterical hypnosis can be unmistakably demonstrated upon a newly arrived experimental subject even when the most scrupulous behaviour is maintained by the investigator; and no doubt such proof will not be long in coming. For already the description of major hypnotism offers symptoms which tend most definitely against their being regarded as mental. I refer to the increase in neuro-muscular excitability during the lethargic stage. Anyone who has seen how, during lethargy, light pressure upon a muscle (even if it is a facial muscle or one of the three external muscles of the ear which are never contracted during life) will throw the whole fasciculus concerned into tonic contraction, or how pressure upon a superficial nerve will reveal its terminal distribution—anyone who has seen this will inevitably assume that the effect must be attributed to physiological reasons or to deliberate training and will without hesitation exclude unintentional suggestion as a possible cause. For suggestion cannot produce anything which is not contained in consciousness or introduced into it. But our consciousness knows only of the end-result of a movement; it knows nothing of the operation and arrangement of the individual muscles and nothing of the anatomical distribution of the nerves in relation to them. I shall show in detail in a work which is shortly to appear[1] that the characteristics of hysterical par-alyses are bound up with this fact and that this is why hysteria shows no paralyses of individual muscles, no peripheral paralyses and no facial paralyses of a central nature. Dr. Bernheim should not have neglected to produce the phenomenon of neuro-muscular hyper-excitability by means of suggestion; the omission con-stitutes a serious gap in his argument against the three stages.

Thus physiological phenomena do occur at all events in hysterical major hypnotism. But in normal, minor hypnotism, which, as Bernheim justly insists, is of greater importance for our understanding of the prob-lem, every manifestation—so it is maintained—comes about by means of suggestion, by mental means. Even hypnotic sleep, it seems, is itself a result of suggestion: sleep sets in owing to normal human suggestibility, because Bernheim arouses an expectation of sleep. But there are other occasions, on which the mechanism of hypnotic sleep seems nevertheless to be a different one. Anyone who has hypnotized much will sometimes have come upon subjects who can only be put to sleep with difficulty by talking, while, on the contrary, it can be done quite easily if they are made to stare at something for a little. Indeed, who has not had the experience of a patient falling into a hypnotic sleep whom he has had

---

[1] [In fact not published till five years later, in 1893: 'Some Points in a Comparative Study of Organic and Hysterical Paralyses', *Collected Papers*, **1**, 42.]

no intention of hypnotizing and who certainly had no previous conception of hypnosis? A female patient takes her place for the purpose of having her eyes or throat examined; there is no expectation of sleep either on the part of the physician or of the patient; but no sooner does the beam of light fall on her eyes than she goes to sleep and, perhaps for the first time in her life, she is hypnotized. Here, surely, any conscious mental connecting link could be excluded. Our natural sleep, which Bernheim compares so happily with hypnosis, behaves in a similar fashion. As a rule we bring on sleep by suggestion, by mental preparedness and expectation of it; but occasionally it comes upon us without any effort on our part as a result of the physiological condition of fatigue. So too when children are rocked to sleep or animals hypnotized by being held in a fixed position it can hardly be a question of mental causation. Thus we have reached the position adopted by Preyer and Binswanger in Eulenburg's *Realencyclopädie*: there are both mental and physiological phenomena in hypnotism, and hypnosis itself can be brought about in the one manner or the other. Indeed, in Bernheim's own description of his hypnoses there is unmistakably one objective factor independent of suggestion. If this were not so, then, as Jendrássik (*Archives de Neurologie*, XI, 1886) logically insists, hypnosis would bear a different appearance according to the individuality of each experimenter: it would be impossible to understand why increase of suggestibility should follow a regular sequence, why the musculature should invariably be influenced only in the direction of catalepsy, and so on.

We must agree with Bernheim, however, that the partitioning of hypnotic phenomena under the two headings of physiological and mental leaves us with a most unsatisfied feeling: a connecting link between the two classes is urgently needed. Hypnosis, whether it is produced in the one way or in the other, is always the same and shows the same appearances. The symptomatology of hysteria[1] hints in many respects at a psychological mechanism, though this need not be the mechanism of suggestion. And, finally, suggestion is at an advantage over the physiological conditions, since its mode of operation is incontestable and relatively clear, while we have no further knowledge of the mutual influences of the nervous excitability to which the physiological phenomena must go back. In the remarks which follow, I hope to be able to give some indication of the connecting link between the mental and physiological phenomena of hypnosis of which we are in search.

In my opinion the shifting and ambiguous use of the word 'suggestion' lends to the antithesis a deceptive sharpness which it does not in reality possess. It is worth while considering what it is which we can legitimately call a 'suggestion'. No doubt some kind of mental influence is implied by the term; and I should like to put forward the view that what distinguishes a suggestion from other kinds of mental influence, such as a command or the giving of a piece of information or instruction, is that in the case of a suggestion an idea is aroused in another person's brain which is not examined in regard to its origin but is accepted just as though it had arisen spontaneously in that brain. A classical example of a suggestion of this kind occurs when a physician says to a hypnotized subject: 'Your arm must stay where I put it' and the phenomenon of catalepsy thereupon sets in; or again when the physician raises the subject's arm time after time after it has

[1] The relations between hysteria and hypnotism are no doubt very intimate, but they are not so close as to justify one in representing an ordinary hysterical attack as a hypnotic state with several stages, as Meynert has done before the Vienna Society of Medicine (reported in *Wiener medic. Blätter*, No. 23, 1888). In this paper, indeed, a general confusion seems to have been made of our knowledge about these two conditions. For Charcot is spoken of as distinguishing *four* stages of hypnosis, whereas in fact he only distinguishes *three*, and the fourth stage, the so-called 'somniant' stage, is nowhere mentioned except by Meynert. On the other hand, Charcot does ascribe *four* stages to the hysterical attack.

dropped, until the subject guesses that the physician wants it to be held up. But on other occasions we speak of suggestion where the mechanism of origin is evidently a different one. For instance, in the case of many hypnotized subjects catalepsy sets in without any injunction being given: the arm that has been raised remains raised of its own accord, or the subject maintains the posture in which he went to sleep unaltered unless there is some interference. Bernheim calls this result too a suggestion, saying that the posture itself suggests its maintenance. But in this case the part played by external stimulus is evidently smaller and the part played by the physiological condition of the subject, which disallows any impulse for altering his posture, is greater than in the former cases. The distinction between a directly mental and an indirect (physiological) suggestion may perhaps be seen more clearly in the following example. If I say to a hypnotized subject: 'Your right arm is paralysed; you can't move it', I am making a directly mental suggestion. Instead of this, Charcot gives the subject a light blow on his arm; [the subject finds he is unable to move it]. Or Charcot says to him: 'Look at that hideous face! Hit out at it!'; the subject hits out and his arm drops down paralysed. In these two last cases an external stimulus has to begin with produced a feeling of painful exhaustion in the arm; and this in turn, spontaneously and independently of any intervention on the part of the physician, has suggested paralysis—if such an expression is still applicable here. In other words, it is a question in these cases not so much of suggestions as of stimulation to *autosuggestions*. And these, as anyone can see, contain an objective factor, independent of the physician's will, and they reveal a connection between various conditions of innervation or excitation in the nervous system. It is autosuggestions such as these that lead to the production of spontaneous hysterical paralyses and it is an inclination to such autosuggestions rather than suggestibility which, from the point of view of the physician, characterizes hysteria; nor do the two seem by any means to run parallel.

I need not insist on the fact that Bernheim too works to a very large extent with indirect suggestions of this sort—that is, with stimulations to autosuggestion. His procedure for bringing about sleep, as described in the opening pages of the present volume, is essentially a mixed one: suggestion pushes open the doors which are in fact slowly opening of themselves by auto-suggestion.

Indirect suggestions, in which a series of intermediate links arising from the subject's own activity are inserted between the external stimulus and the result, are none the less mental processes; but they are no longer exposed to the full light of consciousness which falls upon direct suggestions. For we are far more accustomed to bring our attention to bear upon external perceptions than upon internal processes. Indirect suggestions or autosuggestions can accordingly be described equally as physiological or as mental phenomena, and the term 'suggestion' has the same meaning as the reciprocal provocation of mental states according to the laws of association. Shutting the eyes leads to sleep because it is linked to the concept of sleep through being one of its most regular accompaniments: one portion of the manifestations of sleep suggests the other manifestations which go to make up the phenomenon as a whole. This linking-up lies in the nature of the nervous system and not in any arbitrary decision by the physician; it cannot occur unless it is based upon alterations in the excitability of the relevant portions of the brain, in the innervation of the vasomotor centres, etc., and it thus presents alike a psychological and a physiological aspect. As is the case wherever states of the nervous system are linked together, it may run its course in either direction. The idea of sleep may lead to feelings of fatigue in the eyes and muscles and to a corresponding condition of the vasomotor nerve centres; or on the other hand the condition of the musculature or a stim-

ulus acting on the vasomotor nerves may in itself cause
the sleeper to wake, and so on. All that can be said is
that it would be just as one-sided to consider only the
psychological side of the process as to attribute the whole
responsibility for the phenomena of hypnosis to the vas-
cular innervation.

How does this affect the antithesis between the
mental and the physiological phenomena of hypnosis?
There was a meaning in it so long as by suggestion was
understood a directly mental influence exercised by the
physician which forced any symptomatology he liked
upon the hypnotized subject. But this meaning disappears as soon as it is realized that even suggestion
only releases sets of manifestations which are based
upon the functional peculiarities of the subject's nervous system, and that in hypnosis characteristics of the
nervous system other than suggestibility make themselves felt.. The question might still be asked whether all
the phenomena of hypnosis must *at some point* pass
through the mental sphere; in other words—for the
question can have no other sense—whether the changes
in excitability which occur in hypnosis invariably affect
only the region of the cerebral cortex. By thus putting
the question in this other form we seem to have decided
the answer to it. There is no justification for making
such a contrast as is here made between the cerebral
cortex and the rest of the nervous system: it is improbable that so profound a functional modification of
the cerebral cortex could occur unaccompanied by
significant alterations in the excitability of the other
parts of the brain. We possess no criterion which
enables us to distinguish exactly between a mental process and a physiological one, between an act occurring
in the cerebral cortex and one occurring in the sub-
cortical substance; for 'consciousness', whatever that
may be, is not attached to every activity of the cerebral
cortex, nor is it always attached in an equal degree to
any particular one of its activities; it is not a thing
which is bound up with any locality in the nervous

system.[1] It therefore seems to me that the question whether hypnosis exhibits mental or physiological phenomena cannot be accepted in this general form and that the decision in the case of each individual phenomenon must be made dependent upon a special investigation.

To this extent I feel justified in saying that, whereas on the one hand Bernheim's work goes outside the field of hypnosis, on the other hand it leaves a portion of its subject-matter out of account. But it is to be hoped that German readers of Bernheim will now have the opportunity of recognizing what an instructive and valuable contribution he has made in thus describing hypnotism from the standpoint of suggestion.

VIENNA, *August*, 1888

[1] [In this connection, it is relevant to quote a footnote added by Freud by way of criticism to a passage in his translation of Bernheim's book (p. 116): 'It appears to me unjustifiable, and unnecessary, to assume that an executive act changes its localization in the nervous system if it is begun consciously and continued later unconsciously. It is, on the contrary, probable that the portion of the brain concerned can operate with a varying amount of attention (or consciousness).']

II

EARLY STUDIES ON THE PSYCHICAL MECHANISM OF HYSTERICAL PHENOMENA[1]

(1892)

(A) LETTER TO JOSEPH BREUER[2]

29.6.92

MY DEAR BREUER,

The innocent satisfaction I felt when I handed you over those few pages of mine has given way to the uneasiness which is so apt to go along with the unremitting pains of thinking. I am tormented by the problem of how it will be possible to give a two-dimensional picture of anything that is so much of a solid as our theory of hysteria. No doubt the main question is whether we are to give an historical account of it and lead off with all the case histories, or the two best ones, or whether we should start with a dogmatic statement of the theories we have devised by way of explanation. I am inclined to decide in favour of the second course and would arrange the material thus: [3]

[These three posthumously published fragments all date from the months immediately preceding the publication of Breuer and Freud's first paper on hysteria, 'On the Psychical Mechanism of Hysterical Phenomena' (1893), *Collected Papers*, **1**, 24. All three drafts had been in Breuer's possession but were returned to Freud in 1909, as is shown by a letter from Freud acknowledging their receipt and dated October 8, 1909: 'Very many thanks for letting me have the old drafts and sketches which seem to me most interesting. As regards the notes on hysterical attacks, it must be as you say; but I did not keep the manuscript after it was printed.' A discussion of some of the terminology used in these early papers will be found in Bernfeld (1944). Translation by James Strachey.]

[2] [This letter, dated June 29, 1892, was first published in *Schriften aus dem Nachlass*, (*Ges. W.*, **17**, 5) in 1941.]

[3] [In the original, the five numbered paragraphs which follow are no more than exceedingly condensed jottings. They are here translated literally. Their meaning can be gathered from the much fuller explanations given below in Drafts (B) and (C). The words in paragraph (2) which are printed in italics and enclosed in square brackets are deleted in the manuscript.]

(1) Our theories:
  (*a*) The theorem which deals with the constancy of the sums of excitation.
  (*b*) The theory of memory.
  (*c*) The theorem which lays it down that the contents of different states of consciousness are not associated with one another.

(2) The origin of chronic hysterical symptoms: dreams, auto-hypnosis, affect and the results of the absolute trauma. The first three factors relate to disposition, the last relates to aetiology. The chronic symptoms would correspond to normal mechanism; they are [*attempts at reaction, partly by abnormal methods, their hysterical feature being that they persist. The reason for their persistence lies in theorem* (*c*)] displacements, partly by an abnormal method (internal modification), of sums of excitation [*Subsidiary Topic*] which have not been released. Reason for displacement: attempt at reaction; reason for persistence: theorem (*c*), which deals with associative isolation. Comparison with hypnosis.

  Subsidiary Topic. On the nature of displacement: localization of chronic hysterical symptoms.

(3) *The hysterical attack:* also an attempt at reaction by the method of recollection, etc.

(4) *The origin of hysterical stigmata:* highly obscure, a few hints.

(5) *The pathological formula of hysteria:* Dispositional and accidental hysteria. The series proposed by me. The magnitude of the sums of excitation, concept of trauma, the second state of consciousness.

(B) ON THE THEORY OF HYSTERICAL ATTACKS[1]

So far as we are aware, no theory of hysterical attacks has yet been put forward. All we have is Charcot's description of them, which relates to the rare, unshortened *'grande attaque hystérique'*. A 'typical' attack of this kind consists, according to Charcot, of four phases: (1) the epileptoid phase, (2) the large movements, (3) the phase of *'attitudes passionnelles'* and (4) the *'délire terminal'*. All the numerous forms of hysterical attacks which the physician comes across more frequently than the typical *grande attaque* arise, Charcot tells us, when one or more of these phases appear independently, or are prolonged or modified or omitted.

This description throws no light at all upon any possible connection between the different phases, upon the significance of the attack in the general picture of hysteria or upon the way in which attacks are modified in individual patients. Perhaps we are not wrong in supposing that the majority of physicians are inclined to regard the hysterical attack as 'a periodic discharge of the motor and psychical centres of the cerebral cortex'.

We have arrived at our opinions on hysterical attacks by treating hysterical subjects by means of hypnotic suggestion and by questioning them under hypnosis and thus investigating their psychical processes during the attack. Before proceeding to state our views, we must point out that we consider it essential for the explanation of hysterical phenomena to assume the presence of a dissociation—a splitting of the content of consciousness.

(1) The regular and essential content of a (recurrent) hysterical attack is the recurrence of a psychical state

---

[1] [Written jointly with Breuer. The manuscript, in Freud's handwriting, is dated 'Vienna, end of November, 1892', and was first published in *Int. Z. Psychoanal. Imago*, **25**, (1940), 107. Reprinted *Ges. W.*, **17**, 9.]

which the patient has experienced earlier, in other words, the recurrence of a *memory*.

We believe, accordingly, that the essential part of an hysterical attack is comprised in Charcot's phase of *attitudes passionnelles*. In some cases it is quite obvious that this phase involves a memory from the patient's life, and frequently the memory involved in any one case is always the same one. But in other cases this phase seems absent and the attack appears to consist only of motor phenomena—of epileptoid spasms or of a cataleptic or sleeplike state of quiescence—but even in such cases examination under hypnosis provides definite evidence of a psychical mnemic process such as is otherwise openly betrayed in the *phase passionnelle*.

The motor phenomena of an attack are never unrelated to its psychical content; they either give a general expression of the accompanying emotion or they correspond exactly to the actions involved in the hallucinatory mnemic process.

(2) The memory which forms the content of an hysterical attack is not any chance one; it is the recurrence of the event which caused the outbreak of hysteria—the psychical trauma.

Once again, this is quite obviously true in the classical cases of traumatic hysteria which Charcot demonstrated in male patients, where a person who was not previously hysterical succumbed to a neurosis after some single major fright (such as a railway accident, a fall, etc.). In such cases the content of the attack consists in an hallucinatory reproduction of the event which endangered the subject's life, accompanied perhaps by the train of thought and sense impressions which passed through his mind at the time. But the behaviour of these patients differs in no respect from that of common female hysterics; it is an exact model of it. If we examine the content of the attacks of one of the latter by the method that has been indicated, we come upon events which by their nature are equally well calculated to operate as traumas (e.g. frights, mortifications, disappointments). Here, however ,the single major trauma is as a rule replaced by a series of minor ones, which are united by their similarity or by the fact of forming part of a single unhappy story. In such cases, accordingly, the patients often have attacks of different kinds, each with a particular mnemic content. This fact makes it necessary to extend the concept of traumatic hysteria considerably.

In a third group of cases one finds that the content of the attacks consists of memories which one would not have judged likely in themselves to constitute traumas. They evidently owe their position to the fact that they happened by chance to coincide with a moment at which the subject's hysterical disposition was pathologically intensified and they have thus been promoted into traumas.

(3) The memory which forms the content of an hysterical attack is an *unconscious* one, or, more correctly, it is part of the second state of consciousness which is present in a more or less highly organized shape in every hysteria. Accordingly that memory is either wholly absent from the patient's recollection when he is in his normal state, or is present only in a summary way. If we can succeed in bringing such a memory entirely into normal consciousness, it ceases to be capable of producing attacks. During an actual attack, the patient is partly or wholly in the second state of consciousness. In the latter case the whole attack is covered by amnesia during his normal life; in the former case he is aware of the change in his state and of his motor behaviour, but the psychical events during his attack remain hidden from him. They can, however, be awakened at any time by hypnosis.

(4) The question of the origin of the mnemic content of an hysterical attack coincides with the question of what it is that determines whether a particular experience (idea, intention, etc.) shall be received into the second consciousness instead of into the normal one. We have discovered two of these determinants with certainty in cases of hysteria:

If an hysterical patient intentionally seeks to forget an experience, or forcibly repudiates, inhibits and suppresses an intention or idea, these psychical acts, as a consequence, enter the second state of consciousness; from there they produce permanent effects and the memory of them returns in the form of hysterical attacks. (*Cf.* the occurrence of hysteria in nuns, continent women, well-brought-up boys, persons with a hankering for art or the stage, etc.)

Impressions received during unusual psychical states (such as affective states, states of ecstasy or auto-hypnosis) also enter the second state of consciousness.

It may be added that these two determinants are often connected by internal links; it is to be supposed, moreover, that there are other determinants besides these.

(5) The nervous system endeavours to keep constant something in its functional condition that may be described as the 'sum of excitation'. It seeks to establish this necessary precondition of health by dealing with every sensible increase of excitation along associative lines or by discharging it by an appropriate motor reaction. Starting from this theorem, with its far-reaching implications, we find that the psychical experiences forming the content of hysterical attacks have a common characteristic. They are all of them *impressions that have failed to find an adequate discharge*, either because the patient refuses to deal with them for fear of distressing mental conflicts, or because (as in the case of sexual impressions) he is forbidden to do so by modesty or by social circumstances, or finally because he received these impressions in a state in which his nervous system was incapable of dealing with them.

In this way, too, we arrive at a definition of psychical trauma which can be employed in the theory of hysteria: any impression which the nervous system has difficulty in dealing with by means of associative thinking or by motor reaction becomes a psychical trauma.

(C) DRAFT 'III'[1]

IN what we have written above we have been obliged to point out as a fact of observation that the memories lying behind hysterical phenomena are absent from the patients' accessible recollections, though they can be awakened under hypnosis with hallucinatory vividness. We have also pointed out that a number of such memories relate to events that occurred in peculiar states, such as cataplexy due to fright, half-dreaming conditions, auto-hypnosis, and so on, the content of which is not connected associatively with normal consciousness. It was thus impossible for us to discuss the question of what determines the occurrence of hysterical phenomena without first considering a particular hypothesis. This hypothesis seeks to characterize the hysterical disposition by supposing that in hysteria a temporary dissociation of the content of consciousness can easily occur and particular ideational complexes which are not associatively connected can easily fly apart. Thus we look for the essence of the hysterical disposition in the fact that states of this kind either arise in it spontaneously (for internal causes) or are easily provoked in it by external influences, the relative size of the part played by the two factors being a variable one.

We describe these states as 'hypnoid'. We insist that it is an essential characteristic of them that their content is more or less cut off from the remaining content of consciousness and is thus deprived of the possibility of being dealt with associatively. In just the same way, in the case of dreaming and waking—models of two differing psychical states—we are not inclined to make associations between them but only within each.[2]

[1] [The manuscript of this fragment bears the heading 'III'. It is undated but was almost certainly written in 1892. It was first published in *Schriften aus dem Nachlass*, 1941 (*Ges. W.*, **17**, 17).]

[2] [The exact wording of this sentence is obscure in the original manuscript owing to the omission of a word. But the general sense seems clear enough.]

In persons of an hysterical disposition any affect can give rise to a split of this kind, and an impression received during the affect would thus become a trauma even though it was not in itself appropriate for such a purpose. Moreover, the impression could itself produce the affect. In their fully developed form these hypnoid states, between which there can be associative connections, form the *condition seconde* so well known to us from case histories. But rudiments of such a disposition are, it seems, present everywhere, and may be developed by suitable traumas even in non-disposed subjects. Sexual life is especially well suited to provide the content [of such traumas] owing to the very great contrast it presents to the rest of the personality and to the fact that its ideas cannot be abreacted.

It will be understood that our therapy consists in putting an end to the effects of the unabreacted ideas, either by reviving the trauma in a state of somnambulism and then abreacting and correcting it, or by bringing it into normal consciousness under lighter hypnosis.

III

A CASE OF SUCCESSFUL TREATMENT BY HYPNOTISM

WITH SOME REMARKS ON THE ORIGIN OF HYSTERICAL SYMPTOMS THROUGH 'COUNTER-WILL' [1]

(1893)

IPROPOSE in the following pages to publish an isolated case of a successful treatment by hypnotic suggestion because, owing to a number of attendant circumstances, it was more convincing and more lucid than the majority of our successful treatments.

I have been acquainted for many years with the woman whom I was thus able to assist at an important moment of her existence, and she remained under my observation for several years afterwards. The disorder from which she was relieved by hypnotic suggestion had made its first appearance some time earlier. She had struggled against it in vain and been driven by it to an act of renunciation which, with my help, she was spared on a second occasion. A year later the same disorder appeared yet again, and was once more overcome in the same manner. The therapeutic success was of value to the patient and persisted as long as she desired to carry out the function affected by the disorder. Finally, it was possible in this case to trace the simple psychical mechanism of the disorder and to bring it into relation with similar processes in the field of neuropathology.

It was a case, if I may now cease talking in riddles, of a mother who was unable to feed her new-born child till hypnotic suggestion intervened, and whose experiences with an earlier and a later child provided controls of the therapeutic success such as are seldom obtainable.

---

[1] ['Ein Fall von hypnotischer Heilung.' First published *Z. Hypnotismus, Suggestionstherapie, Suggestionslehre und verwandte psycholog. Forsch.*, **1**, (1892–3); reprinted *Ges. Schr.*, **1**, 258, and *Ges. W.*, **1**. Translation by James Strachey.]

The subject of the following case history is a young woman between twenty and thirty years of age with whom I happen to have been acquainted from her childhood. Her capability, her quiet common sense and her naturalness made it impossible for anyone, including her family doctor, to regard her as neurotic. Taking the circumstances that I am about to narrate into account, I must describe her, in Charcot's happy phrase, as an *hystérique d'occasion*. This category, as we know, does not exclude the most admirable of qualities and otherwise uninterrupted nervous health. As regards her family, I am acquainted with her mother, who is not in any way neurotic, and a younger sister who is similarly healthy. A brother suffered from a typical neurasthenia of early manhood, and this ruined his career. I am familiar with the aetiology and course of this form of illness, which I come across repeatedly every year in my medical practice. Starting originally with a good constitution, the patient is haunted by the usual sexual difficulties at puberty; there follow years of overwork as a student, preparation for examinations, and an attack of gonorrhea, followed by a sudden onset of dyspepsia accompanied by obstinate and inexplicable constipation. After some months the constipation is replaced by pressure in the head, depression and incapacity for work. Thenceforward the patient grows increasingly self-centred and his character more and more restricted, till he becomes a torment to his family. I am not certain whether it is not possible to *acquire* this form of neurasthenia with all its elements and therefore, especially as I am not acquainted with my patient's other relatives, I leave it an open question whether we are to assume the presence in her family of a hereditary predisposition to neurosis.

When the time approached for the birth of the first child of her marriage (which was a happy one) the patient intended to feed the infant herself. The delivery was not more difficult than is usual with a primiparous mother who is no longer very youthful; it was terminated with the forceps. Nevertheless, though her bodily build seemed favourable, she did not succeed in feeding the infant satisfactorily. There was a poor flow of milk, pains were brought on when the baby was put to the breast, the mother lost appetite and showed an alarming unwillingness to take nourishment, her nights were agitated and sleepless. At last, after a fortnight, in order to avoid any further risk to the mother and infant, the attempt was abandoned as a failure and the child was transferred to a wet-nurse. Thereupon all the mother's troubles immediately cleared up. I must add that I am not able to give a medical or eye-witness account of this first attempt at lactation.

Three years later a second baby was born; and on this occasion external circumstances added to the desirability of avoiding a wet-nurse. But the mother's attempts at feeding the child herself seemed even less successful and to provoke even more painful symptoms than the first time. She vomited all her food, became agitated when it was brought to her bedside and was completely unable to sleep. She became so much depressed at her incapacity that her two family doctors —physicians of such wide repute in Vienna as Dr. Breuer and Dr. Lott—would not hear of any prolonged attempt being made on this occasion. They recommended that one more effort should be made—with the help of hypnotic suggestion—and, on the evening of the fourth day, arranged for me to be brought in professionally, since I was already personally acquainted with the patient.

I found her lying in bed with flushed cheeks and furious at her inability to feed the baby—an inability which increased at every attempt but against which she struggled with all her strength. In order to avoid the vomiting, she had taken no nourishment the whole day. Her epigastrium was distended and sensitive to pressure; manual palpation showed morbid peristalsis of the stomach; there was odourless eructation from time to time and the patient complained of having a constant bad taste in her mouth. The area of gastric resonance was considerably increased. Far from being welcomed as a saviour in the hour of need, it was obvious that I was being received with a bad grace and that I could not count on the patient having much confidence in me.

I at once attempted to induce hypnosis by ocular fixation, at the same time making constant suggestions of the symptoms of sleep. After three minutes the patient was lying back with the peaceful expression of a person in profound sleep. I cannot recollect whether I made any tests for catalepsy and other symptoms of pliancy. I made use of suggestion to contradict all her fears and the feelings on which those fears were based: 'Do not be afraid. You will make an excellent nurse and the baby will thrive. Your stomach is perfectly quiet, your appetite is excellent, you are looking forward to your next meal, etc.' The patient went on sleeping while I left her for a few minutes, and when I had woken her up showed amnesia for what had occurred. Before I left the house I was also under the necessity of contradicting a worried remark by the patient's husband to the effect that his wife's nerves might be ruined by hypnosis.

Next evening I was told something which seemed to me a guarantee of success but which, oddly enough, had made no impression on the patient or her relations. She had had a meal the evening before without any ill effects, had slept peacefully and in the morning had taken nourishment herself and fed the baby irreproachably. The rather abundant midday meal, however, had been too much for her. No sooner had it been brought in than her former disinclination returned; vomiting set in even before she had touched it. It was impossible to put the child to her breast and all the objective signs were the same as they had been when I had arrived the previous evening. I produced no effect by my argument that, since she was now convinced that her disorder *could* disappear and in fact *had* disappeared for half a day, the battle was already won. I now brought on the second hypnosis, which led to a state of somnambulism as quickly as the first, and I acted with greater energy and confidence. I told the patient that five minutes after my departure she would break out against her family with some acrimony: what had happened to her dinner? did they mean to let her starve? how could she feed the baby if she had nothing to eat herself? and so on.

When I returned on the third evening the patient refused to have any further treatment. There was nothing more wrong with her, she said: she had an excellent appetite and plenty of milk for the baby, there was not the slightest difficulty when it was put to her breast, and so on. Her husband thought it rather queer, however, that after my departure the evening before she had clamoured violently for food and had remonstrated with her mother in a way quite unlike herself. But since then, he added, everything had gone all right.

There was nothing more for me to do. The mother fed her child for eight months; and I had many opportunities of satisfying myself in a friendly way that they were both doing well. I found it hard to understand, however, as well as annoying, that no reference was ever made to my remarkable achievement.

But my time came a year later, when a third child made the same demands on the mother and she was as unable to meet them as on the previous occasions. I found the patient in the same condition as the year before and positively embittered against herself because her will could do nothing against her disinclination for food and her other symptoms; and the first evening's hypnosis only had the result of making her feel more hopeless. Once again after the second hypnosis the symptoms were so completely cut short that a third was not required. This child too, which is now eighteen months old, was fed without any trouble and has enjoyed uninterrupted good health.

In face of this renewed success the patient and her husband unbent and admitted the motive that had governed their behaviour towards me. 'I felt ashamed', the woman said to me, 'that a thing like hypnosis should be successful where I myself, with all my will-power, was helpless.' Nevertheless, I do not think either she or her husband have overcome their dislike of hypnosis.

I shall now pass on to consider what may have been the psychical mechanism of this disorder of my patient's which was thus removed by suggestion. I have not, as in certain other cases which I shall discuss elsewhere [Breuer and Freud, 1893], direct information on the subject; and I am thrown back upon the alternative of deducing it.

There are certain ideas which have an affect of expectancy attached to them. They are of two kinds: ideas of my doing this or that—what we call *intentions* —and ideas of this or that happening to me—*expectations* proper. The affect attached to them is dependent on two factors, first on the degree of importance which the outcome has for me, and secondly on the degree of uncertainty inherent in the expectation of that outcome. The subjective uncertainty, the counter-expectation, is itself represented by a collection of ideas to which I shall give the name of 'distressing antithetic ideas' ['*peinliche Kontrastvorstellungen*']. In the case of an intention, these antithetic ideas will run: 'I shall not succeed in carrying out my intentions because this or that is too difficult for me and I am unfit to do it; I know, too, that certain other people have also failed in a similar situation.' The other case, that of an expectation, needs no comment: the antithetic idea consists in enumerating all the things that could possibly happen to me other than the one I desire. Further along this line we should reach the *phobias*, which play so great a part in the symptomatology of the neuroses. But let us return to the first category, the intentions. How does a person with a healthy ideational life deal with antithetic ideas against an intention? With the powerful self-confidence of health, he suppresses and inhibits them so far as possible, and excludes them from his associations. This often succeeds to such an extent that the antithetic ideas against an intention are as a rule not manifestly visible; their existence only becomes probable when neuroses are taken into account. On the other hand, where a neurosis is present—and I am explicitly referring not to hysteria alone but to the *status nervosus* in general—we have to assume that there exists a *primary* tendency to depression and to a lowering of self-confidence, such as we find very highly developed and in isolation in melancholia. In neuroses, then, great attention is paid to antithetic ideas against intentions, perhaps because the subject-matter of such ideas fits in with the mood of the neurosis, or perhaps because antithetic ideas, which would otherwise have been absent, flourish in the soil of a neurosis.

When this intensification of antithetic ideas relates to *expectations*, if the case is one of a simple *status nervosus*, the effect is shown in a generally pessimistic frame of mind ; in case of neurasthenia, associations from the most accidental sensations occasion the numerous phobias of neurasthenics. If the intensification attaches to *intentions*, it gives rise to the disturbances which are summed up under the description of *folie du doute*, and which have as their subject-matter distrust of the subject's own capacity. Precisely at this point the two major neuroses, neurasthenia and hysteria, each behave in a characteristic manner. In neurasthenia the pathologically intensified antithetic idea becomes attached, along with the volitional idea, to a *single* act of consciousness; it detracts from the volitional idea and brings about the weakness of will which is so striking in neurasthenics and of which they themselves are aware. The process in hysteria differs from this in two respects, or possibly only in one. [Firstly,] in accordance with the tendency to a dissociation of consciousness in hysteria, the distressing antithetic idea, which has the appearance of being inhibited, is removed from association with the intention and continues to exist as a disconnected idea, often unconsciously to the patient himself. [Secondly,] it is supremely characteristic of hysteria that, if it should come to the carrying out of the intention, the inhibited antithetic idea can put itself into effect through the agency of the somatic innervations just as easily as does a volitional idea in normal circumstances. The antithetic idea establishes itself, so to speak, as a *'counter-will'*, while the patient is aware with astonishment of having a will which is resolute but powerless. Perhaps, as I have said, these two factors are at bottom one and the same: it may be that the antithetic idea is only able to put itself into effect because it is not inhibited by its connection with the intention in the same way as it itself inhibits the intention.[1]

If in our present case the mother who was prevented by neurotic difficulties from feeding her child had been a neurasthenic, her behaviour would have been different. She would have felt conscious dread of the task before her, she would have been greatly concerned with the various possible accidents and dangers and, after much temporizing with anxieties and doubts, would after all have carried out the feeding without any difficulty; or, if the antithetic idea had gained the upper hand, she would have abandoned the task because she felt afraid of it. But the hysteric behaves quite otherwise. She may not be conscious of her fear, she is quite determined to carry her intention through and sets about it without hesitating. Then, however, she behaves as though it was her will not to feed the child on any account. Moreover, this will evokes in her all the subjective symptoms which a malingerer would put forward as an excuse for not feeding her child: loss of appetite, aversion to food, pains when the child is put to her breast. And, since the counter-will exercises greater control over the body than does conscious simulation, it also produces a

---

[1] In the interval between writing this and correcting the proofs, I have come across a work by H. Kaan (1893) containing similar arguments.

number of objective signs in the digestive tract which malingering would be unable to bring about. Here, in contrast to the *weakness* of will shown in neurasthenia, we have a *perversion* of will; and, in contrast to the resigned irresoluteness shown in the former case, here we have astonishment and embitterment at a disunity which is incomprehensible to the patient.

I therefore consider that I am justified in describing my patient as an *hystérique d'occasion*, since she was able, as a result of a fortuitous cause, to produce a complex of symptoms with a mechanism so supremely characteristic of hysteria. It may be assumed that in this instance the fortuitous cause was the patient's excited state before the first confinement or her exhaustion after it. A first confinement is, after all, the greatest shock to which the female organism is subject, and as a result of it a woman will as a rule produce any neurotic symptoms that may be latent in her disposition.

It seems probable that the case of this patient is a typical one and throws light upon a large number of other cases in which breast-feeding or some similar function is prevented by neurotic influences. Since, however, in the case I have reported I have only arrived at the psychical mechanism by inference, I hasten to add an assurance that I have frequently been able to establish the operation of a similar psychical mechanism in hysterical symptoms *directly*, by investigating the patient under hypnosis.[1]

Here I will mention only one of the most striking instances.[2] Some years ago I treated an hysterical lady who showed great strength of will in those of her dealings which were unaffected by her illness; but in those which *were* so affected she showed no less clearly the weight of the burden imposed on her by her numerous

[1] See the preliminary statement by J. Breuer and S. Freud on 'The Psychical Mechanism of Hysterical Phenomena', which is appearing at the same time as the present paper in Mendel's *Zentralblatt*, Nos. 1 and 2, 1893. [*Collected Papers*, 1, 24.]

[2] [This patient was subsequently made the subject of the second case history in Breuer and Freud's *Studies in Hysteria* (1895).]

and oppressive hysterical impediments and incapacities. One of her striking characteristics was a peculiar noise which intruded, like a *tic*, into her conversation. I can best describe it as a singular clicking of the tongue accompanied by a sudden spasmodic closing of the lips. After observing it for some weeks, I once asked her when and how it had first originated. 'I don't know when it was,' she replied, 'oh! a long time ago.' This led me to regard it as a genuine *tic*, till it occurred to me one day to ask the patient the same question in deep hypnosis. This patient had access in hypnosis (without there being any necessity to suggest the idea to her) to the whole store of her memories—or, as I should prefer to put it, to the whole extent of her consciousness, which was restricted in her waking life. She promptly answered: 'It was when my younger girl was so ill and had been having convulsions all day but had fallen asleep at last in the evening. I was sitting beside her bed and thought to myself: "Now you must be absolutely quiet, so as not to wake her." It was then that the clicking came on for the first time. Afterwards it passed off. But once, some years later, when we were driving through the forest near ——, a violent thunderstorm came on and a tree beside the road just ahead of us was struck by lightning, so that the coachman had to rein in the horses suddenly, and I thought to myself: "Now, whatever you do, you mustn't scream, or the horses will bolt." And at that moment it came on again, and has persisted ever since.' I was able to convince myself that the noise she made was not a genuine *tic*, since, from the moment it was in this way traced back to its origin, it disappeared and never returned during all the years I remained in contact with the patient. This however was the first occasion on which I was able to observe the origin of hysterical symptoms through the putting into effect of a distressing antithetic idea, that is, through counter-will. The mother, worn out by anxieties and her duties as a nurse, made a decision not to let a sound pass her lips for fear of disturbing her child's sleep, which had been so long in coming. But in her exhausted state the attendant antithetic idea that she nevertheless *would* do it proved to be the stronger; it made its way to the innervation of the tongue, which her decision to remain silent may perhaps have forgotten to inhibit, broke through her closed lips and produced a noise which thenceforward remained fixated for many years, especially after the same procedure had been gone through on a second occasion.

There is one objection that must be met before we can fully understand this process. It may be asked how it comes about that it is the *antithetic* idea that gains the upper hand as a result of general exhaustion (which is what constitutes the predisposing situation for the event). I should reply by putting forward the theory that the exhaustion is in fact only a *partial* one. What are exhausted are those elements of the nervous system which form the material foundation of the ideas associated with *primary* consciousness; the ideas that are excluded from that chain of associations—that is, from the normal ego—, the inhibited and suppressed ideas, are *not* exhausted, and they consequently predominate at the moment when the disposition to hysteria emerges.

Anyone who is well acquainted with hysteria will observe that the psychical mechanism which I have been describing offers an explanation not merely of isolated hysterical occurrences but of major portions of the symptomatology of hysteria as well as of one of its most striking characteristics. Let us keep firmly in mind the fact that it is the distressing antithetic ideas (inhibited and rejected by normal consciousness) which press forward at the moment of the emergence of the disposition to hysteria and find their way to the somatic innervation, and we shall then hold the key to an understanding of the peculiarity of the deliria of hysterical attacks as well. It is owing to no chance coincidence that the hysterical deliria of nuns during the epidemics of the Middle Ages took the form of violent blasphemies and unbridled erotic language or that (as Charcot remarked in the first volume of his *Leçons du Mardi*) it is precisely well-brought-up and well-behaved boys who suffer from hysterical attacks in which they give free play to every kind of rowdiness, every kind of wild escapade and bad conduct. It is the suppressed—the laboriously suppressed—groups of ideas that are brought into action in these cases, by the operation of a sort of counter-will, when the subject has fallen a victim to hysterical exhaustion. Perhaps, indeed, the connection may be a more intimate one, for the hysterical condition may perhaps be *produced* by the laborious suppression; but in the present paper I have not been considering the psychological features of that condition. Here I am merely concerned with explaining why—assuming the presence of the disposition to hysteria—the symptoms take the particular form in which we in fact observe them.

This emergence of a counter-will is chiefly responsible for the characteristic which often gives to hysterics the appearance almost of being possessed by an evil spirit— the characteristic, that is, of not being able to do something precisely at the moment when they want to most passionately, of doing the exact opposite of what they have been asked to do, and of being obliged to cover what they most value with abuse and contempt. The perversity of character shown by hysterics, their itch to do the wrong thing, to appear to be ill just when they most want to be well—compulsions such as these (as anyone will know who has had to do with these patients) may often affect the most irreproachable characters when for a time they become the helpless victims of their antithetic ideas.

The question of what becomes of inhibited intentions seems to be meaningless in regard to normal ideational life. We might be tempted to reply that they simply do not occur. The study of hysteria shows that nevertheless they *do* occur, that is to say that the physical modification corresponding to them is retained, and that they are stored up and enjoy an unsuspected existence in a sort of shadow kingdom, till they emerge like bad spirits and take control of the body, which is as a rule under the orders of the predominant ego-consciousness.

I have already said that this mechanism is supremely characteristic of hysteria; but I must add that it does not occur only in hysteria. It is present in striking fashion in *tic convulsif*, a neurosis which has so much symptomatic similarity with hysteria that its whole picture may occur as a part-manifestation of hysteria. So it is that Charcot, if I have not completely misunderstood his teachings on the subject, after keeping the two separate for some time, could only find one distinguishing mark between them—that hysterical *tic* disappears sooner or later, while genuine *tic* persists. The picture of a severe *tic convulsif* is, as we know, made up of involuntary movements (frequently, according to Charcot and Guinon, in the nature of grimaces or of performances which have at one time had a meaning), of coprolalia, of echolalia and of obsessive ideas belonging to the range covered by *folie du doute*. Now it is surprising to learn that Guinon, who had no notion whatever of going into the psychical mechanism of these symptoms, tells us that some of his patients arrived at their spasms and grimaces because an antithetic idea had put itself into effect. These patients reported that on some particular occasion they had seen a similar *tic*, or a comedian intentionally making a similar grimace, and felt afraid that they might be obliged to imitate the ugly movement. Thenceforward they had actually begun imitating it. No doubt only a small proportion of the involuntary movements occurring in *tics* originate in this way. On the other hand, it would be tempting to attribute this mechanism to the origin of coprolalia, a term used to describe the involuntary, or rather, the unwilling ejaculation of the foulest words which occurs in *tics*. If so, the root of coprolalia would be the patient's perception that he cannot prevent himself from producing some particular sound, probably an 'ahem'. He would then become afraid of losing control over other sounds as well, especially over words such as any well-brought-up man avoids using, and this fear would lead to what he feared coming true. No anamnesis confirming this suspicion is quoted by Guinon, and I myself have never had occasion to question a patient suffering from coprolalia. On the other hand I have found in the same writer's work a report upon another case of *tic* in which the word that was involuntarily spoken did not, exceptionally enough, belong to the coprolalic vocabulary. This was the case of an adult man who was afflicted with the necessity of calling out 'Maria!'. When he was a schoolboy he had had a sentimental attachment to a girl of that name; he had been completely absorbed in her, and this, it may be supposed, predisposed him to a neurosis. He began at that time to call out his idol's name in the middle of his school classes, and the name persisted with him, as a *tic* half a lifetime after he had got over his love-affair. I think the explanation must be that his most determined endeavour to keep the name secret was reversed, at a moment of special excitement, into the counter-will and that thereafter the *tic* persisted as it did in the case of my second patient. If my explanation of this instance is correct, it would be tempting to derive coprolalic *tic* proper from the same mechanism, since obscene words are secrets that we all know and the knowledge of which we try to conceal from one another.[1]

[1] I will merely add a suggestion that it would be repaying to study elsewhere than in hysteria and *tic* the way in which the counter-will puts itself into effect—an event which very frequently occurs within the limits of the normal.

IV

SCREEN MEMORIES[1]

(1899)

I N the course of my psycho-analytic treatment of cases of hysteria, obsessional neurosis, etc., I have often had to deal with fragmentary recollections which were all that remained in the patient's memory from the earliest years of his childhood. As I have elsewhere shown,[2] great pathogenic importance must be attributed to the impressions of that time of life. But the subject of childhood memories is in any case bound to be of psychological interest, for they bring into striking relief a fundamental difference between the mental functioning of children and of adults. No one calls in question the fact that the experiences of the earliest years of our childhood leave ineradicable traces in the depths of our minds. If, however, we seek in our memories to ascertain what were the impressions that were destined to influence us to the end of our lives, the outcome is either nothing at all or a relatively small number of isolated recollections which are often of dubious or enigmatic importance. It is only from the sixth or seventh year onwards—in many cases only after the tenth year—that our lives can be reproduced in memory as a connected chain of events. From that time on, however, there is also a direct relation between the psychical significance of an experience and its retention in the memory. Whatever seems important on account of its immediate or directly subsequent effects is recollected; whatever is judged to be inessential is forgotten. If I can remember an event for a long time after its occurrence, I regard the fact of having retained

---

[1] ['Über Deckerinnerungen.' First published in *Mschr. Psychiat. Neurol.*, 1899; reprinted *Ges. Schr.*, **1**, 465, and *Ges. W.*, **1**. The topic of this paper was further developed by Freud in Chapter IV of his *Psychopathology of Everyday Life* (1904). Translation by James Strachey.]

[2] [Cf., for instance, Freud (1896b).]

it in my memory as evidence of its having made a deep impression on me at the time. I feel surprised at forgetting something important; but I feel even more surprised, perhaps, at remembering something apparently indifferent.

It is only in certain pathological mental conditions that the relation holding in normal adults between the psychical significance of an event and its retention in memory once more ceases to apply. For instance, an hysteric habitually shows amnesia for some or all of the experiences which led to the onset of his illness and which from that very fact have become important to him and, apart from that fact, may have been important on their own account. The analogy between pathological amnesia of this kind and the normal amnesia affecting our early years seems to me to give a valuable hint at the intimate connection that exists between the psychical content of neuroses and our infantile life.

We are so much accustomed to this lack of memory of the impressions of childhood that we are apt to overlook the problem underlying it and are inclined to explain it as a self-evident consequence of the rudimentary character of the mental activities of children. Actually, however, a normally developed child of three or four exhibits an enormous amount of organized mental functioning in the comparisons and inferences which he makes and in the expression of his feelings; and there is no obvious reason why amnesia should overtake these mental acts, which carry no less weight than those of a later age.

Before dealing with the psychological problems attaching to the earliest memories of childhood, it would of course be essential to make a collection of material by circularizing a fairly large number of normal adults and discovering what kind of recollections they are able to produce from these early years. A first step in this direction was taken in 1895 by V. and C. Henri, who sent round a paper of questions drawn up by them.

The highly suggestive results of their questionnaire, which brought in replies from 123 persons, were published by the two authors in 1897. I have no intention at present of discussing the subject as a whole, and I shall therefore content myself with emphasizing the few points which have led me to introduce the notion of what I have termed 'screen memories'.

The age to which the content of the earliest memories of childhood are usually referred back is the period between the ages of two and four. (This is the case with 88 persons in the series observed by the Henris.) There are some, however, whose memory reaches back further—even to the time before the completion of the first year; and, on the other hand, there are some whose earliest recollections go back only to their sixth, seventh, or even eighth year. There is nothing at the moment to show what else is related to these individual differences; but it is to be noticed, say the Henris, that a person whose earliest recollection goes back to a very tender age, to the first year of his life, perhaps, will also have at his disposal further detached memories from the following years, and that he will be able to reproduce his experiences as a continuous chain from an earlier point of time—from about his fifth year—than is possible for other people, whose first recollection dates from a later time. Thus not only the date of the appearance of the first recollection but the whole function of memory may, in the case of some people, be advanced or retarded.

Quite special interest attaches to the question of what is the usual subject-matter of these earliest memories of childhood. The psychology of adults would necessarily lead us to expect that those experiences would be selected as worth remembering which had aroused some powerful emotion or which, owing to their consequences, had been recognized as important soon after their occurrence. And some indeed of the observations collected by the Henris appear to fulfil this expectation. They report that the most frequent subject-matter of the first memories of childhood are on the one hand occasions of fear, shame, physical pain, etc., and on the other hand important events such as illnesses, deaths, fires, births of brothers and sisters, etc. We might therefore be inclined to assume that the principle governing the choice of memories is the same in the case of children as in that of adults. It is intelligible—though the fact deserves to be explicitly mentioned—that the memories retained from childhood should necessarily show evidence of the difference between what attracts the interest of a child and of an adult. This easily explains why, for instance, one woman reports that she remembers a number of accidents that occurred to her dolls when she was two years old but has no recollection of the serious and tragic events she might have observed at the same period.

Now, however, we are met by a fact that is diametrically opposed to our expectations and cannot fail to astonish us. We hear that there are some people whose earliest recollections of childhood are concerned with everyday and indifferent events which could not produce any emotional effect even in children, but which are recollected (*too* clearly, one is inclined to say) in every detail, while approximately contemporary events, which on the evidence of their parents moved them intensely at the time, have not been retained in their memory. Thus the Henris mention a professor of philology whose earliest memory, dating back to between the ages of three and four, showed him a table laid for a meal and on it a basin of ice. At the same period there occurred the death of his grandmother which, according to his parents, was a severe blow to the child. But the professor of philology, as he now is, has no recollection of this bereavement; all that he remembers of those days is the basin of ice. Another man reports that his earliest memory is an episode upon a walk in which he broke off the branch of a tree. He thinks he can still identify the spot where this happened. There were several other people present, and one of them helped him.

The Henris describe such cases as rare. In my experience, based for the most part, it is true, upon neurotics, they are quite frequent. One of the subjects of the Henris' investigation made an attempt at explaining the occurrence of these memories, whose innocence makes them so mysterious, and his explanation seems to me very much to the point. He thinks that in such cases the relevant scene may perhaps have been only *incompletely* retained in the memory, and that that may be why it seems so unenlightening: the parts that have been forgotten probably contained everything that made the experience noteworthy. I am able to confirm the truth of this view, though I should prefer to speak of these elements of the experience being *omitted* rather than forgotten. I have often succeeded, by means of psycho-analytic treatment, in uncovering the missing portions of a childhood experience and in thus proving that when the impression, of which no more than a torso was retained in the memory, had been restored to completion, it did in fact agree with the presumption that it is the most important things that are recollected. This, however, provides no explanation of the remarkable choice which memory has made among the elements of the experience. We must first enquire why it should be that precisely what is important is suppressed and what is indifferent retained; and we shall not find an explanation of this until we have thoroughly investigated the mechanism of these processes. We shall then form a notion that two psychical forces are concerned in bringing about memories of this sort. One of these forces takes the importance of the experience as a motive for seeking to remember it, while the other—a resistance—tries to prevent any such preference from being shown. These two opposing forces do not cancel each other out, nor does one of them (whether with or without loss to itself) overpower the other. Instead, a compromise is brought about, somewhat on the analogy of the resultant in a parallelogram of forces. And the compromise is this. What is recorded in the memory is not the relevant experience itself—in this respect the resistance gets its way; what is recorded is another psychical element closely associated with the objectionable one—and in this respect the *first* principle shows its strength, the principle which endeavours to fix important impressions by establishing reproducible memory pictures. The result of the conflict is therefore that, instead of the memory which would have been justified by the original event, another memory is produced which has been to some degree associatively *displaced* from the former one. And since the elements of the experience which aroused objection were precisely the important ones, the substituted memory will necessarily lack those important elements and will in consequence most probably strike us as trivial. It will seem incomprehensible to us because we are inclined to look for the reason for its retention in its own subject-matter, whereas in fact that retention is due to the relation holding between its own subject-matter and a different one which has been suppressed. There is a common saying among us about shams, that they are not made of gold themselves but have lain beside something that *is* made of gold. The same simile might well be applied to some of the experiences of childhood which have been retained in the memory.

There are numerous possible types of case in which one piece of psychical material is replaced by another, and these come about in a variety of psychological constellations. One of the simplest of these cases is that occurring in the childhood memories with which we are here concerned—the case, that is, where the essential elements of an experience are represented in memory by the inessential elements of the same experience. It is a case of displacement on to something associated by contiguity; or, looking at the process as a whole, a case of repression accompanied by replacement by something in the neighbourhood (whether in space or time).

I have elsewhere [1896a, 177] had occasion to describe a very similar instance of replacement which occurred in the analysis of a patient suffering from paranoia. The woman in question hallucinated voices, which used to repeat long passages from Otto Ludwig's novel *Die Heiterethei*. But the passages they chose were the most trifling and irrelevant in the book. The analysis showed, however, that there were other passages in the same work which had stirred up the most distressing thoughts in the patient. The distressing affect was a motive for putting up a defence against them, but the motive in favour of pursuing them further was not to be suppressed. The result was a compromise by which the innocent passages emerged in the patient's memory with pathological strength and clarity. The process which we here see at work—conflict, repression, replacement involving a compromise—returns again and again in all psychoneurotic symptoms and gives us the key to understanding their formation. Thus it is not without importance that we should be able to show the same process operating in the mental life of normal persons; and the fact that what it influences in normal people is precisely their choice of childhood memories seems to afford one more indication of the intimate relations which have already been insisted upon between the mental life of children and the psychical material of the neuroses.

The processes of normal and pathological defence and the effects of displacement to which they lead are clearly of great importance. But to the best of my knowledge no study whatever has hitherto been made of them by psychologists; and it remains to be ascertained in what strata of psychical activity and under what conditions they come into operation. The reason for this neglect may well be that our mental life, so far as it is the object of our *conscious* internal perception, shows nothing of these processes, apart from instances which we classify as 'errors of thought' and some mental operations which aim at producing a comic effect. The assertion that a psychical intensity can be displaced from one presentation (which is then abandoned) on to another (which thenceforward plays the psychological part of the former one) is as bewildering to us as certain features of Greek mythology—as, for instance, when the gods are said to clothe someone with beauty as though it were with a veil, whereas *we* should think of it only as a face transfigured by a change of expression.

Further investigation of these indifferent childhood memories has taught me that they can originate in other ways as well and that an unsuspected wealth of meaning lies concealed behind their apparent innocence. But on this point I shall not content myself with a mere assertion but shall give a detailed report of one particular instance which seems to me the most instructive out of a considerable number of similar ones. Its value is certainly increased by the fact that it relates to someone who is not at all or only very slightly neurotic.

The subject of this observation is a man of university education, aged thirty-eight. Though his own profession lies in a very different field, he has taken an interest in psychological questions ever since I was able to relieve him of a slight phobia by means of psychoanalysis. Last year he drew my attention to his childhood memories, which had already played some part in his analysis. After studying the investigation made by V. and C. Henri, he gave me the following summarized account of his own experience.

'I have at my disposal a fair number of early memories of childhood which I can date with great certainty. For at the age of three I left the small place where I was born and moved to a large town; and all these memories of mine relate to my birthplace and therefore date from my second and third years. They are mostly short scenes, but they are very well preserved and furnished with every detail of sense-perception, in complete contrast to my memories of adult years, which are entirely lacking in the visual element. From my third year onwards my recollections grow scantier and less clear; there are gaps in them which must cover more than a year; and it is not, I believe, until my sixth or seventh year that the stream of my memories becomes continuous. My memories up to the time of my leaving my first place of residence fall into three groups. The first group consists of scenes which my parents have repeatedly since described to me. As regards these, I feel uncertain whether I have had their picture in my memory from the beginning or whether I only constructed it after hearing one of these descriptions. I may remark, however, that there are also events of which I have no picture in my memory in spite of their having been frequently retailed by my parents. I attach more importance to the second group. It comprises scenes which have not (so far as I know) been described to me and some of which, indeed, *could* not have been described to me, as I have not met the other participants in them (my nursemaid and play-mates) since their occurrence. I shall come to the third group presently. As regards the subject-matter of these scenes and their consequent claim to being recollected, I should like to say that I am not entirely at sea. I cannot maintain, indeed, that what I have retained are memories of the most important events of the period, or what I should to-day judge to be the most important. I have no knowledge of the birth of a sister, who is two and a half years younger than I am; my departure, my first sight of the railway and the long carriage-drive before it—none of these has left a trace in my memory. On the other hand, I can remember two small occurrences during the railway-journey; these, as you will recollect, came up in the analysis of my phobia. But what must have made most impression on me was an injury to my face which caused a considerable loss of blood so that I had to have some stitches put in by a surgeon. I can still feel the scar resulting from this accident, but I know of no recollection which points to it, either directly or indirectly. It is true that I may perhaps have been under two years old at the time.

'It follows from this that I feel no surprise at the pictures and scenes of these first two groups. No doubt they are displaced memories from which the essential element has for the most part been omitted. But in a few of them it is at least hinted at, and in others it is easy for me to complete them by following certain pointers. By doing so I can establish a sound connection between the separate fragments of memories and arrive at a clear understanding of what the childish interest was that recommended these particular occurrences to my memory. This does not apply, however, to the subject-matter of the third group, which I have not so far discussed. There I am met by material—one rather long scene and several smaller pictures—with which I can make no headway at all. The scene appears to me fairly indifferent and I cannot understand why it should have become fixed in my memory. Let me describe it to you. I see a rectangular, rather steeply sloping piece of meadow-land, green and thickly grown; in the green there are great number of yellow flowers— evidently common dandelions. At the top end of the meadow there is a cottage and in front of the cottage door two women are standing chatting busily, a peasant-woman with a handkerchief on her head and a nursemaid. Three children are playing in the grass. One of them is myself (between the age of two and three); the two others are my boy cousin, who is a year older, and his sister, who is almost exactly the same age as I am. We are picking the yellow flowers and each of us is holding a bunch of flowers we have already picked. The little girl has the best bunch; and, as though by mutual agreement, we—the two boys—fall on her and snatch away her flowers. She runs up the meadow in tears and as a consolation the peasant-woman gives her a big piece of black bread. Hardly have we seen this than we throw the flowers away, hurry to the cottage and ask to be given some bread too. And we are in fact given some; the peasant-woman cuts the loaf with a long knife. In my memory the bread tastes quite delicious—and at that point the scene breaks off.

'Now what is there in this occurrence to justify the expenditure of memory which it has occasioned me? I have racked my brains in vain over it. Does the emphasis lie on our disagreeable behaviour to the little girl? Did the yellow colour of the dandelions—a flower which I am, of course, far from admiring to-day—so greatly please me? Or, as a result of my careering round the grass, did the bread taste so much nicer than usual that it made an unforgettable impression on me? Nor can I find any connection between this scene and the interest which (as I was able to discover without any difficulty) bound together the other scenes from my childhood. Altogether, there seems to me something not quite right about this scene. The yellow of the flowers is a disproportionately prominent element in the situation as a whole, and the nice taste of the bread seems to me exaggerated in an almost hallucinatory fashion. I cannot help being reminded of some pictures that I once saw in a burlesque exhibition. Certain portions of these pictures, and of course the most inappropriate ones, instead of being painted, were built up in three dimensions—for instance, the ladies' bustles. Well, can you point out any way of finding an explanation or interpretation of this redundant memory of my childhood?'

I thought it advisable to ask him since when he had been occupied with this recollection: whether he was of opinion that it had recurred to his memory periodically since his childhood, or whether it had perhaps emerged at some later time on some occasion that could be recalled. This question was all that it was necessary for me to contribute to the solution of the problem; the rest was found by my collaborator himself, who was no novice at jobs of this kind.

'I have not yet considered that point,' he replied. 'Now that you have raised the question, it seems to me almost a certainty that this childhood memory never occurred to me at all in my earlier years. But I can also recall the occasion which led to my recovering this and many other recollections of my earliest childhood. When I was seventeen and a secondary schoolboy, I returned for the first time to my birthplace for the holidays, to stay with a family who had been our friends ever since that remote date. I know quite well what a wealth of impressions overwhelmed me at that time. But I see now that I shall have to tell you a whole big piece of my history: it fits in here, and you have brought it upon yourself by your question. So listen. I was the child of people who were originally well-to-do and who, I fancy, lived comfortably enough in that little corner of the provinces. When I was about three, the branch of industry in which my father was concerned met with a catastrophe. He lost all his means and we were forced to leave the place and move to a large town. Long and difficult years followed, of which, as it seems to me, nothing was worth remembering. I never felt really comfortable in the town. I believe now that I was never free from a longing for the beautiful woods near our home, in which (as one of my memories from those days tells me) I used to be able to run away too fast for my father to catch me, almost before I had learnt to walk. Those holidays, when I was seventeen, were my first holidays in the country, and, as I have said, I stayed with a family with whom we were friends and who had risen greatly in the world since our move. I could compare the comfort reigning there with our own style of living at home in the town. It is no use evading the subject any longer: I must admit that there was something else that excited me powerfully. I was seventeen, and in the family where I was staying there was a daughter of fifteen, with whom I immediately fell in love. It was my first calf-love and sufficiently intense, but I kept it completely secret. After a few days the girl went off to her school (from which she too was home for the holidays) and it was this separation after such a short acquaintance that first brought my longings to a really high pitch. I passed many hours in solitary walks through the lovely woods that I had found once more and spent my time building castles in the air. These, strangely enough, were not concerned with the future but sought to improve the past. If only the smash had not occurred! If only I had stopped at home and grown up in the country and grown as strong as the young men in the house, the brothers of my love! And then if only I had followed my father's profession and had married her at last—for I should have known her intimately all those years! I had not the slightest doubt, of course, that in the circumstances created by my imagination I should have loved her just as passionately as I really seemed to then. A strange thing. For when I see her now from time to time—she happens to have married someone here—she is quite exceptionally indifferent to me. Yet I can remember quite well for what a long time afterwards I was affected by the yellow colour of the dress she was wearing when we first met, whenever I saw the same colour anywhere else.'

That sounds very much like your parenthetical remark to the effect that you are no longer fond of the common dandelion. Do you not suspect that there may be a connection between the yellow of the girl's dress and the unnaturally distinct yellow of the flowers in your childhood scene?

'Possibly. But it was not the same yellow. The dress was more of a yellowish brown, more like the colour of wall-flowers. However, I can at least let you have an intermediate idea which may serve your purpose. At a later date, while I was in the Alps, I saw how certain flowers which have light colouring in the lowlands take on darker shades at high altitudes. Unless I am greatly mistaken, there is frequently to be found in mountainous regions a flower which is very similar to the dandelion but which is dark yellow and would exactly agree in colour with the dress of the girl I was so fond of. But I have not finished yet. I now come to a

second occasion which stirred up in me the impressions
of my childhood and which dates from a time not far
distant from the first. I was seventeen when I revisited
my birthplace. Three years later during my holidays I
visited my uncle and met once again the children who
had been my first playmates, the same two cousins, the
boy a year older than I am, and the girl of the same age
as myself, who appear in the childhood scene with the
dandelions. This family had left my birthplace at the
same time as we did and had become prosperous in a
far-distant city.'

And did you once more fall in love—with your
cousin this time—and indulge in a new set of phantasies?

'No, things turned out differently. By then I was at
the University and I was a slave to my books. I had
nothing left over for my cousin. So far as I know I had
no similar phantasies on that occasion. But I believe
that my father and my uncle had concocted a plan by
which I was to exchange the abstruse subject of my
studies for one of more practical value, settle down, after
my studies were completed, in the place where my uncle
lived, and marry my cousin. No doubt when they saw
how absorbed I was in my own intentions the plan was
dropped; but I fancy I must certainly have been aware
of its existence. It was not until later, when I was a
newly-fledged man of science and hard pressed by the
burdens of life and when I had to wait so long before
finding a post here, that I must sometimes have reflected
that my father had meant well in planning this marriage
for me to make good the loss in which the original
catastrophe had involved my whole existence.'

Then I am inclined to believe that the childhood
scene we are considering emerged at this time, when you
were struggling for your daily bread—provided, that is,
that you can confirm my idea that it was during this same
period that you first made the acquaintance of the Alps.

'Yes, that is so: mountaineering was the one enjoyment that I allowed myself at that time. But I still
cannot grasp your point.'

I am coming to it at once. The element on which you put most stress in your childhood scene was the fact of the country-made bread tasting so delicious. It seems clear that this idea, which amounted almost to an hallucination, corresponded to your phantasy of the comfortable life you would have led if you had stayed at home and married this girl [in the yellow dress]—or, in symbolic language, of how sweet the bread would have tasted for which you had to struggle so hard in your later years. The yellow of the flowers, too, points to the same girl. But there are also elements in the childhood scene which can only be related to the *second* phantasy —of being married to your cousin. Throwing away the flowers in exchange for bread strikes me as not a bad disguise for the scheme your father had for you: you were to give up your unpractical ideals and take on a 'bread and butter' occupation, were you not?

'It seems then that I amalgamated the two sets of phantasies of how my life could have been more comfortable—the "yellow" and the "country-made bread" from the one and the throwing-away of the flowers and the actual persons concerned from the other.'

Yes. You projected the two phantasies on to one another and made a childhood memory of them. The element about the alpine flowers is as it were a stamp giving the date of manufacture. I can assure you that people often construct such things unconsciously— almost like works of fiction.

'But if that is so, there was *no* childhood memory, but only a phantasy projected back into childhood. A feeling tells me, though, that the scene is genuine. How is that to be accounted for?'

There is in general no guarantee of the data produced by our memory. But I am ready to agree with you that the scene is genuine. If so, you selected it from innumerable others of a similar or different kind because, on account of its subject-matter (which in itself was indifferent) it was well adapted to represent the two phantasies, which were important enough to you. A recollection of this kind, whose value lies in the fact that it represents in the memory impressions and thoughts of a later date whose subject-matter is connected with its own by symbolic or similar links, may appropriately be called a *'screen memory'*. In any case you will cease to feel any surprise that this scene should so often recur to your mind. It can no longer be regarded as an innocent one since, as we have discovered, it is calculated to illustrate the most momentous turning-points in your life, the influence of the two most powerful motive forces—hunger and love.

'Yes, it represented hunger well enough. But what about love?'

In the yellow of the flowers, I mean. But I cannot deny that in this childhood scene of yours love is represented far less prominently than I should have expected from my previous experience.

'No. You are mistaken. The essence of it is its representation of love. Now I understand for the first time. Think for a moment! Taking flowers away from a girl means to deflower her. What a contrast between the boldness of this phantasy and my bashfulness on the first occasion and my indifference on the second.'

I can assure you that youthful bashfulness habitually has as its complement bold phantasies of that sort.

'But in that case the phantasy would not be a conscious one that I can remember, but an unconscious one that has transformed itself into these childhood memories?'

Unconscious thoughts which are a prolongation of conscious ones. You think to yourself 'If I had married so-and-so', and behind the thought there is an impulse to form a picture of what the 'being married' really is.

'I can go on with it now myself. The most seductive part of the whole subject for a young scapegrace is the picture of the marriage night. (What does he care about what comes afterwards?) But that picture cannot venture out into the light of day: the dominating mood of diffidence and of respect towards the girl keeps it suppressed. So it remains unconscious—'

And is toned down into the childhood memory. You are quite right. It is precisely the coarsely sensual element in the phantasy which explains why it does not develop into a *conscious* phantasy but must be content to find its way allusively and under a flowery disguise into a childhood scene.

'But why precisely into a *childhood* scene, I should like to know?'

On account of its innocence, perhaps. Can you imagine a greater contrast to these designs for gross sexual aggression than childish pranks? However, there are more general grounds that have a decisive influence in bringing about the toning down of repressed thoughts and wishes into childhood memories, for you will find the same thing invariably happening in hysterical patients. It seems, moreover, as though the recollection of the remote past is in itself facilitated by some pleasurable motive: *forsan et haec olim meminisse juvabit.*

'If that is so, I have lost all faith in the genuineness of the dandelion scene. This is how I look at it: On the two occasions in question, and with the support of very comprehensible realistic motives, the thought occurred to me: "If you had married this or that girl, your life would have become much pleasanter." The sensual current in my mind took the thought contained in the conditional clause or protasis and repeated it in images of a kind capable of giving that same sensual current satisfaction. This second version of the thought remained unconscious on account of its incompatibility with the dominant sexual disposition; but this very fact of its remaining unconscious enabled it to persist in my mind long after changes in the real situation had quite got rid of the first version. In accordance, as you say, with a general law, the clause that had remained un-

conscious. With this end in view it had to undergo a
fresh transformation, or rather two fresh transformations. One of these removed the objectionable element
from the protasis by expressing it figuratively; the
second forced the apodosis into a shape capable of
visual representation—using for the purpose the intermediary ideas of "bread" and "bread-and-butter occupation". I see that by producing a phantasy like this I
was providing, as it were, a fulfilment of the two
suppressed wishes—for deflowering a girl and for
material comfort. But now that I have given such a
complete account of the motives that led to my producing the dandelion phantasy, I cannot help conclud-
ing that what I am dealing with is something that never
happened at all but has been unjustifiably smuggled in
among my childhood memories.'

I see that I must take up the defence of its genuineness. You are going too far. You have accepted my
assertion that every suppressed phantasy of this kind
tends to be toned down into a childhood scene. But
suppose now that this cannot occur unless there is a
memory-trace the subject-matter of which offers the
phantasy a point of contact—comes, as it were, halfway to meet it. Once a point of contact of this kind has
been found—in the present instance it was the deflowering, the taking away of the flowers—the remaining subject-matter of the phantasy is remodelled with
the help of every legitimate intermediate idea—take the
bread as an example—till it can find further points of
contact with the subject-matter of the childhood scene.
It is very possible that in the course of this process the
childhood scene itself also undergoes changes; I regard
it as certain that falsifications of memory may be
brought about in this way. In your case the childhood
scene seems only to have had some of its lines engraved
more deeply: think of the over-emphasis on the yellow
and the exaggerated niceness of the bread. But the raw
material was utilizable. If that had not been so, it would
not have been possible for this particular memory,

rather than any others, to force its way forward into consciousness. No such scene would have occurred
to you as a childhood memory, or perhaps some other
one would have—for you know how easily your intelligence can build connecting bridges from any one point
to any other. And apart from your own subjective feeling, which I am not inclined to undervalue, there is
another thing that speaks in favour of the genuineness
of your dandelion memory. It contains elements which
have not been solved by what you have told me and
which do not in fact fit in with the scene required by the
phantasy. For instance, your boy cousin helping you to
rob the little girl of her flowers—can you make any
sense of the idea of being helped in deflowering someone? or of the peasant-woman and the nursemaid in
front of the cottage?

'Not that I can see.'

So the phantasy does not coincide completely with
the childhood scene. It is only based upon it at certain
points. That argues in favour of the childhood memory
being genuine.

'Do you think an interpretation like this of an apparently innocent childhood memory is often applicable?'

Very often, in my experience. Shall we amuse ourselves by seeing whether the two examples given by the
Henris can be interpreted as screen memories concealing subsequent experiences and wishes? I mean the
memory of a table laid for a meal with a basin of ice on
it, which was supposed to have some connection with
the death of the subject's grandmother, and the other
memory of a child breaking off the branch of a tree
while he was on a walk and of his being helped to do it
by someone.

He reflected for a little and then answered: 'I can
make nothing of the first one. It is most probably a case
of displacement at work; but the intermediate steps are
beyond conjecture. As for the second case, I should
be prepared to give an interpretation, if only the person
concerned had not been a Frenchman.'

c

Now it is my turn not to understand. What difference would that make?

'A great deal of difference, since what provides the intermediate step between a screen memory and what it conceals is likely to be a verbal expression. In German "to pull one off" is a very common vulgar term for masturbation. The scene would then be putting back into early childhood a seduction to masturbation—someone was helping him to do it—which in fact occurred at a later period. But even so, it does not fit, for in the childhood scene there were a number of other people present.'

Whereas his seduction to masturbate must have occurred in solitude and secrecy. It is just that contrast that inclines me to accept your view: it serves once again to make the scene innocent. Do you know what it means when in a dream we see 'a lot of strangers', as happens so often in dreams of nakedness in which we feel so terribly embarrassed? Nothing more nor less than—secrecy, which there again is expressed by its opposite. However, our interpretation remains a joke, since we have no idea whether a Frenchman would recognize an allusion to masturbation in the words *casser une branche d'un arbre* or in some suitably emended phrase.

This analysis, which I have reproduced as accurately as possible, will, I hope, have to some extent clarified the concept of a 'screen memory' as one which owes its value as a memory not to its own subject-matter but to the relation existing between that subject-matter and some other, suppressed psychical material. Different classes of screen memories can be distinguished according to the nature of that relation. We have found examples of two of these classes among what are described as the earliest memories of childhood—that is, if we include under the heading of screen memories the incomplete childhood scenes which are innocent by very reason of their incompleteness. It is to be anticipated that screen memories will also be formed from remnants of memories relating to later life as well. Anyone who bears in mind their distinctive feature—namely that they are extremely well remembered but that their subject-matter is completely indifferent—will easily recall a number of examples of the sort from his own memory. Some of these screen memories dealing with events later in life owe their importance to a connection with experiences in early youth which have remained suppressed. The connection, that is, is the reverse of the one in the case which I have analysed, where a childhood memory was accounted for by later experiences. A screen memory may be described as 'retrogressive' or 'prospective' according as the one chronological relation or the other holds between the screen and the thing screened-off. From another point of view, we can distinguish positive screen memories from negative ones (or refractory memories) whose subject-matter stands in a contrary relation to the suppressed material. The whole subject deserves a thorough examination; but I must content myself with pointing out what complicated processes—processes, incidentally, which are altogether analogous to the formation of hysterical symptoms—are involved in the building up of our store of memories.

Our earliest childhood memories will always be a subject of special interest because the problem mentioned at the beginning of this paper (of how it comes about that the impressions which are of most significance for our whole future usually leave no pictures behind in our memory) leads us to reflect upon the origin of conscious memories in general. We shall no doubt be inclined at first to separate off the screen memories which are the subject of this study as heterogeneous elements among the traces of childhood recollections. As regards the remaining pictures, we shall probably adopt the simple view that they arise simultaneously with an experience as an immediate consequence of the impression it makes and that thereafter they recur from time to time in accordance with the familiar laws of reproduction. Closer observation, however, reveals certain features which do not altogether tally with this view. Above all, there is the following point. In the majority of significant and in other respects unimpeachable childhood scenes the subject sees himself in the recollection as a child, with the knowledge that this child is himself; he sees this child, however, as an observer from outside the scene would see him. The Henris duly draw attention to the fact that many of those taking part in their investigation expressly emphasized this peculiarity of their childhood scenes. Now it is evident that such a picture cannot be an exact repetition of the impression that was originally received. For the subject was then in the middle of the situation and was attending not to himself but to the external world.

Whenever in a memory the subject himself appears in this way as an object among other objects, this contrast between the acting and the recollecting ego may be taken as evidence that the original impression has been worked over. It looks as though a memory trace from childhood had here been retrospectively translated into a plastic and visual state at a later date—the date of the memory's 'revival'. But no reproduction of the original impression has ever entered the subject's consciousness.

There is another fact that affords even more convincing evidence in favour of this second view. Out of a number of childhood memories of significant experiences, all of them of similar distinctness and clarity, there will be some scenes which, when they are tested (for instance by the recollections of adults), turn out to have been falsified. Not that they are complete inventions; they are false in the sense that they have shifted an event to a place where it did not occur—this is the case in one of the instances quoted by the Henris—or that they have merged two people into one or substituted one for the other, or the scenes as a whole give signs of being combinations of two separate experiences. Simple inaccuracy of recollection does not play any

considerable part here, in view of the high degree of
sensory intensity shown by the pictures and the
efficiency of the function of memory in the young; close
investigation shows rather that these falsifications of
memory are tendentious, that is, they serve the purposes of the repression and replacement of objectionable or disagreeable impressions. It follows, therefore,
that these falsified memories too must have originated
at a period of life when it has become possible for conflicts of this kind and impulses towards repression to
have made a place for themselves in mental life—far
later, therefore, than the period to which their subject-
matter belongs. But in these cases too the falsified
memory is the first that we become aware of: the raw
material of memory-traces out of which it was forged
remains unknown to us in its original form.

The recognition of this fact must diminish the distinction we have drawn between screen memories and
other memories derived from our childhood. It may
indeed be questioned whether we have any memories at
all *from* our childhood: memories *relating to* our childhood may be all that we possess. Our childhood memories show us our earliest years not as they were but as
they appeared at the later periods when the memories
were revived. In these periods of revival, the childhood
memories did not, as people are accustomed to say,
emerge; they were *formed* at that time. And a number of
motives, which had no concern with historical accuracy,
had their part in thus forming them as well as in the
selection of the memories themselves.

V

A PREMONITORY DREAM FULFILLED[1]

(1899)

FRAU B., an estimable woman who moreover possesses a critical sense, told me in another connection and without the slightest *arrière pensée* that once some years ago she dreamt she had met Dr. K., a friend and former family doctor of hers, in the Kärntnerstrasse[2] in front of Hies's shop. The next morning, while she was walking along the same street, she in fact met the person in question at the very spot she had dreamt of. So much for my theme. I will only add that no subsequent event proved the importance of this miraculous coincidence, which cannot therefore be accounted for by what lay in the future.

Analysis of the dream was helped by questioning, which established the fact that there was no evidence of her having had any recollection at all of the dream on the morning after she dreamt it, until after her walk— evidence such as her having written the dream down or told it to someone before it was fulfilled. On the contrary, she was obliged to accept the following account of what happened, which seems to me more plausible, without raising any objection to it. She was walking along the Kärntnerstrasse one morning and met her old family doctor in front of Hies's shop. On seeing him she felt convinced that she had dreamt the night before of having this very meeting at that precise spot. According-ing to the rules that apply to the interpretation of neurotic symptoms, her conviction must have been

---

[1] [The manuscript is dated November 10, 1899, six days after the publication of *The Interpretation of Dreams*. First published posthumously in *Schriften aus dem Nachlass*, 1941 (*Ges. Schr.*, **17**, 21). The same incident is reported very much more briefly in Chapter XII of *The Psychopathology of Everyday Life* (1904). Translation by James Strachey.]

[2] [The principal street in Vienna.]

justified; its content may, however, require to be re-
interpreted.

The following is an episode with which Dr. K. is connected from Frau B.'s earlier life. When she was young
she was married, without her wholehearted consent, to
an elderly but wealthy man. A few years later he lost
his money, fell ill of tuberculosis and died. For many
years the young woman supported herself and her sick
husband by giving music lessons. Among her friends in
misfortune was her family doctor, Dr. K., who devoted
himself to looking after her husband and helped her in
finding her first pupils. Another friend was a barrister,
also a Dr. K., who put the chaotic affairs of the ruined
merchant in order, while at the same time he made love
to the young woman and—for the first and last time—
set her passion aflame. This love affair brought her no
real happiness, for the scruples created by her upbringing
and her cast of mind interfered with her complete surrender while she was married and later when she was a
widow. In the same connection in which she told me
the dream, she also told me of a real occurrence dating
from this unhappy period of her life, an occurrence
which in her opinion was a remarkable coincidence.
She was in her room, kneeling on the floor with her head
buried in a chair and sobbing in passionate longing for
her friend and helper the barrister, when at that very
moment the door opened and he came in to visit her.
We shall find nothing at all remarkable in this coincidence when we consider how often she thought of
him and how often he probably visited her. Moreover,
accidents which seem preconcerted like this are to be
found in every love story. Nevertheless this coincidence
was probably the true content of her dream and the sole
basis of her conviction that it had come true.

Between the scene in which her wish had been fulfilled and the time of the dream more than twenty-five
years elapsed. In the meantime Frau B. had become the
widow of a second husband who left her with a child and
a fortune. The old lady's affection was still centred on

Dr. K., who was now her adviser and the administrator of her estate and whom she saw frequently. Let us suppose that during the few days before the dream she had been expecting a visit from him, but that this had not taken place—he was no longer so pressing as he used to be. She may then have quite well had a nostalgic dream one night which took her back to the old days. Her dream was probably of a *rendez-vous* at the time of her love affair, and the chain of her dream-thoughts carried her back to the occasion when, without any pre-arrangement, he had come in at the very moment at which she had been longing for him. She probably had dreams of this kind quite often now; they were a part of the belated punishment with which a woman pays for her youthful cruelty. But such dreams—derivatives of a suppressed current of thought, filled with memories of *rendez-vous* of which, since her second marriage, she no longer liked to think—such dreams were put aside on waking. And that was what happened to our ostensibly prophetic dream. She then went out, and in the Kärntnerstrasse, at a spot which was in itself indifferent, she met her old family doctor, Dr. K. It was a very long time since she had seen him. He was intimately associated with the excitements of that happy-unhappy time. He too had been a helper, and we may suppose that he had been used in her thoughts, and perhaps in her dreams as well, as a screen figure behind which she concealed the better-loved figure of the other Dr. K. This meeting now revived her recollection of the dream. She must have thought: 'Yes, I had a dream last night of my *rendez-vous* with Dr. K.' But this recollection had to undergo the distortion which the dream escaped only because it had been completely forgotten. She inserted the indifferent K. (who had reminded her of the dream) in place of the beloved K. The content of the dream—the *rendez-vous*—was transferred to a belief that she had dreamt of that particular spot, for a *rendez-vous* consists in two people coming to the same spot at the same time. And if she then had an impression that a dream had been fulfilled, she was only giving effect in that way to her memory of the scene in which she had longed in her misery for him to come and her longing had at once been fulfilled.

Thus the creation of a dream after the event, which alone makes prophetic dreams possible, is nothing other than a form of censoring, which enables the dream to make its way through into consciousness.

10 *Nov.* 99.

VI

FAMILY ROMANCES[1]

(1909)

THE freeing of an individual, as he grows up, from the authority of his parents is one of the most necessary though one of the most painful results brought about by the course of his development. It is quite essential that that liberation should occur and it may be presumed that it has been to some extent achieved by everyone who has reached a normal state. Indeed, the whole progress of society rests upon the opposition between successive generations. On the other hand, there is a class of neurotics whose condition is recognizably determined by their having failed in this task.

For a small child his parents are at first the only authority and the source of all belief. The child's most intense and most momentous wish during these early years is to be like his parents (that is, the parent of his own sex) and to be big like his father and mother. But as intellectual growth increases, the child cannot help discovering by degrees the category to which his parents belong. He gets to know other parents and compares them with his own, and so comes to doubt the incomparable and unique quality which he has attributed to them. Small events in the child's life which make him feel dissatisfied afford him provocation for beginning to criticize his parents, and for using, in order to support his critical attitude, the knowledge which he has acquired that other parents are in some respects preferable to them. The psychology of the neuroses teaches us that, among other factors, the most intense impulses of sexual rivalry contribute to this result. A

---

[1] [Otto Rank's book *Der Mythus von der Geburt des Helden* (1909) included this note by Freud, which was reprinted under the title of 'Der Familienroman der Neurotiker', *Ges. Schr.*, **12**, 367, and *Ges. W.*, **7**, 227. Rank's book appeared in English as *The Myth of the Birth of the Hero* (1914). Present translation by James Strachey.]

feeling of being slighted is obviously what constitutes the subject-matter of such provocations. There are only too many occasions on which a child is slighted, or at least *feels* he has been slighted, on which he feels he is not receiving the whole of his parents' love, and, most of all, on which he feels regrets at having to share it with brothers and sisters. His sense that his own affection is not being fully reciprocated then finds a vent in the idea, which is often consciously recollected from early childhood, of being a step-child or an adopted child. People who have not developed neuroses very frequently remember occasions of this kind on which— usually as a result of something they have read—they thus interpreted and responded to their parents' hostile behaviour. But at this point the influence of sex is already in evidence, for a boy is far more inclined to feel hostile impulses towards his father than towards his mother and has a far more intense desire to get free from *him* than from *her*. In this respect the imagination of girls is apt to show itself much weaker. These consciously remembered mental impulses of childhood embody the factor which enables us to understand the nature of hero-myths.

The later stage in the development of the neurotic's estrangement from his parents, begun in this manner, might be described as 'the neurotic's family romance'. It is seldom remembered consciously but can almost always be revealed by psycho-analysis. For a quite specific form of imaginative activity is one of the essential characteristics of neurotics and also of all comparatively highly gifted people. This activity emerges first in children's play, and then, starting roughly from the period before puberty, takes over the topic of family relations. A characteristic example of this particular kind of phantasy is to be seen in the familiar day-dreams[1] which persist far beyond puberty. If these

---

[1] Cf. 'Hysterical Phantasies and their Relation to Bisexuality' (1908), *Collected Papers*, **2**, 51, where a reference will be found to the literature of the subject.

day-dreams are carefully examined, they are found to serve as the fulfilment of wishes and as a correction of actual life. They have two principal aims, erotic and ambitious—though an erotic aim is usually concealed behind the latter too. At about the period I have mentioned, then, the child's imagination becomes engaged in the task of getting free from the parents of whom he now has such a low opinion and of replacing them by others, occupying, as a rule, a higher social station. He will make use in this connection of any opportune coincidences from his actual experience, such as his becoming acquainted with the Lord of the Manor or some landed proprietor if he lives in the country or with some member of the aristocracy if he lives in town. Chance occurrences of this kind arouse the child's envy, which finds expression in a phantasy in which both his parents are replaced by others of better birth. The technique used in carrying out phantasies like this (which are, of course, conscious at this period) depends upon the ingenuity and the material which the child has at his disposal. There is also the question of whether the phantasies are worked out with greater or less effort to obtain verisimilitude. This stage is reached at a time at which the child is still in ignorance of the sexual determinants of procreation.

When presently the child comes to know of the various kinds of sexual relations between fathers and mothers and realizes that *'pater semper incertus est'*, while the mother is *'certissima'*, the family romance undergoes a peculiar curtailment: it contents itself with exalting the child's father, but no longer casts any doubts on his maternal origin, which is regarded as something unalterable. This second (sexual) stage of the family romance is actuated by another motive as well, which is absent in the first (asexual) stage. The child, having learnt about sexual processes, tends to picture to himself erotic situations and relations, the motive force behind this being his desire to bring his mother (who is the subject of the most intense sexual curiosity) into situations of secret infidelity and into secret love-affairs. In this way the child's phantasies, which started by being, as it were, asexual, are brought up to the level of his later knowledge.

Moreover the motive of revenge and retaliation, which was in the background at the earlier stage, is also to be found at the later one. It is, as a rule, precisely these neurotic children who were punished by their parents for sexual naughtiness and who later revenge themselves on their parents by means of phantasies of this kind.

A younger child is very specially inclined to use imaginative stories such as these in order to rob those born before him of their prerogatives—in a way which reminds one of historical intrigues; and he often has no hesitation in attributing to his mother as many fictitious love-affairs as he himself has competitors. An interesting variant of the family romance may then appear, in which the hero and author returns to legitimacy himself while his brothers and sisters are got out of the way by being bastardized. So too if there are any other particular interests at work they can direct the course to be taken by the family romance; for its many-sidedness and its great range of applicability enable it to meet every sort of requirement. In this way, for instance, the young phantasy-builder can get rid of his forbidden degree of kinship with one of his sisters if he finds himself sexually attracted by her.

If anyone is inclined to turn away in horror from this depravity of the childish heart or feels tempted, indeed, to dispute the possibility of such things, he should observe that these works of fiction, which seem so full of hostility, are none of them really so badly intended, and that they still preserve, under a slight disguise, the child's original affection for his parents. The faithlessness and ingratitude are only apparent. If we examine in detail the commonest of these imaginative romances, the replacement of both parents or of the father alone by grander people, we find that these new and aristocratic parents are equipped with attributes that are derived entirely from real recollections of the actual and humble ones; so that in fact the child is not getting rid of his father but exalting him. Indeed the whole effort at replacing the real father by a superior one is only an expression of the child's longing for the happy, vanished days when his father seemed to him the noblest and strongest of men and his mother the dearest and loveliest of women. He is turning away from the father whom he knows to-day to the father in whom he believed in the earlier years of his childhood; and his phantasy is no more than the expression of a regret that those happy days have gone. Thus in these phantasies the over-valuation that characterizes a child's earliest years comes into its own again. An interesting contribution to this subject is afforded by the study of dreams. We learn from their interpretation that even in later years, if the Emperor and Empress appear in dreams, those exalted personages stand for the dreamer's father and mother.[1] So that the child's over-valuation of his parents also survives in the dreams of normal adults.

[1] Cf. my *Interpretation of Dreams* (1900). [English translation, revised ed. (1932), 336.]

VII

ON TRANSIENCE[1]

(1915)

NOT long ago I went on a summer walk through a smiling countryside in the company of a taciturn friend and of a young but already famous poet. The poet admired the beauty of the scene around us but felt no joy in it. He was disturbed by the thought that all this beauty was fated to extinction, that it would vanish when winter came, like all human beauty and all the beauty and splendour that men have created or may create. All that he would otherwise have loved and admired seemed to him to be shorn of its worth by the transience which was its doom.

The proneness to decay of all that is beautiful and perfect can, as we know, give rise to two different impulses in the mind. The one leads to the aching despondency felt by the young poet, while the other leads to rebellion against the fact asserted. No! it is impossible that all this loveliness of Nature and Art, of the world of our sensations and of the world without, will really fade away into nothing. It would be too senseless and too presumptuous to believe it. Somehow or other this loveliness must be able to persist and to escape all the powers of destruction.

But this demand for immortality is a product of our wishes too unmistakable to lay claim to reality: what is painful may none the less be true. I could not see my way to dispute the transience of all things, nor could I insist upon an exception in favour of what is beautiful

[1] ['Vergänglichkeit' was written in November, 1915, at the request of the Berlin Goethebund, as a contribution to a volume of collected essays by various writers to raise a fund for establishing public libraries in East Prussia. The volume was published in 1916 under the title of *Das Land Goethes*. The present essay was reprinted *Ges. Schr.*, **11**, 291, and *Ges. W.*, **10**, 358. Translation, reprinted from *Int. J. Psycho-Anal.*, **23** (1942), 84, by James Strachey.]

and perfect. But I did dispute the pessimistic poet's view that the transience of what is beautiful involves any loss in its worth.

On the contrary, an increase! Transience value is scarcity value in time. Limitation in the possibility of an enjoyment raises the value of the enjoyment. It was incomprehensible, I declared, that the thought of the transience of beauty should interfere with our joy in it. As regards the beauty of Nature, each time it is destroyed by winter it comes again next year, so that in relation to the length of our lives it can in fact be regarded as eternal. The beauty of the human form and face vanish for ever in the course of our own lives, but their evanescence only lends them a fresh charm. A flower that blossoms only for a single night does not seem to us on that account less lovely. Nor can I understand any better why the beauty and perfection of a work of art or of an intellectual achievement should lose its worth because of its temporal limitation. A time may indeed come when the pictures and statues which we admire to-day will crumble to dust, or a race of men may follow us who no longer understand the works of our poets and thinkers, or a geological epoch may even arrive when all animate life upon the earth ceases; but since the value of all this beauty and perfection is determined only by its significance for our own emotional lives, it has no need to survive us and is therefore independent of absolute duration.

These considerations appeared to me incontestable; but I noticed that I had made no impression either upon the poet or upon my friend. My failure led me to infer that some powerful emotional factor was at work which was disturbing their judgement, and I believed later that I had discovered what it was. What spoilt their enjoyment of beauty must have been a revolt in their minds against mourning. The idea that all this beauty was transient was giving these two sensitive minds a foretaste of mourning over its decease; and, since the mind instinctively recoils from anything that is painful, they felt their enjoyment of beauty interfered with by thoughts of its transience.

Mourning over the loss of something that we have loved or admired seems so natural to the layman that he regards it as self-evident. But to psychologists mourning is a great riddle, one of those phenomena which cannot themselves be explained but to which other obscurities can be traced back. We possess, as it seems, a certain amount of capacity for love—what we call libido—which in the earliest stages of development is directed towards our own ego. Later, though still at a very early time, this libido is diverted from the ego on to objects, which are thus in a sense taken into our ego. If the objects are destroyed or if they are lost to us, our capacity for love (our libido) is once more liberated; and it can then either take other objects instead or can temporarily return to the ego. But why it is that this detachment of libido from its objects should be such a painful process is a mystery to us and we have not hitherto been able to frame any hypothesis to account for it. We only see that libido clings to its objects and will not renounce those that are lost even when a substitute lies ready to hand. Such then is mourning.

My conversation with the poet took place in the summer before the war. A year later the war broke out and robbed the world of its beauties. It destroyed not only the beauty of the countrysides through which it passed and the works of art which it met with on its path but it also shattered our pride in the achievements of our civilization, our admiration for many philosophers and artists and our hopes of a final triumph over the differences between nations and races. It tarnished the lofty impartiality of our science, it revealed our instincts in all their nakedness and let loose the evil spirits within us which we thought had been tamed for ever by centuries of continuous education by the noblest minds. It made our country small again and made the rest of the world far remote. It robbed us of very much that we had loved, and showed us how

ephemeral was much that we had regarded as immutable.

We cannot be surprised that our libido, thus bereft
of so many of its objects, has clung with all the greater
intensity to what is left to us, that our love of our
country, our affection for those nearest us and our pride
in what is common to us have suddenly grown stronger.
But have those other possessions, which we have now
lost, really ceased to have any worth for us because they
have proved so perishable and so unresistant? To many
of us this seems to be so, but once more wrongly, in my
view. I believe that those who think thus, and seem
ready to make a permanent renunciation because what
was precious has proved not to be lasting, are simply in
a state of mourning for what is lost. Mourning, as we
know, however painful it may be, comes to a spontaneous end. When it has renounced everything that has
been lost, then it has consumed itself, and our libido is
once more free (in so far as we are still young and active)
to replace the lost objects by fresh ones equally or still
more precious. It is to be hoped that the same will be
true of the losses caused by this war. When once the
mourning is over, it will be found that our high opinion
of the riches of civilization has lost nothing from our
discovery of their fragility. We shall build up again all
that war has destroyed, and perhaps on firmer ground
and more lastingly than before.

VIII

FOUR PREFACES

(A) PSYCHO-ANALYSIS AND WAR NEUROSES[1]
(1919)

THIS small book on the war neuroses—the opening volume of our 'Internationale Psychoanalytische Bibliothek'—deals with a subject which until recently enjoyed the advantage of being in the highest degree topical. When it came up for discussion at the Fifth Psycho-Analytical Congress, which was held in Budapest in September, 1918, official representatives of the highest quarters of the Central European Powers were present as observers at the papers and other proceedings. The hopeful result of this first contact was that the establishment of psycho-analytical Centres was approved, at which analytically trained physicians would have leisure and opportunity for studying the nature of these puzzling disorders and the therapeutic effect exercised on them by psycho-analysis. Before these proposals could be put into effect, the war came to an end, the state organizations collapsed and interest in the war neuroses gave place to other concerns. It is, however, a significant fact that, when war conditions ceased to operate, the greater number of the neurotic disturbances brought about by the war simultaneously vanished. The opportunity for a thorough investigation of these affections was thus unluckily lost—though, we must add, the early recurrence of such an opportunity is not a thing to be desired.

But this episode, though it is now closed, was not without an important influence on the spread of psycho-

[1] [*Zur Psychoanalyse der Kriegsneurosen*, to which this is the preface and which also contained contributions by Ferenczi, Abraham, Simmel and Ernest Jones, was published by the Internationaler Psychoanalytischer Verlag in 1919. In 1921 it appeared in English under the title of *Psycho-Analysis and the War Neuroses*. This paper was reprinted *Ges. Schr.*, 11, 252, and *Ges. W.*, 12, 321. Present translation by James Strachey.]

analysis. Medical men who had hitherto held back from
any approach to psycho-analytic theories were brought
into closer contact with them when, in the course of
their duties as army doctors, they were obliged to deal
with war neuroses. The reader will be able to gather
from Ferenczi's paper with what hesitations and under
what disguises these closer contacts were made. Some
of the factors which psycho-analysis had recognized
and described long before as being at work in peace-
time neuroses—the psychogenic origin of the symptoms,
the importance of *unconscious* instinctual impulses, the
part played in dealing with mental conflicts by the
primary benefit from being ill ('the flight into illness')—
were observed to be present equally in the war neuroses
and were accepted almost universally. Simmel's studies
show, too, what successes could be achieved by treating
war neurotics by the method of catharsis, which, as we
know, was the first step towards the psycho-analytic
technique.

There is, however, no need to consider that these
approaches to psycho-analysis imply any reconciliation
or any appeasement of opposition. Suppose someone has
hitherto rejected the whole of a complex of inter-
dependent propositions, but now suddenly finds himself
in a position to convince himself of the truth of one
portion of the whole. It might be expected that he
will begin to hesitate about his opposition in general and will permit himself some degree of polite
expectation that the other portion (upon which he has
had no personal experience and can consequently
form no judgement of his own) may also turn out to be
true. This other portion of psycho-analytic theory,
with which the study of the war neuroses did not come
into contact, is to the effect that the motive forces
which are expressed in the formation of symptoms are
sexual and that neuroses arise from a conflict between
the ego and the sexual instincts which it repudiates.
'Sexuality' in this context is to be understood in the
extended sense in which it is used in psycho-analysis

and is not to be confounded with the narrower concept of 'genitality'. Now it is quite true, as Ernest Jones remarks in his contribution to this volume, that this portion of the theory has not yet been proved to apply to the war neuroses. The work that might prove it has not yet been taken in hand. It may be that the war neuroses are altogether unsuitable material for the purpose. But the opponents of psycho-analysis, whose dislike of sexuality is evidently stronger than their logic, have been in a hurry to proclaim that the investigation of the war neuroses has finally disproved this portion of psycho-analytic theory. They have been guilty here of a slight confusion. If the investigation of the war neuroses (and a very superficial one at that) has *not shown* that the sexual theory of the neuroses is *correct*, that is something very different from its *showing* that that theory is *incorrect*. With the help of an impartial attitude and a little good will, it should not be hard to find the way to a further clarification of the subject.

The war neuroses, in so far as they are distinguished from the ordinary neuroses of peace-time by special characteristics, are to be regarded as traumatic neuroses whose occurrence has been made possible or has been promoted by a conflict in the ego. Abraham's paper affords good evidence for this conflict, which has also been recognized by the English and American writers quoted by Jones. The conflict is between the soldier's old peaceful ego and his new warlike one, and it becomes acute as soon as the peace-ego realizes what danger it runs of losing its life owing to the rashness of its newly formed, parasitic double. It would be equally true to say that the old ego is protecting itself from a mortal danger by taking flight into a traumatic neurosis or that it is defending itself against the new ego which it sees is threatening its life. Thus the precondition of the war neuroses, the soil that nourishes them, would seem to be a national [conscript] army; there would be no possibility of their arising in an army of professional soldiers or mercenaries.

Apart from this, the war neuroses are only traumatic neuroses, which, as we know, occur in peace-time too after terrifying experiences or severe accidents, without any reference to a conflict in the ego.

The theory of the sexual aetiology of the neuroses, or, as we prefer to say, the libido theory of the neuroses, was originally put forward only in relation to the trans-ference neuroses of peace-time and is easy to demon-strate in their case by the use of the technique of analysis. But its application to the other disorders which we later grouped together as the narcissistic neuroses already met with difficulties. An ordinary dementia praecox, a paranoia or a melancholia are essentially quite unsuitable material for demonstrating the validity of the libido theory or for serving as a first introduction to an understanding of it; and it is for that reason that psychiatrists, who neglect the transference neuroses, are unable to come to terms with it. But the traumatic neuroses of peace-time have always been regarded as the most refractory material of all in this respect; so that it was impossible for the emergence of the war neuroses to introduce any new factor into the situation that already existed.

It only became possible to extend the libido theory to the narcissistic neuroses after the concept of a 'nar-cissistic libido' had been put forward and applied—a concept, that is, of a quantity of sexual energy attached to the ego itself and finding satisfaction in the ego just as satisfaction is usually found only in objects. This en-tirely legitimate development of the concept of sexuality promises to accomplish as much for the severer neuroses and for the psychoses as can be expected of a theory which is feeling its way forwards on an empirical basis. The traumatic neuroses of peace will also be fitted into the scheme as soon as a successful outcome has been reached of our investigations into the relations which undoubtedly exist between fright, anxiety and nar-cissistic libido.

The traumatic neuroses and war neuroses may

proclaim too loudly the effects of mortal danger and may be silent or speak only in muffled tones of the effects of frustration in love. But, on the other hand, the ordinary transference neuroses of peace-time set no aetiological store by the factor of mortal danger which, in the former class of neuroses, plays so mighty a part. It is even held that the peace-time neuroses are promoted by indulgence, good living and inactivity—which would afford an interesting contrast to the living-conditions under which the war neuroses develop. If they were to follow the example of their opponents, psycho-analysts, finding that their patients had fallen ill owing to frustration in love (owing to the claims of the libido being unsatisfied) would have to maintain that there can be no such things as danger-neuroses or that the disorders that appear after terrifying experiences are not neuroses. They have, of course, no notion of maintaining any such thing. On the contrary, a convenient possibility occurs to them of bringing the two apparently divergent sets of facts together under a single hypothesis. In traumatic and war neuroses the human ego is defending itself from a danger which threatens it from without or which is embodied in a shape assumed by the ego itself. In the transference neuroses of peace the enemy from which the ego is defending itself is actually the libido, whose demands seem to it to be menacing. In both cases the ego is afraid of being damaged—in the latter case by the libido and in the former by external violence. It might, indeed, be said that in the case of the war neuroses, in contrast to the pure traumatic neuroses and in approximation to the transference neuroses, what is feared is nevertheless an internal enemy. The theoretical difficulties standing in the way of a unifying hypothesis of this kind do not seem insuperable: it would after all be right and proper to describe repression, which lies at the basis of every neurosis, as a reaction to a trauma—as an elementary traumatic neurosis.

(B) THE EXCRETORY FUNCTIONS IN PSYCHO-ANALYSIS AND FOLKLORE[1]

(1913)

WHILE I was living in Paris in 1885 as a pupil of Charcot, what chiefly attracted me, apart from the great man's own lectures, were the demonstrations and addresses given by Brouardel. He used to show us from post-mortem material at the morgue how much there was which deserved to be known by doctors but of which science preferred to take no notice. On one occasion he was discussing the indications which enabled one to judge the social rank, character and origin of an unidentified body, and I heard him say: '*Les genoux sales sont le signe d'une fille honnête.*' He was suggesting that a girl's dirty knees bore witness to her virtue!

This lesson, that bodily cleanliness is far more readily associated with vice than with virtue, often occurred to me later on, when psycho-analytic work made me acquainted with the way in which civilized men to-day deal with the problem of their physical nature. They are evidently embarrassed by anything that reminds them too much of their animal origin. They feel like the 'more perfected angels' in the last scene of *Faust*, who complain:

> 'Uns bleibt ein Erdenrest
> zu tragen peinlich,
> und wär' er von Asbest,
> er ist nicht reinlich.'[2]

Since, however, they must necessarily remain far removed from such perfection, men have chosen to

---

[1] [This first appeared as a preface to a German translation of John G. Bourke's *Scatalogic Rites of All Nations* (Washington, 1891) which was issued under the title of *Der Unrat in Sitte, Brauch, Glauben und Gewohnheitsrecht der Völker* by F. S. Krauss and H. Ihm (Leipzig, 1913). Freud's preface was reprinted *Ges. Schr.*, **11**, 249, and *Ges. W.*, **10**, 453. Translation by James Strachey.]

[2] [Literally: 'We still have a trace of the Earth, which is distressing to bear; and though it were of asbestos it is not cleanly.']

evade the predicament by so far as possible denying the very existence of this inconvenient 'trace of the Earth', by concealing it from one another, and by withholding from it the attention and care which it might claim as an integrating component of their essential being. The wiser course would undoubtedly have been to admit it and to make as much improvement in it as its nature would allow.

It is far from being a simple matter to survey or describe the consequences involved in this way of treating the 'distressing trace of the Earth', of which the sexual and excretory functions may be considered the nucleus. It will be enough to mention a single one of these consequences, the one with which we are most concerned here: the fact that science is prohibited from dealing with these proscribed aspects of human life, so that anyone who studies such things is regarded as scarcely less 'improper' than someone who actually *does* improper things.

Nevertheless, psycho-analysis and folklore have not allowed themselves to be deterred from transgressing these prohibitions and have been able as a result to teach us all kinds of things that are indispensable for an understanding of human nature. If we limit ourselves here to what has been learnt about the excretory functions, it may be said that the chief finding from psycho-analytic research has been the fact that the human infant is obliged to recapitulate during the early part of his development the fluctuations in the attitude of the human race towards excremental matters which probably had their start when *homo sapiens* first raised himself off Mother Earth. In the earliest years of infancy there is as yet no trace of shame about the excretory functions or of disgust at excreta. Small children show great interest in these, just as they do in others of their bodily secretions; they like occupying themselves with them and can derive many kinds of pleasure from doing so. Excreta, regarded as parts of a child's own body and as products of his own organism,

have a share in the esteem—the narcissistic esteem, as
we should call it—with which he regards everything
relating to his self. Children are proud, as it were, of
their own excretions and make use of them to help in
asserting themselves against adults. Under the influence of education the coprophilic instincts and inclinations of children give way to repression; they learn to
keep them secret, to be ashamed of them and to feel
disgust at the objects themselves. Strictly speaking,
the disgust never goes so far as to apply to a child's own
excretions, but is content with repudiating them when
they are the products of other people. The interest
which has hitherto been attached to excrement is
carried over on to other objects—for instance, from
faeces on to money, which is late in acquiring significance for children. Important constituents in the formation of character are developed, or strengthened,
from the repression of coprophilic desires.

Psycho-analysis further shows that, to begin with,
excremental and sexual instincts are not distinct in
children. The divorce between them only occurs late
and it remains incomplete. Their original affinity,
which is established by the anatomy of the human body,
still makes itself felt in many ways in normal adults.
Finally, it should not be forgotten that these developments can no more be expected to yield a perfect result
than any others. Some portion of the old preferences
persist, some part of the coprophilic inclinations continue to operate in later life and are expressed in the
neuroses, perversions and bad habits of adults.

Folklore has adopted a quite different method of
research, and yet it has reached the same results as
psycho-analysis. It shows us how incompletely the
repression of coprophilic inclinations has been carried
out among various peoples at various times and how
closely at other cultural levels the treatment of excretory substances approximates to that practised by
children. It also demonstrates the persistent and indeed
ineradicable nature of coprophilic interests, by display-

ing to our astonished gaze the multiplicity of applications—in magical ritual, in tribal customs, in observ-
ances of religious cults and in the art of healing—by
which the old esteem for human excretions has found
new expression. The connection with sexual life also
seems to be fully preserved. This expansion of our
knowledge clearly involves no risk to our morality. The
major part of what is known of the role played by
excretions in human life has been brought together in
J. G. Bourke's *Scatalogic Rites of All Nations*. To make
it accessible to German readers is therefore not only a
courageous but also a meritorious undertaking.

(C) PSYCHO-ANALYSIS AND RELIGIOUS ORIGINS[1]

(1919)

PSYCHO-ANALYSIS was born out of medical necessity. It sprang from the need for bringing help to neurotic patients, who had found no relief from rest-cures, from the arts of hydropathy or from electricity. A most remarkable observation made by Josef Breuer had excited a hope that the more one understood of the hitherto unexplored origin of their symptoms the more extensive would be the help one could afford them. Thus it came about that psycho-analysis, which was originally a purely medical technique, was from the first led along the pathway of research, towards the discovery of causal chains at once far-reaching and recondite.

Its further course led it away from the study of the somatic determinants of nervous disease to an extent that was bewildering to physicians. Instead, it was brought into contact with the mental substance of human lives—the lives not only of the sick, but of the healthy, the normal and the supernormal. It had to deal with emotions and passions, and most of all with those which the poets never tire of depicting and celebrating—the emotions of love. It learnt to recognize the power of memories, the unsuspected importance of the years of childhood in shaping the adult, and the strength of wishes, which falsify human judgements and lay down fixed lines for human endeavour.

For a time psycho-analysis seemed fated to merge into psychology without being able to show why the

---

[1] [This first appeared as a preface to *Das Ritual*, the first volume, and the only one which has been published, of Theodor Reik's *Probleme der Religionspsychologie* (Vienna, 1919); reprinted *Ges. Schr.*, **11**, 256, and *Ges. W.*, **12**, 325. Reik's book (including this preface) appeared in English under the title of *Ritual* (London, 1931). Present translation by James Strachey.]

psychology of the sick differed from that of the normal. In the course of its advance, however, it came up against the problem of dreams, which are abnormal products of the mind created by normal men under regularly recurrent physiological conditions. When psycho-analysis had solved the problem of dreams, it had discovered in *unconscious* psychical processes the common ground in which the highest and the lowest of mental impulses have their roots and from which spring the most normal as well as the most morbid and erratic of mental achievements. The new picture of the workings of the mind began to grow ever clearer and more complete. It was a picture of obscure instinctual forces of organic origin striving towards inborn aims, and, above them, of an agency comprising more highly organized mental structures—acquisitions of human evolution made under the impact of human history—an agency which has taken over portions of the instinctual impulses, has developed them further or has even directed them towards higher aims, but which in any case holds them under firm restraints and manipulates their energy to suit its own purposes. This higher organization, however, which is known to us as the ego, has rejected another portion of these same elementary instinctual impulses as being unserviceable because they cannot be fitted into the organic unity of the individual or because they rebel against the individual's cultural aims. The ego is not in a position to exterminate these unsubdued mental forces, but it turns its back on them, allows them to remain at the lowest psychological level, defends itself from their demands by the energetic erection of protective and antithetical barriers or seeks to appease them with substitutive satisfactions. These instincts which have fallen victim to repression— uncontrolled and indestructible, yet inhibited from any kind of activity—together with their primitive mental representatives, constitute the mental underworld, the nucleus of the true unconscious, and are at every moment ready to make good their demands and, by hook or by crook, to force their way forward to satisfaction. To this is due the instability of the proud superstructure of the mind, the emergence at night of the proscribed and repressed material in the form of dreams, and the tendency to fall ill with neuroses and psychoses as soon as the balance of power between the ego and the repressed shifts to the disadvantage of the ego.

A little reflection was bound to show that it would be impossible to restrict to the provinces of dreams and nervous disorders a view such as this of the life of the human mind. If that view has hit upon a truth, it must apply equally to normal mental events, and even the highest achievements of the human spirit must bear a demonstrable relation to the factors found in pathology —to repression, to the efforts at mastering the unconscious and to the possibilities of satisfying the primitive instincts. There was thus an irresistible temptation and, indeed, a scientific duty, to apply the research methods of psycho-analysis, in regions far remote from its native soil, to the various mental sciences. And indeed psycho-analytic work upon patients pointed persistently in the direction of this new task, for it was obvious that the forms assumed by the different neuroses echoed the most highly admired productions of our culture. Thus hysterics are undoubtedly imaginative artists, even if they express their phantasies *mimetically* in the main and without considering their intelligibility to other people; the ceremonials and prohibitions of obsessional neurotics drive us to suppose that they have created a private religion of their own; and the delusions of paranoics have an unpalatable external similarity and internal kinship to the systems of our philosophers. It is impossible to escape the conclusion that these patients are, in an *asocial* fashion, making the very attempts at solving their conflicts and appeasing their pressing needs which, when they are carried out in a fashion that has binding force for the majority, go by the names of poetry, religion and philosophy.

In 1913 Otto Rank and Hanns Sachs, in an extremely interesting work, brought together the results which had been achieved up to that time in the application of psycho-analysis to the mental sciences. The most easily accessible branches of those sciences seem to be mythology and the history of literature and religion. No final formula has yet been found enabling us to give an appropriate place to myths in this connection. Otto Rank, in a large volume on the incest complex (1912), has produced evidence of the surprising fact that the choice of subject-matter, especially for dramatic works, is principally determined by the ambit of what psycho-analysis has termed the 'Oedipus complex'. By working it over with the greatest variety of modifications, distortions and disguises, the dramatist seeks to deal with his own most personal relations to this emotional theme. It is in attempting to master the Oedipus complex—that is to say, a person's emotional attitude towards his family, or in a narrower sense towards his father and mother—that individual neurotics come to grief, and for this reason that complex habitually forms the nucleus of their neuroses. It does not owe its importance to any unintelligible conjunction; the emphasis laid upon the relation of children to their parents is an expression of the biological facts that the young of the human race pass through a long period of dependence and are slow in reaching maturity, as well as that their capacity for love undergoes a complicated course of development. Consequently, the overcoming of the Oedipus complex coincides with the most efficient way of mastering the archaic, animal heritage of humanity. It is true that that heritage comprises all the forces that are required for the subsequent cultural development of the individual, but they must first be sorted out and worked over. This archaic heirloom is not fit to be used for the purposes of civilized social life in the form in which it is inherited by the individual.

To find the starting-point for the psycho-analytic opinions upon religious life we must go a step further.

What is to-day the heritage of the individual was once a new acquisition and has been handed on from one to another of a long series of generations. Thus the Oedipus complex too may have had stages of development, and the study of prehistory may enable us to trace them out. Investigation suggests that life in the human family took a quite different form in those remote days from that with which we are now familiar. And this idea is supported by findings based on observations of contemporary primitive races. If the prehistoric and ethnological material on this subject is worked over psycho-analytically, we arrive at an unexpectedly precise result: namely that God the Father once walked upon earth in bodily form and exercised his sovereignty as chieftain of the primal human horde until his sons united to slay him. It emerges further that this crime of liberation and the reactions to it had as their result the appearance of the first social ties, the basic moral restrictions and the oldest form of religion, totemism. But the later religions too have the same content, and on the one hand they are concerned with obliterating the traces of that crime or with expiating it by bringing forward other solutions of the struggle between the father and sons, while on the other hand they cannot avoid repeating once more the elimination of the father. Incidentally, an echo of this monstrous event, which overshadowed the whole course of human development, is also to be found in myths.

This hypothesis, which is founded upon the observations of Robertson Smith and was developed by me in *Totem and Taboo* [1912-1913] has been taken by Theodor Reik as the basis of his studies upon the problems of the psychology of religion, of which this is the first volume. In accordance with psycho-analytic technique these studies start out from hitherto unexplained details of religious life, the elucidation of which makes it possible to gain access to the fundamental postulates and ultimate aims of religion; moreover they keep steadily in view the relation between prehistoric man and contemporary primitive societies as well as the connection between the products of culture and the substitutive structures of neurotics. In conclusion, I would draw attention to the author's own introduction and express my belief that his work will be its own recommendation to the notice of specialists in the branch of knowledge with which it deals.

D

(D) PSYCHO-ANALYSIS AND DELINQUENCY

(1925)

NONE of the applications of psycho-analysis has excited so much interest and aroused so many hopes, and none, consequently, has attracted so many capable workers as its use in the theory and practice of education. It is easy to understand why; for children have become the main subject of psycho-analytic research and have thus replaced in importance the neurotics upon whom its studies began. Analysis has shown how the child lives on, almost unchanged, in the sick man as well as in the dreamer and the artist; it has thrown light upon the motive forces and impulses which set its characteristic stamp upon the childish nature; and it has traced the stages through which a child grows to maturity. It is not surprising, therefore, that an expectation should have arisen that psycho-analytic concern with children would benefit the work of education, whose aim it is to guide and assist children upon their forward path and to shield them from going astray.

My personal share in this application of psycho-analysis has been very slight. At an early stage I had accepted the *bon mot* which lays it down that there are three impossible professions—educating, healing and governing—and I was already fully occupied with the second of them. But this does not mean that I overlook the high social value of the work done by those of my friends who are engaged in education.

The present volume by August Aichhorn is concerned with one department of the great problem—with the educational influencing of juvenile delinquents. The author had worked for many years in an official

---

[1] [*Verwahrloste Jugend*, by August Aichhorn, to which this is the preface, was published in Vienna in 1925. Freud's preface was reprinted *Ges. Schr.*, **11**, 267, and *Ges. W.*, **14**, 565. An English translation of the book, including this preface, was published (under the title of *Wayward Youth*) in New York in 1935 and in London in 1936. Present translation by James Strachey.]

capacity as a director of municipal institutions for delinquents before he became acquainted with psycho-analysis. His attitude to his charges sprang from a warm sympathy with the fate of those unfortunates and was correctly guided by an intuitive perception of their mental needs. Psycho-analysis could teach him little that was new of a practical kind, but it brought him a clear theoretical insight into the justification of his way of acting and put him in a position to explain its basis to other people.

It must not be assumed that this gift of intuitive understanding will be found in everyone concerned with the bringing-up of children. Two lessons may be derived, it seems to me, from the experience and the success of August Aichhorn. One is that every such person should receive a psycho-analytic training, since without it children, the object of his endeavours, must remain an inaccessible problem to him. A training of this kind is best carried out if the student himself under-goes an analysis and experiences it on his own person: theoretical instruction in analysis fails to penetrate deep enough and carries no conviction.

The second lesson has a somewhat conservative ring. It is to the effect that the work of education is some-thing *sui generis*: it is not to be confounded with psycho-analytic influence and cannot be replaced by it. Psycho-analysis can be called in by education as an auxiliary means of treating a child; but it is not a suitable substitute for education. Not only is such a substitu-tion impossible on practical grounds but it is also to be disrecommended for theoretical reasons. The relation between education and psycho-analytic treatment will probably before long be the subject of a detailed investi-gation. Here I will only give a few hints. One should not be misled by the statement—incidentally a per-fectly true one—that the psycho-analysis of an adult neurotic is equivalent to a re-education. A child, even a wayward and delinquent child, is not as yet a neurotic; and re-education is something quite different from the education of the immature. The possibility of analytic influence rests upon quite definite preconditions which can be summed up under the term 'analytic situation'; it requires the development of certain psychical structures and a particular attitude to the analyst. Where these are lacking—as in the case of children, of juvenile delinquents, and, as a rule, of impulsive criminals—something other than analysis must be employed, though something which will be at one with analysis in its *purpose*. The theoretical chapters of the present volume will give the reader a preliminary grasp of the multiplicity of the decisions involved.

I will end with a further conclusion, and this time one which is important not for the theory of education but for the status of those who are engaged in education. If one of these has learnt analysis by experiencing it on his own person and has reached the stage of being able to employ it in borderline and mixed cases to assist him in his work, he should obviously be given the right to practise analysis, and narrow-minded motives should not be allowed to put obstacles in his way.

IX

A NOTE ON THE PREHISTORY OF THE TECHNIQUE OF ANALYSIS[1]

(1920)

ARECENT book by Havelock Ellis (so justly admired for his researches into sexual science, and an eminent critic of psycho-analysis), which bears the title of *The Philosophy of Conflict* (1919), includes an essay on 'Psycho-Analysis in Relation to Sex'. The aim of this essay is to show that the writings of the creator of analysis should be judged not as a piece of scientific work but as an artistic production. We cannot but regard this view as a fresh turn taken by resistance and as a repudiation of analysis, even though it is disguised in a friendly, indeed in too flattering a manner. We are inclined to meet it with a most decided contradiction.

It is not, however, with a view to contradicting him on this point that we are now concerned with Havelock Ellis's essay, but for another reason. His wide reading has enabled him to bring forward an author who practised and recommended free association as a technique, though for purposes other than ours, and thus has a claim to be regarded as a forerunner of psycho-analysis.

'In 1857, Dr. J. J. Garth Wilkinson, more noted as a Swedenborgian mystic and poet than as a physician, published a volume of mystic doggerel verse written by what he considered "a new method", the method of "Impression". "A theme is chosen or written down," he stated; "as soon as this is done the first impression upon the mind which succeeds the act of writing the title is the beginning of the evolution of that theme, no matter how strange or alien the word

[1] ['Zur Vorgeschichte der analytischen Technik.' First published anonymously, over the signature 'F', *Int. Z. Psychoanal.*, **6** (1920), 79; reprinted *Ges. Schr.*, **6**, 148, and *Ges. W.*, **12,** 309. Translation by James Strachey.]

or phrase may seem." "The first mental movement, the first word that comes" is "the response to the mind's desire for the unfolding of the subject." It is continued by the same method, and Garth Wilkinson adds: "I have always found it lead by an infallible instinct into the subject." The method was, as Garth Wilkinson viewed it, a kind of exalted *laissez-faire*, a command to the deepest unconscious instincts to express themselves. Reason and will, he pointed out, are left aside; you trust to "an influx", and the faculties of the mind are "directed to ends they know not of". Garth Wilkinson, it must be clearly understood, although he was a physician, used this method for religious and literary, and never for scientific or medical ends; but it is easy to see that essentially it is the method of psycho-analysis applied to oneself, and it is further evidence how much Freud's method is an artist's method.'

Those who are familiar with psycho-analytic literature will recall at this point the interesting passage in Schiller's correspondence with Körner[1] in which (1788) the great poet and thinker recommends anyone who desires to be productive to adopt the method of free association. It is to be suspected that what is alleged to be Garth Wilkinson's new technique had already occurred to the minds of many others and that its systematic application in psycho-analysis is not evidence so much of Freud's artistic nature as of his conviction, amounting almost to a prejudice, that all mental events are completely determined. It followed from this view that the first and most likely possibility was that a free association would be related to the subject designated; and this was confirmed by experience in analysis except in so far as too great resistances made the suspected connection unrecognizable.

Meanwhile it is safe to assume that neither Schiller nor Garth Wilkinson had in fact any influence on the

---

[1] Pointed out by Otto Rank and quoted in my *Interpretation of Dreams* (1900) [English translation, revised ed. (1932), 111-12].

choice of psycho-analytic technique. It is from another direction that there are indications of a personal influence at work.

A short time ago in Budapest Dr. Hugo Dubowitz drew Dr. Ferenczi's attention to a short essay covering only four and a half pages, by Ludwig Börne. This was written in 1823 and was reprinted in the first volume of the 1862 edition of his collected works. It is entitled 'The Art of Becoming an Original Writer in Three Days', and shows the familiar stylistic features of Jean Paul, of whom Börne was at that time a great admirer. He ends the essay with the following sentences:

'And here follows the practical application that was promised. Take a few sheets of paper and for three days on end write down, without fabrication or hypocrisy, everything that comes into your head. Write down what you think of yourself, of your wife, of the Turkish War, of Goethe, of Fonk's trial, of the Last Judgement, of your superiors—and when three days have passed you will be quite out of your senses with astonishment at the new and unheard-of thoughts you have had. This is the art of becoming an original writer in three days.'

When Professor Freud came to read this essay of Börne's, he brought forward a number of facts that may have an important bearing on the question that is under discussion here as to the prehistory of the psycho-analytic use of free associations. He said that when he was fourteen he had been given Börne's works as a present, that he still possessed the book now, fifty years later, and that it was the only one that had survived from his boyhood. Börne, he said, had been the first author into whose writings he had penetrated deeply. He could not remember the essay in question, but some of the others that were contained in the same volume—such as 'A Tribute to the Memory of Jean Paul', 'The Artist in Eating', and 'The Fool at the White Swan Inn' —kept on recurring to his mind for no obvious reason over a long period of years. He was particularly astonished to find expressed in the advice to the original writer some opinions which he himself had always cherished and vindicated. For instance : 'A disgraceful cowardliness in regard to thinking holds us all back. The censorship of governments is less oppressive than the censorship exercised by public opinion over our intellectual productions.' (Moreover there is a reference here to a 'censorship', which reappears in psycho-analysis as the dream-censorship.) 'It is not lack of intellect but lack of character that prevents most writers from being better than they are. . . . Sincerity is the source of all genius, and men would be cleverer if they were more moral. . . .'

Thus it seems not impossible that this hint may have brought to light the fragment of cryptomnesia which in so many cases may be suspected to lie behind apparent originality

X

MEDUSA'S HEAD[1]

(1922)

W E have not often attempted to interpret individual mythological themes, but an interpretation suggests itself easily in the case of the horrifying decapitated head of Medusa.

To decapitate = to castrate. The terror of Medusa is thus a terror of castration that is linked to the sight of something. Numerous analyses have made us familiar with the occasion for this: it occurs when a boy, who has hitherto been unwilling to believe the threat of castration, catches sight of the female genitals, probably those of an adult, surrounded by hair, and essentially those of his mother.

The hair upon Medusa's head is frequently represented in works of art in the form of snakes, and these once again are derived from the castration complex. It is a remarkable fact that, however frightening they may be in themselves, they nevertheless serve actually as a mitigation of the horror, for they replace the penis, the absence of which is the cause of the horror. This is a confirmation of the technical rule according to which a multiplication of penis symbols signifies castration.

The sight of Medusa's head makes the spectator stiff with terror, turns him to stone. Observe that we have here once again the same origin from the castration complex and the same transformation of affect! For becoming stiff means an erection. Thus in the original situation it offers consolation to the spectator: he is still in possession of a penis, and the stiffening reassures him of the fact.

[1] ['Das Medusenhaupt.' First published posthumously *Int. Z. Psychoanal. Imago*, **25** (1940), 105; reprinted *Ges. W.*, **17,** 47. The manuscript is dated May 14, 1922, and appears to be a sketch for a more extensive work. Translation, reprinted from *Int. J. Psycho-Anal.*, **22** (1941), 69, by James Strachey.]

This symbol of horror is worn upon her dress by the virgin goddess Athena. And rightly so, for thus she becomes a woman who is unapproachable and repels all sexual desires—since she displays the terrifying genitals of the Mother. Since the Greeks were in the main strongly homosexual, it was inevitable that we should find among them a representation of woman as a being who frightens and repels because she is castrated.

If Medusa's head takes the place of a representation of the female genitals, or rather if it isolates their horrifying effects from their pleasure-giving ones, it may be recalled that displaying the genitals is familiar in other connections as an apotropaic act. What arouses horror in oneself will produce the same effect upon the enemy against whom one is seeking to defend oneself. We read in Rabelais of how the Devil took to flight when the woman showed him her vulva.

The erect male organ also has an apotropaic effect, but thanks to another mechanism. To display the penis (or any of its surrogates) is to say: 'I am not afraid of you. I defy you. I have a penis.' Here, then, is another way of intimidating the Evil Spirit.

In order seriously to substantiate this interpretation it would be necessary to investigate the origin of this isolated symbol of horror in Greek mythology as well as parallels to it in other mythologies.[1]

[1] [The same topic was dealt with by Ferenczi (1923) in a very short paper which was itself briefly commented upon by Freud in his 'Infantile Genital Organization of the Libido' (1923a), *Collected Papers*, **2**, 247. The whole subject has been treated at greater length by Flugel (1924).]

XI
TWO ENCYCLOPÆDIA ARTICLES[1]
(1922)
(A) PSYCHO-ANALYSIS

PSYCHO-ANALYSIS is the name (1) of a procedure for the investigation of mental processes which are almost inaccessible in any other way, (2) of a method (based upon that investigation) for the treatment of neurotic disorders and (3) of a collection of psychological information obtained along those lines, which is gradually being accumulated into a new scientific discipline.

History.—The best way of understanding psychoanalysis is still by tracing its origin and development. In 1880 and 1881 Dr. Josef Breuer of Vienna, a well-known physician and experimental physiologist, was occupied in the treatment of a girl who had fallen ill of a severe hysteria while she was nursing her sick father. The clinical picture was made up of motor paralyses, inhibitions and disturbances of consciousness. Following a hint given him by the patient herself, who was a person of great intelligence, he put her into a state of hypnosis and contrived that, by describing to him the moods and thoughts that were uppermost in her mind, she returned on each particular occasion to a normal mental condition. By consistently repeating the same wearisome process, he succeeded in freeing her from all

---

[1] ['Psychoanalyse' and 'Libidotheorie' were two articles designed for Max Marcuse's *Handwörterbuch für Sexualwissenschaft*, which was first published in 1923, and were reprinted *Ges. Schr.*, **11**, 201, and *Ges. W.*, **13**, 211. They were actually written during the summer of 1922, that is to say before Freud's final re-casting of his views upon the topography of the mind in *The Ego and the Id* (1923*b*). But the new views, though unexpressed in these articles, must already have been clearly present in his thoughts while he was writing them, for it was in September, 1922, at the Berlin Psycho-Analytical Congress (which is actually mentioned in one of the articles) that he first made public his newly defined conceptions of ego, super-ego and id. Translation, reprinted from *Int. J. Psycho-Anal.*, **23** (1942), 97, by James Strachey.]

her inhibitions and paralyses, so that in the end he found his trouble rewarded by a great therapeutic success as well as by an unexpected insight into the nature of the puzzling neurosis. Nevertheless, Breuer refrained from following up his discovery or from publishing anything about the case until some ten years later, when the personal influence of the present writer (Freud, who had returned to Vienna in 1886 after studying in the school of Charcot) prevailed upon him to take up the subject afresh and embark upon a joint study of it. These two, Breuer and Freud, published a preliminary paper 'On the Psychical Mechanism of Hysterical Phenomena' in 1893, and in 1895 a volume entitled *Studien über Hysterie* (which reached its fourth edition in 1922), in which they described their therapeutic procedure as '*cathartic*'.

Catharsis.—The investigations which lay at the root of Breuer and Freud's studies led above all to two results, and these have not been shaken by subsequent experience: first, that hysterical symptoms have sense and meaning, being substitutes for normal mental acts; and secondly, that the uncovering of this unknown meaning is accompanied by the removal of the symptoms—so that in this case scientific research and therapeutic effort coincide. The observations were carried out upon a series of patients who were treated in the same manner as Breuer's first patient, that is to say, put into a state of deep hypnosis; and the results seemed brilliant, until later their weak side became evident. The theoretical ideas put forward at that time by Breuer and Freud were influenced by Charcot's theories upon traumatic hysteria and could find support in the findings of his pupil Pierre Janet, which, though they were published earlier than the *Studien*, were in fact subsequent to Breuer's first case. From the very beginning the factor of *affect* was brought into the foreground: hysterical symptoms, the authors maintained, came into existence when a mental process with a heavy charge of affect was in any way prevented from equalizing that charge by passing along the normal paths leading to consciousness and movement (*i.e.* from being '*abreacted*'), as a result of which the affect, which was in a sense '*strangulated*', was diverted on to the wrong paths and found its discharge into the somatic innerva tion (a process named '*conversion*'). The occasions upon which 'pathogenic ideas' of this kind arose were described by Breuer and Freud as '*psychical traumas*', and, since these often dated back to the very remote past, it was possible for the authors to say that hysterics suffered to a large extent from reminiscences (which had not been dealt with). Under the treatment, therefore, '*catharsis*' came about when the path to consciousness was opened and there was a normal discharge of affect. It will be seen that an essential part of this theory was the assumption of the existence of *unconscious* mental processes. Janet too had made use of unconscious acts in mental life; but, as he insisted in his later polemics against psycho-analysis, to him the phrase was no more than a make-shift expression, '*une manière de parler*', and he intended to suggest no new point of view by it.

In a theoretical section of the *Studien* Breuer brought forward some speculative ideas upon the processes of excitation in the mind. These ideas determined the direction of future lines of thought and even to-day have not received sufficient appreciation. But they brought his contributions to this branch of science to an end, and soon afterwards he withdrew from the common work.

The Transition to Psycho-analysis.—Contrasts between the views of the two authors had been visible even in the *Studien*. Breuer supposed that the pathogenic ideas produced their traumatic effect because they arose during '*hypnoid states*', in which mental functioning was subject to special limitations. The present writer rejected this explanation and inclined to the belief that an idea became pathogenic if its content was in opposition to the predominant trend of the subject's mental life so that it provoked him into '*defence*'. (Janet had attributed to hysterical patients a constitutional incapacity for holding together the contents of their minds; and it was at this point that his path diverged from that of Breuer and Freud.) Moreover, both of the innovations which led the present writer to move away from the cathartic method had already been mentioned in the *Studien*. After Breuer's withdrawal they became the starting-point of fresh developments.

Abandonment of Hypnosis.—The first of these innovations was based upon practical experience and led to a change in technique. The second consisted in an advance in the clinical understanding of neuroses. It soon appeared that the therapeutic hopes which had been placed upon cathartic treatment in hypnosis were to some extent unfulfilled. It was true that the disappearance of the symptoms went hand-in-hand with the catharsis, but total success turned out to be entirely dependent upon the patient's relation to the physician and thus resembled the effect of 'suggestion'. If that relation was disturbed, all the symptoms reappeared, just as though they had never been cleared up. In addition to this, the small number of people who could be put into a deep state of hypnosis involved a very considerable limitation, from the medical standpoint, of the applicability of the cathartic procedure. For these reasons the present writer decided to give up the use of hypnosis. But at the same time the impressions he had derived from hypnosis afforded him the means of replacing it.

Free Association.—The effect of the hypnotic condition upon the patient had been so greatly to increase his ability to make associations that he was able to find straightaway the path—inaccessible to his conscious reflection—which led from the symptom to the thoughts and memories connected with it. The abandonment of hypnosis seemed to make the situation hopeless, until the writer recalled a remark of Bernheim's to the effect that things that had been experienced in a state of somnambulism were only *apparently* forgotten and that

they could be brought into recollection at any time if
the physician insisted forcibly enough that the patient
knew them. The writer therefore endeavoured to press
his *unhypnotized* patients into giving him their associations, so that from the material thus provided he might
find the path leading to what had been forgotten or
warded off. He noticed later that such pressure was
unnecessary and that copious ideas almost always arose
in the patient's mind, but that they were held back from
being communicated and even from becoming conscious
by certain objections put by the patient in his own way.
It was to be expected—though this was still unproved
and not until later confirmed by wide experience—that
everything that occurred to a patient setting out from a
particular starting-point must also stand in an internal
connection with that starting-point; hence arose the
technique of educating the patient to give up the whole
of his critical attitude and of making use of the material
which was thus brought to light for the purpose of uncovering the connections that were being sought. A
strong belief in the strict determination of mental events
certainly played a part in the choice of this technique
as a substitute for hypnosis.

The '*Fundamental Technical Rule*' of this procedure
of 'free association' has from that time on been maintained in psycho-analytic work. The treatment is begun
by the patient being required to put himself in the
position of an attentive and dispassionate self-observer,
merely to read off all the time the surface of his consciousness, and on the one hand to make a duty of the
most complete candour while on the other not holding
back any idea from communication, even if (1) he feels
that it is too disagreeable or if (2) he judges that it is
nonsensical or (3) too unimportant or (4) irrelevant to
what is being looked for. It is uniformly found that
precisely those ideas which provoke these last-men-
tioned reactions are of particular value in discovering
the forgotten material.

Psycho-analysis as an Interpretative Art.—The new

technique altered the picture of the treatment so greatly, brought the physician into such a new relation to the patient and produced so many surprising results that it seemed justifiable to distinguish the procedure from the cathartic method by giving it a new name. The present writer gave this method of treatment, which could now be extended to many other forms of neurotic disorder, the name of *psycho-analysis*. Now, in the first resort, this psycho-analysis was an art of *interpretation* and it set itself the task of carrying deeper the first of Breuer's great discoveries—namely, that neurotic symptoms are significant substitutes for other mental acts which have been omitted. It was now a matter of regarding the material produced by the patients' associations as though it hinted at a hidden meaning and of discovering that meaning from it. Experience soon showed that the attitude which the analytical physician could most advantageously adopt was to surrender himself to his own unconscious mental activity, in a state of *easy and impartial attention*, to avoid so far as possible reflection and the construction of conscious expectations, not to try to fix anything that he heard particularly in his memory, and by these means to catch the drift of the patient's unconscious with his own unconscious. It was then found that, except under conditions that were too unfavourable, the patient's associations emerged like allusions, as it were, to one particular theme and that it was only necessary for the physician to go a step further in order to guess the material which was concealed from the patient himself and to be able to communicate it to him. It is true that this work of interpretation was not to be brought under strict rules and left a great deal of play to the physician's tact and skill; but, with impartiality and practice, it was usually possible to obtain trustworthy results—that is to say, results which were confirmed by being repeated in similar cases. At a time when so little was as yet known of the unconscious, the structure of the neuroses and the pathological processes underlying them, it was a matter for satisfaction that a technique of this kind should be available, even if it had no better theoretical basis. Moreover it is still employed in analyses at the present day in the same manner, though with a sense of greater assurance and with a better understanding of its limitations.

The Interpretation of Parapraxes and Chance Actions. —It was a triumph for the interpretative art of psycho-analysis when it succeeded in demonstrating that certain common mental acts of normal people, for which no one had hitherto attempted to put forward a psychological explanation, were to be regarded in the same light as the symptoms of neurotics: that is to say, they had a *meaning*, which was unknown to the subject but which could easily be discovered by analytic means. The phenomena in question were such events as the temporary forgetting of familiar words and names, forgetting to carry out prescribed tasks, everyday slips of the tongue and of the pen, misreadings, losses and mislayings of objects, certain mistakes, instances of apparently accidental self-injury, and finally habitual movements carried out seemingly without intention or in play, tunes hummed 'thoughtlessly', and so on. All of these were shorn of their physiological explanation, if any such had ever been attempted, and were shown to be strictly determined and were revealed as an expression of the subject's suppressed intentions or as a result of a clash between two intentions one of which was permanently or temporarily unconscious. The importance of this contribution to psychology was of many kinds. The range of mental determinism was extended by it in an unforeseen manner; the supposed gulf between normal and pathological mental events was narrowed; in many cases a useful insight was afforded into the play of mental forces that must be suspected to lie behind the phenomena. Finally, a class of material was brought to light which is calculated better than any other to stimulate a belief in the existence of unconscious mental acts even in people to whom the hypothesis of something at once mental and unconscious seems strange and even absurd. The study of one's own parapraxes and chance actions, for which most people have ample opportunities, is even to-day the best preparation for an approach to psycho-analysis. In analytic treatment, the interpretation of parapraxes retains a place as a means of uncovering the unconscious, alongside the immeasurably more important interpretation of associations.

The Interpretation of Dreams.—A new approach to the depths of mental life was opened when the technique of free association was applied to dreams, whether one's own or those of patients in analysis. In fact, the greater and better part of what we know of the processes in the unconscious levels of the mind is derived from the interpretation of dreams. Psycho-analysis has restored to dreams the importance which was generally ascribed to them in ancient times, but it treats them differently. It does not rely upon the cleverness of the dream-interpreter but for the most part hands the task over to the dreamer himself by asking him for his associations to the separate elements of the dream. By pursuing these associations further we obtain knowledge of thoughts which coincide entirely with the dream but which can be recognized—up to a certain point—as genuine and completely intelligible portions of waking mental activity. Thus the recollected dream emerges as the *manifest dream-content*, in contrast to the *latent dream-thoughts* discovered by interpretation. The process which has transformed the latter into the former, that is to say into 'the dream', and which is undone by the work of interpretation, may be called '*dream-work*'.

We also describe the latent dream-thoughts, on account of their connection with waking life, as '*residues of the* [*previous*] *day*'. By the operation of the dream-work (to which it would be quite incorrect to ascribe any 'creative' character) the latent dream-thoughts are *condensed* in a remarkable way, they are *distorted* by the *displacement* of psychical intensities, they are arranged with a view to being *represented in visual pictures*; and, besides all this, before the manifest dream is arrived at, they are submitted to a process of *secondary elaboration* which seeks to give the new product something in the nature of sense and coherence. But, strictly speaking, this last process does not form a part of dream-work.

The Dynamic Theory of Dream-Formation.—An understanding of the dynamics of dream-formation did not involve any very great difficulties. The motive power for the formation of dreams is not provided by the latent dream-thoughts or day's residues, but by an unconscious impulse, repressed during the day, with which the day's residues have been able to establish contact and which contrives to make a *wish-fulfilment* for itself out of the material of the latent thoughts. Thus every dream is on the one hand the fulfilment of a wish on the part of the unconscious and on the other hand (in so far as it succeeds in guarding the state of sleep against being disturbed) the fulfilment of the normal wish to sleep which set the sleep going. If we disregard the unconscious contribution to the formation of the dream and limit the dream to its latent thoughts, it can represent anything with which waking life has been concerned—a reflection, a warning, an intention, a preparation for the immediate future or, once again, the satisfaction of an unfulfilled wish. The unrecognizability, strangeness and absurdity of the manifest dream are partly the result of the translation of the thoughts into a different, so to say *archaic*, method of expression, but partly the effect of a restrictive, critically disapproving agency in the mind, which does not entirely cease to function during sleep. It is plausible to suppose that the '*dream-censorship*', which we regard as being responsible in the first instance for the distortion of the dream-thoughts into the manifest dream, is a manifestation of the same mental forces which during the day-time had held back or *repressed* the unconscious wishful impulse.

It has been worth while to enter in some detail into the explanation of dreams, since analytical work has shown that the dynamics of the formation of dreams are the same as those of the formation of symptoms. In both cases we find a struggle between two trends, of which one is unconscious and ordinarily repressed and strives towards satisfaction—that is, wish-fulfilment—while the other, belonging probably to the conscious ego, is disapproving and repressive. The outcome of this conflict is a *compromise-formation* (the dream or the symptom) in which both trends have found an incomplete expression. The theoretical importance of this conformity between dreams and symptoms is illuminating. Since dreams are not pathological phenomena, the fact shows that the mental mechanisms which produce the symptoms of illness are equally present in normal mental life, that the same uniform law embraces both the normal and the abnormal and that the findings of research into neurotics or psychotics cannot be without significance for our understanding of the healthy mind.

Symbolism.—In the course of investigating the form of expression brought about by dream-work, the surprising fact emerged that certain objects, arrangements and relations are represented, in a sense indirectly, by 'symbols', which are used by the dreamer without his understanding them and to which as a rule he offers no associations. Their translation has to be provided by the analyst, who can himself only discover it empirically by experimentally fitting it into the context. It was later found that linguistic usage, mythology and folklore afford the most ample analogies to dream-symbols. Symbols, which raise the most interesting and hitherto unsolved problems, seem to be a fragment of extremely ancient inherited mental equipment. The use of a common symbolism extends far beyond the use of a common language.

The Aetiological Significance of Sexual Life.—The second novelty which emerged after the hypnotic technique had been replaced by free associations was of a clinical nature. It was discovered in the course of the prolonged search for the traumatic experiences from which hysterical symptoms appeared to be derived. The more carefully the search was pursued the more extensive seemed to be the network of aetiologically significant impressions, but the further back, too, did they reach into the patient's puberty or childhood. At the same time they assumed a uniform character and eventually it became inevitable to bow before the evidence and recognize that at the root of the formation of every symptom there were to be found traumatic experiences from early sexual life. Thus a sexual trauma stepped into the place of an ordinary trauma and the latter was seen to owe its aetiological significance to an associative or symbolic connection with the former, which had preceded it. An investigation of cases of common nervousness (falling into the two classes of *neurasthenia* and *anxiety neurosis*) which was simultaneously undertaken led to the conclusion that these disorders could be traced to *contemporary* abuses in the patients' sexual life and could be removed if these were brought to an end. It was thus easy to infer that neuroses in general are an expression of disturbances in sexual life, the so-called *actual-neuroses* being the consequences (by chemical agency) of *contemporary* injuries and the *psycho-neuroses* the consequences (by psychical modification) of *bygone* injuries to a biological function which had hitherto been gravely neglected by science. None of the theses of psycho-analysis has met with such tenacious scepticism or such embittered resistance as this assertion of the preponderating aetiological significance of sexual life in the neuroses. It should, however, be expressly remarked that, in its development up to the present day, psycho-analysis has found no reason to retreat from this opinion.

Infantile Sexuality.—As a result of its aetiological researches, psycho-analysis found itself in the position of dealing with a subject the very existence of which had scarcely been suspected previously. Science had become accustomed to consider sexual life as beginning with puberty and regarded manifestations of sexuality in children as rare signs of abnormal precocity and degeneracy. But now psycho-analysis revealed a wealth of phenomena, remarkable, yet of regular occurrence, which made it necessary to date back the beginning of the sexual function in children almost to the commencement of extra-uterine existence; and it was asked with astonishment how all this could have come to be overlooked. The first glimpses of sexuality in children had indeed been obtained through the analytic examination of adults and were consequently saddled with all the doubts and sources of error that could be attributed to such a belated retrospect; but subsequently (from 1908 onwards) a beginning was made with the analysis of children themselves and with the unembarrassed observation of their behaviour, and in this way direct confirmation was reached for the whole factual basis of the new view.

Sexuality in children showed a different picture in many respects from that in adults, and, surprisingly enough, it exhibited numerous traces of what, in adults, were condemned as *'perversions'*. It became necessary to enlarge the concept of what was sexual, till it covered more than the impulsion towards the union of the two sexes in the sexual act or towards provoking particular pleasurable sensations in the genitals. But this enlargement was rewarded by the new possibility of grasping infantile, normal and perverse sexual life as a single whole.

The analytic researches carried out by the writer fell, to begin with, into the error of greatly overestimating the importance of *seduction* as a source of sexual manifestations in children and as a root for the formation of neurotic symptoms. This misapprehension was corrected when it became possible to appreciate the extraordinarily large part played in the mental life of neurotics by the activities of *phantasy*, which clearly carried more weight in neurosis than did the external world. Behind these phantasies there came to light the material which allows us to draw the picture which follows of the development of the sexual function.

The Development of the Libido.—The sexual instinct, the dynamic manifestation of which in mental life we shall call '*libido*', is made up of component instincts into which it may once more break up and which are only gradually united into well-defined organizations. The sources of these component instincts are the organs of the body and in particular certain specially marked *erotogenic zones*; but contributions are made to libido from every important functional process in the body. At first the individual component instincts strive for satisfaction independently of one another, but in the course of development they become more and more convergent and concentrated. The first (pre-genital) stage of organization to be discerned is the *oral* one, in which —in conformity with the suckling's predominant interest—the oral zone plays the leading part. This is followed by the *sadistic-anal* organization, in which the *anal* zone and the component instinct of *sadism* are particularly prominent; at this stage the difference between the sexes is represented by the contrast between active and passive. The third and final stage of organization is that in which the majority of the component instincts converge under the *primacy of the genital zones*. As a rule this development is passed through swiftly and unobtrusively; but some individual portions of the instincts remain behind at the prodromal stages of the process and thus give rise to *fixations* of libido, which are important as constituting predispositions for subsequent irruptions of repressed impulses and which stand in a definite relation to the later development of neuroses and perversions. (See the article upon the Libido Theory [page 131 below].)

The Process of Finding an Object and the Oedipus Complex.—In the first instance the oral component instinct finds satisfaction by attaching itself to the sating of the desire for nourishment; and its object is the mother's breast. It then detaches itself, becomes independent and at the same time *auto-erotic*, that is, it finds an object in the child's own body. Others of the component instincts also start by being auto-erotic and are not until later diverted on to an external object. It is a particularly important fact that the component instincts belonging to the genital zone habitually pass through a period of intense auto-erotic satisfaction. The component instincts are not all equally serviceable in the final genital organization of libido; some of them (for instance, the anal components) are consequently left aside and suppressed, or undergo complicated transformations.

In the very earliest years of childhood (approximately between the ages of two and five) a convergence of the sexual impulses occurs of which, in the case of boys, the object is the mother. This choice of an object, in conjunction with a corresponding attitude of rivalry and hostility towards the father, provides the content of what is known as the *Oedipus complex*, which in every human being is of the greatest importance in determining the final shape of his erotic life. It has been found to be characteristic of a normal individual that he has learnt how to master his Oedipus complex, whereas the neurotic subject remains involved in it.

The Diphasic Onset of Sexual Development.—Towards the end of the fifth year this early period of sexual life normally comes to an end. It is succeeded by a period of more or less complete *latency*, during which ethical restraints are built up, to act as defences against the desires of the Oedipus complex. In the subsequent period of *puberty*, the Oedipus complex is revivified in the unconscious and embarks upon further modifications. It is only at puberty that the sexual instincts develop to their full intensity; but the direction of that development, as well as all the predispositions for it, have already been determined by the early efflorescence of sexuality during childhood which preceded it. This diphasic development of the sexual function—in two stages, interrupted by the latency period—appears to be a biological peculiarity of the human species and to contain the determining factor for the origin of neuroses.

The Theory of Repression.—These theoretical considerations, taken together with the immediate impressions derived from analytic work, lead to a view of the neuroses which may be described in the roughest outline as follows. The neuroses are the expression of conflicts between the ego and such of the sexual impulses as seem to the ego incompatible with its integrity or with its ethical standards. Since these impulses are not *ego-syntonic*, the ego has *repressed* them: that is to say, it has withdrawn its interest from them and has shut them off from becoming conscious as well as from obtaining satisfaction by motor discharge. If in the course of analytic work one attempts to make these repressed impulses conscious, one becomes aware of the repressive forces in the form of *resistance*. But the achievement of repression fails particularly easily in the case of the sexual instincts. Their dammed-up libido finds other ways out from the unconscious: for it *regresses* to earlier phases of development and earlier attitudes towards objects, and, at weak points in the libidinal development where there are infantile fixations, it breaks through into consciousness and obtains discharge. What results is a *symptom* and consequently in its essence a substitutive sexual satisfaction. Nevertheless the symptom cannot entirely escape from the repressive forces of the ego and must therefore submit to modifications and displacements—exactly as happens with dreams—by means of which its characteristic of being a sexual satisfaction becomes unrecognizable. Thus symptoms are in the nature of compromise-formations between the repressed sexual instincts and the repressive ego instincts; they represent a wish-fulfilment for both partners to the conflict simultaneously, but one which is incomplete for each of them. This is quite strictly true of the symptoms of hysteria, while in the symptoms of obsessional neurosis there is often a stronger emphasis upon the side of the repressive function owing to the erection of reaction-formations, which are assurances against sexual satisfaction.

Transference.—If further proof were needed of the truth that the motive forces behind the formation of neurotic symptoms are of a sexual nature, it would be found in the fact that in the course of analytic treatment a special emotional relation is regularly formed between the patient and the physician. This goes far beyond rational limits. It varies between the most affectionate devotion and the most obstinate enmity and derives all of its characteristics from earlier emotional erotic attitudes of the patient's which have become unconscious. This *transference* alike in its positive and in its negative form is used as a weapon by the resistance; but in the hands of the physician it becomes the most powerful therapeutic instrument and it plays a part that can scarcely be overestimated in the dynamics of the process of cure.

The Corner-stones of Psycho-analytic Theory.—The assumption that there are unconscious mental processes, the recognition of the theory of resistance and repression, the appreciation of the importance of sexuality and of the Oedipus complex—these constitute the principal subject-matter of psycho-analysis and the foundations of its theory. No one who cannot accept them all should count himself a psycho-analyst.

Later History of Psycho-analysis.—Psycho-analysis was carried approximately thus far by the work of the writer of this article, who for more than ten years was its sole representative. In 1906 the Swiss psychiatrist Bleuler and C. G. Jung began to play a lively part in analysis; in 1907 a first conference of its supporters took place at Salzburg; and the young science soon found itself the centre of interest both among psychiatrists and laymen. Its reception in Germany, with her morbid craving for authority, was not precisely to the credit of German science and moved even so cool a partisan as Bleuler to an energetic protest. Yet no condemnation or dismissal at official congresses served to hold up the internal growth or external expansion of psychoanalysis. In the course of the next ten years it extended far beyond the frontiers of Europe and became especially popular in the United States of America, and this was due in no small degree to the advocacy and collaboration of Putnam (Boston), Ernest Jones (Toronto; later London), Flournoy (Geneva), Ferenczi (Budapest), Abraham (Berlin), and many others besides. The anathema which was imposed upon psycho-analysis led its supporters to combine in an international organization which in the present year (1922) is holding its eighth private Congress in Berlin and now includes local groups in Vienna, Budapest, Berlin, Holland, Zurich, London, New York, Calcutta and Moscow. This development was not interrupted even by the World War. In 1918–19 Dr. Anton v. Freund of Budapest founded the Internationaler Psychoanalytischer Verlag, which publishes journals and books concerned with psychoanalysis, and in 1920 Dr. M. Eitingon opened in Berlin the first psycho-analytic clinic for the treatment of neurotics without private means. Translations of the writer's principal works, which are now in preparation, into French, Italian and Spanish, testify to a growing interest in psycho-analysis in the Latin world as well.

Between 1911 and 1913 two movements of divergence from psycho-analysis took place, evidently with the object of mitigating its repellent features. One of these (sponsored by C. G. Jung), in an endeavour to conform to ethical standards, divested the Oedipus complex of its real significance by giving it only a *symbolic* value, and in practice neglected the uncovering of the forgotten and, as we may call it, 'prehistoric' period of childhood. The other (originated by Alfred Adler in Vienna) reproduced many factors from psychoanalysis under other names—repression, for instance, appeared in a sexualized version as the 'masculine protest'. But in other respects it turned away from the unconscious and the sexual instincts, and endeavoured to trace back the development of character and of the neuroses to the 'will to power', which by means of overcompensation strives to check the dangers arising from 'organ inferiority'. Neither of these movements, with their systematic structures, had any permanent influence on psycho-analysis. In the case of Adler's theories it soon became clear that they had very little in common with psycho-analysis, which they were designed to replace.

More Recent Advances in Psycho-analysis.—Since psycho-analysis has become the field of work for such a large number of observers it has made advances, both in extent and depth; but unfortunately these can receive only the briefest mention in the present article.

Narcissism.—The most important theoretical advance has certainly been the application of the libido theory to the repressing ego. The ego itself came to be regarded as a reservoir of what was described as narcissistic libido, from which the libidinal cathexes of objects flowed out and into which they could be once more withdrawn. By the help of this conception it became possible to embark upon the analysis of the ego and to make a clinical distinction of the psychoneuroses into *transference neuroses* and *narcissistic* disorders. In the former the subject has at his disposal a quantity of libido striving to be transferred on to external objects, and use is made of this in carrying out analytic treatment; on the other hand, the narcissistic disorders (dementia praecox, paranoia, melancholia) are characterized by a withdrawal of the libido from objects and they are therefore scarcely accessible to analytic therapy. But their therapeutic inaccessibility has not prevented analysis from making the most fruitful beginnings in the deeper study of these illnesses, which are counted among the psychoses.

Development of Technique.—After the analyst's curiosity had, as it were, been gratified by the elaboration of the technique of interpretation, it was inevitable that interest should turn to the problem of discovering the most effective way of influencing the patient. It soon became evident that the physician's immediate task was to assist the patient in getting to know, and afterwards in overcoming, the resistances which emerged in him during treatment and of which, to begin with, he himself was unaware. And it was found at the same time that the essential part of the process of cure lay in the overcoming of these resistances and that unless this was achieved no permanent mental change could be brought about in the patient. Since the analyst's efforts have in this way been directed upon the patient's resistance, analytic technique has attained a certainty and delicacy rivalling that of surgery. Consequently, everyone is strongly advised against undertaking psycho-analytic treatments without a strict training, and a physician who ventures upon them on the strength of his medical qualification is in no respect better than a layman.

Psycho-analysis as a Therapeutic Procedure.—Psycho-analysis has never set itself up as a panacea and has never claimed to perform miracles. In one of the most difficult spheres of medical activity it is the only possible method of treatment for certain illnesses and for others it is the method which yields the best or the most permanent results—though never without a corresponding expenditure of time and trouble. A physician who is not wholly absorbed in the work of giving help will find his labours amply repaid by obtaining an unhoped-for insight into the complications of mental life and the interrelations between the mental and the physical. Where at present it cannot offer help but only theoretical understanding, it may perhaps be preparing the way for some later, more direct means of influencing neurotic disorders. Its province is above all the two transference neuroses, hysteria and obsessional neurosis, in which it has contributed to the discovery of their internal structure and operative mechanisms; and, beyond them, all kinds of phobias, inhibitions, deformities of character, sexual perversions and difficulties in erotic life. Some analysts (Jelliffe, Groddeck, Felix Deutsch) have reported too that the analytic treatment of gross organic diseases is not unpromising, since a mental factor not infrequently contributes to the origin and continuance of such illnesses. Since psycho-analysis demands a certain amount of psychical plasticity from its patients, some kind of age-limit must be laid down in their selection; and since it necessitates the devotion of long and intense attention to the individual patient, it would be uneconomical to squander such expenditure upon completely worthless persons who happen to be neurotic. Experience upon material in clinics can alone show what modifications may be necessary in order to make psycho-analytic treatment accessible to wider strata of the population or to adapt it to weaker intelligences.

Comparison between Psycho-analysis and Hypnotic and Suggestive Methods.—Psycho-analytic procedure differs from all methods making use of suggestion, persuasion, etc., in that it does not seek to suppress by means of authority any mental phenomenon that may occur in the patient. It endeavours to trace the causation of the phenomenon and to remove it by bringing about a permanent modification in the conditions that led to it. In psycho-analysis the suggestive influence which is inevitably exercised by the physician is diverted on to the task assigned to the patient of overcoming his resistances, that is, of carrying forward the curative process. Any danger of falsifying the products of a patient's memory by suggestion can be avoided by prudent handling of the technique; but in general the arousing of resistances is a guarantee against the misleading effects of suggestive influence. It may be laid down that the aim of the treatment is to remove the patient's resistances and to pass his repressions in review and thus to bring about the most far-reaching unification and strengthening of his ego, to enable him to save the mental energy which he is expending upon internal conflicts, to make the best of him that his inherited capacities will allow and so to make him as efficient and as capable of enjoyment as is possible. The removal of the symptoms of the illness is not specifically aimed at, but is achieved, as it were, as a by-product if the analysis is properly carried through. The analyst respects the patient's individuality and does not seek to remould him in accordance with his own—that is, according to the physician's—personal ideals; he is glad to avoid giving advice and instead to arouse the patient's power of initiative.

Its Relation to Psychiatry.—Psychiatry is at present essentially a descriptive and classificatory science whose orientation is still towards the somatic rather than the psychological and which is without the possibility of giving explanations of the phenomena which it observes. Psycho-analysis does not, however, stand in opposition to it, as the almost unanimous behaviour of the psychiatrists might lead one to believe. On the contrary, as a *depth-psychology*, a psychology of those processes in mental life which are withdrawn from consciousness, it is called upon to provide psychiatry with an indispensable groundwork and to free it from its present limitations. We can foresee that the future will give birth to a scientific psychiatry, to which psycho-analysis has served as an introduction.

Criticisms and Misunderstandings of Psycho-analysis.—Most of what is brought up against psycho-analysis, even in scientific works, is based upon insufficient information which in its turn seems to be determined by emotional resistances. Thus it is a mistake to accuse psycho-analysis of 'pansexualism' and to allege that it derives all mental occurrences from sexuality and traces them all back to it. On the contrary, psycho-analysis has from the very first distinguished the sexual instincts from others which it has provisionally termed 'ego instincts'. It has never dreamt of trying to explain 'everything', and even the neuroses it has traced back not to sexuality alone but to the conflict between the sexual impulses and the ego. In psycho-analysis (unlike the works of C. G. Jung) the term *'libido'* does not mean psychical energy in general but the motive force of the sexual instincts. Some assertions, such as that every dream is the fulfilment of a sexual wish, have never been maintained by it at all. The charge of one-sidedness made against psycho-analysis, which, as *the science of the unconscious mind*, has its own definite and restricted field of work, is as inapplicable as it would be if it were made against chemistry. To believe that psycho-analysis seeks a cure for neurotic disorders by giving a free rein to sexuality is a serious misunderstanding which can only be justified by ignorance. The making conscious of repressed sexual desires in analysis makes it possible, on the contrary, to obtain a mastery over them which the previous repression had been unable to achieve. It can more truly be said that analysis sets the neurotic free from the chains of his sexuality. Moreover, it is quite unscientific to judge analysis by whether it is calculated to undermine religion, authority and morals; for, like all sciences, it is entirely non-tendentious and has only a single aim—namely to arrive at a consistent view of one portion of reality. Finally, one can only characterize as simple-minded the fear which is sometimes expressed that all the highest goods of humanity, as they are called—research, art, love, ethical and social sense—will lose their value or their dignity because psycho-analysis is in a position to demonstrate their origin in elementary and animal instinctual impulses.

The Non-Medical Applications and Correlations of Psycho-analysis.—Any estimate of psycho-analysis would be incomplete if it failed to make clear that, alone among the medical disciplines, it has the most extensive relations with the mental sciences, and that it is in a position to play a part of the same importance in the studies of religious and cultural history and in the sciences of mythology and literature as it is in psychiatry. This may seem strange when we reflect that originally its only object was the understanding and improvement of neurotic symptoms. But it is easy to indicate the starting-point of the bridge that leads over to the mental sciences. The analysis of dreams gave us an insight into the unconscious processes of the mind and showed us that the mechanisms which produce pathological symptoms are also operative in the normal mind. Thus psycho-analysis became a *depth-psychology* and capable as such of being applied to the mental sciences, and it was able to answer a good number of questions with which the academic psychology of consciousness was helpless to deal. At quite an early stage problems of human *phylogenesis* arose. It became clear that pathological function was often nothing more than a *regression* to an earlier stage in the development of normal function. C. G. Jung was the first to draw explicit attention to the striking similarity between the disordered phantasies of sufferers from dementia praecox and the myths of primitive peoples; while the present writer pointed out that the two wishes which combine to form the Oedipus complex coincide precisely with the two principal prohibitions imposed by *totemism* (not to kill the tribal ancestor and not to marry any woman belonging to one's own clan) and drew far-reaching conclusions from this fact. The significance of the Oedipus complex began to grow to gigantic proportions and it looked as though social order, morals, justice and religion had arisen together in the primaeval ages of mankind as reaction-formations against the Oedipus complex. Otto Rank threw a brilliant light upon mythology and the history of literature by the application of psycho-analytical views, as did Theodor Reik upon the history of morals and religions, while Dr. Pfister, of Zurich, aroused the interest of religious and secular teachers and demonstrated the importance of the psycho-analytical standpoint for education. Further discussion of these applications of psycho-analysis would be out of place here, and it is enough to say that the limits of their influence are not yet in sight.

Psycho-analysis an Empirical Science.—Psycho-analysis is not, like philosophies, a system starting out from a few sharply defined basic concepts, seeking to grasp the whole universe with the help of these and, once it is completed, having no room for fresh dis-

E

coveries or better understanding. On the contrary, it keeps close to the facts in its field of study, seeks to solve the immediate problems of observation, gropes its way forward by the help of experience, is always incomplete and always ready to correct or modify its theories. There is no incongruity (any more than in the case of physics or chemistry) if its most general concepts lack clarity and if its postulates are provisional; it leaves their more precise definition to the results of future work.

(B) THE LIBIDO THEORY

LIBIDO is a term used in the theory of the instincts for describing the dynamic manifestation of sexuality. It was already used in this sense by Moll (1898) and was introduced into psycho-analysis by the present writer. What follows is limited to a description of the developments which the theory of the instincts has passed through in psycho-analysis—developments which are still proceeding.

Contrast between Sexual Instincts and Ego Instincts. —Psycho-analysis early became aware that all mental occurrences must be regarded as built upon a basis of the interplay of the forces of the elementary instincts. This, however, led to a difficult predicament, since psychology included no theory of the instincts. No one could say what an instinct really was, the question was left entirely to individual caprice, and every psychologist was in the habit of postulating any instincts in any number that he chose. The first sphere of phenomena to be studied by psycho-analysis comprised what are known as the transference neuroses (hysteria and obsessional neurosis). It was found that their symptoms came about by sexual instinctual impulses being rejected (repressed) by the subject's personality (his ego) and then finding expression by circuitous paths through the unconscious. These facts could be met by drawing a contrast between the sexual instincts and ego instincts (*instincts of self-preservation*), which was in line with the popular saying that hunger and love are what make the world go round: libido was the manifestation of the force of love in the same sense as was hunger of the self-preservative instinct. The nature of the ego instincts remained for the time being undefined and, like all the other characteristics of the ego, inaccessible to analysis. There was no means of deciding whether, and if so what, qualitative differences were to be assumed to exist between the two classes of instincts.

Primal Libido.—C. G. Jung attempted to resolve this obscurity along speculative lines by assuming that there was only a single primal libido which could be either sexualized or desexualized and which therefore coincided in its essence with mental energy in general. This innovation was methodologically disputable, caused a great deal of confusion, reduced the term 'libido' to the level of a superfluous synonym and was still confronted in practice with the necessity for distinguishing between sexual and asexual libido. The difference between the sexual instincts and instincts with other aims was not to be got rid of by means of a new definition.

Sublimation.—An attentive examination of the sexual impulses, which were accessible only to psycho-analysis, had meanwhile led to some remarkable detailed findings. What is described as the sexual instinct turns out to be of a highly composite nature and is liable to disintegrate once more into its component instincts. Each component instinct is unalterably characterized by its *source*, that is, by the region or zone of the body from which its excitation is derived. Each has furthermore as distinguishable features an *object* and an *aim*. The aim is always discharge accompanied by satisfaction, but it is capable of being changed from activity to passivity. The object is less closely attached to the instinct than was at first supposed; it is easily exchanged for another one, and moreover, an instinct which had an external object can be turned round upon the subject's own self. The separate instincts can either remain independent of one another or—in what is still an inexplicable manner—can be combined and merged into one another to perform work in common. They are also able to replace one another and to transfer their libidinal cathexis to one another, so that the satisfaction of one instinct can take the place of the satisfaction of others. The most important vicissitude which an instinct can undergo seems to be *sublimation*; here both object and aim are changed, so that what was originally a sexual instinct finds satisfaction in some achievement

which is no longer sexual but has a higher social or
ethical valuation. These different features do not as yet
combine to form an integral picture.

Narcissism.—A decisive advance was made when the
analysis of dementia praecox and other psychotic disorders was ventured upon and thus the examination of
the ego itself was begun, which had so far been known
only as the agency of repression and opposition. It was
found that the pathogenic process in dementia praecox
is the withdrawal of the libido from objects and its
introduction into the ego, while the clamorous symptoms of the disease arise from the vain struggles of the
libido to find a pathway back to objects. It thus
turned out to be possible for object-libido to change into
cathexis of the ego and *vice versa*. Further reflection
showed that this process must be presumed to occur on
the largest scale and that the ego is to be regarded as a
great reservoir of libido from which libido is sent out *to*
objects and which is always ready to absorb libido flow-
ing back *from* objects. Thus the instincts of self-
preservation were also of a libidinal nature: they were
sexual instincts which, instead of external objects, had
taken the subject's own ego as an object. Clinical experience had made us familiar with people who behaved
in a striking fashion as though they were in love with
themselves and this perversion had been given the
name of *narcissism*. The libido of the self-preservative
instincts was now described as *narcissistic libido* and it
was recognized that a high degree of this self-love con-
stituted the primary and normal state of things. The
earlier formula laid down for the transference neuroses
consequently required to be modified, though not corrected. It was better, instead of speaking of a conflict
between sexual instincts and ego instincts, to speak of a
conflict between object-libido and ego-libido, or, since
the nature of these instincts was the same, between the
object-cathexes and the ego.

Apparent Approach to Jung's Views.—It thus seemed
on the face of it as though the slow process of psycho-

analytic research was following in the steps of Jung's speculation about a primal libido, especially because the transformation of object-libido into narcissism necessarily carries along with it a certain degree of desexualization, or abandonment of the specifically sexual aims. Nevertheless, it has to be borne in mind that the fact that the self-preservative instincts of the ego are recognized as libidinal does not necessarily prove that there are no other instincts operating in the ego.

The Herd Instinct.—It has been maintained in many quarters that there is a special innate and not further analysable 'herd instinct', which determines the social behaviour of human beings and impels individuals to come together into larger communities. Psycho-analysis finds itself in contradiction to this view. Even if the social instinct is innate, it may without any difficulty be traced back to what were originally libidinal object-cathexes and may have developed in the childhood of the individual as a reaction-formation against hostile attitudes of rivalry. It is based upon a peculiar kind of identification with other people.

Aim-inhibited Sexual Impulses.—The social instincts belong to a class of instinctual impulses which need not be described as sublimated, though they are closely related to these. They have not abandoned their directly sexual aims, but they are held back by internal resistances from attaining them; they rest content with certain approximations to satisfaction and for that very reason lead to especially firm and permanent attachments between human beings. To this class belong in particular the affectionate relations between parents and children, which were originally fully sexual, feelings of friendship, and the emotional ties in marriage which had their origin in sexual attraction.

Recognition of Two Classes of Instincts in Mental Life.—Though psycho-analysis endeavours as a rule to develop its theories as independently as possible from those of other sciences, it is nevertheless obliged to seek a basis for the theory of the instincts in biology. On the ground of a far-reaching consideration of the processes which go to make up life and which lead to death, it becomes probable that we should recognize the existence of two classes of instincts, corresponding to the contrary processes of construction and dissolution in the organism. On this view, the one set of instincts, which work essentially in silence, would be those which follow the aim of leading the living creature to death and therefore deserve to be called the *'death instincts'*; these would be directed outwards as the result of the combination of numbers of unicellular elementary organisms, and would manifest themselves as *destructive* or *aggressive* impulses. The other set of instincts would be those which are better known to us in analysis, the libidinal, sexual or life instincts, which are best comprised under the name of *Eros*; their purpose would be to form living substance into ever greater unities, so that life may be prolonged and brought to higher development. The erotic instincts and the death instincts would be present in living beings in regular mixtures or fusions; but defusions would also be liable to occur. Life would consist in the manifestations of the conflict or interaction between the two classes of instincts; death would mean for the individual the victory of the destructive instincts but reproduction would mean for him the victory of Eros.

The Nature of the Instincts.—This view would enable us to characterize instincts as tendencies inherent in living substance towards restoring an earlier state of things: that is to say, they would be historically determined and of a conservative nature and, as it were, the expression of an inertia or elasticity present in what is organic. Both classes of instincts, Eros as well as the death instinct, would, on this view, have been in operation and working against each other from the first origin of life.

XII
REMARKS UPON THE THEORY AND PRACTICE OF DREAM-INTERPRETATION[1]
(1923)

THE accidental circumstance that the last editions of my *Interpretation of Dreams* (1900) have been printed from stereotype plates has led me to issue the following remarks in an independent form, instead of introducing them into the text as modifications or additions.

I

In interpreting a dream during an analysis a choice lies open to one between several technical procedures.

One can (*a*) proceed chronologically and get the dreamer to bring up his associations to the elements of the dream in the order in which those elements occurred in his account of the dream. This is the original, classical method, which I still regard as the best if one is analysing one's own dreams.

Or one can (*b*) start the work of interpretation from some one particular element of the dream which one picks out from the middle of it. For instance, one can choose the most striking piece of it, or the piece which shows the greatest clarity or sensory intensity; or, again, one can start off from some spoken words in the dream, in the expectation that they will lead to the recollection of some spoken words in waking life.

Or one can (*c*) begin by entirely disregarding the manifest content and instead ask the dreamer what events of the previous day are associated in his mind with the dream he has just described.

Finally, one can (*d*) if the dreamer is already familiar

[1] ['Bemerkungen zur Theorie und Praxis der Traumdeutung.' First published *Int. Z. Psychoanal.*, **9**, 1; reprinted *Ges. Schr.*, **3**, 305, and *Ges. W.*, **13**, 301. Translation, reprinted from *Int. J. Psycho-Anal.*, **24** (1943). 66, by James Strachey.]

with the technique of interpretation, avoid giving him any instructions and leave it to him to decide with which associations to the dream he shall begin.

I cannot lay it down that one or the other of these techniques is preferable or in general yields better results.

II

What is of far greater importance is the question of whether the work of interpretation proceeds under a pressure of resistance which is high or low—a point upon which the analyst never remains long in doubt. If the pressure is high, one may perhaps succeed in discovering what the things are with which the dream is concerned, but one cannot make out what it says about these things. It is as though one were trying to listen to a conversation taking place at a distance or in a very low voice. In that case, one can feel confident that there is not much prospect of collaborating with the dreamer, one decides not to bother too much about it and not to give him much help, and one is content to put before him a few translations of symbols that seem probable.

The majority of dreams in a difficult analysis are of this kind; so that one cannot learn much from them about the nature and mechanism of dream-formation. Least of all can one learn anything from them upon the recurring question of where the dream's wish-fulfilment may lie hidden. When the pressure of resistance is quite extremely high, one meets with the phenomenon of the dreamer's associations broadening instead of deepening. In place of the desired associations to the dream that has already been narrated, there appear a constant succession of new fragments of dream, which in their turn remain without associations.

It is only when the resistance is kept within moderate limits that the familiar picture of the work of interpretation comes into view: the dreamer's associations begin by *diverging* widely from the manifest elements, so that a great number of subjects and ranges of ideas are touched upon, after which, a second series of associations suddenly *converge* from these on to the dream-thoughts that are being looked for. When this is so, collaboration between the analyst and the dreamer becomes possible; whereas under a high pressure of resistance it would not even be of any advantage.

A number of dreams which occur during analyses are untranslatable even though they do not actually make much show of the resistance that is there. They exhibit free renderings of the latent dream-thoughts behind them and are comparable to successful creative writings which have been artistically worked over and in which the basic themes are still recognizable though they have been subjected to any amount of re-arrangement and transformation. Dreams of this kind serve in the treatment as an introduction to thoughts and memories of the dreamer without their own actual content coming into account.

III

It is possible to distinguish between dreams *from above* and dreams *from below*, provided the distinction is not made too sharply. Dreams from below are those which are provoked by the strength of an unconscious (repressed) wish which has found a means of being represented in some of the day's residues. They may be regarded as inroads of the repressed into waking life. Dreams from above correspond to thoughts or intentions of the day before which have contrived during the night to obtain reinforcement from repressed material which is debarred from the ego. When this is so, analysis as a rule disregards this unconscious ally and succeeds in inserting the latent dream-thoughts into the complex of waking thought. This distinction calls for no modification in the theory of dreams.

IV

In some analyses, or in some periods of an analysis, a divorce may become apparent between dream-life and

waking life, like the divorce between the activity of
phantasy and waking life which is found in the 'continued story' (a novel in day-dreams). In that case one
dream leads off from another, taking as its central point
some element which was lightly touched upon in its
predecessor, and so on. But we find far more frequently
that dreams are not attached to one another but are
interpolated into a successive series of fragments of
waking thought.

V

The interpretation of a dream falls into two phases:
the phase in which it is translated and the phase in
which it is judged or has its value assessed. During the
first phase one must not allow oneself to be influenced
by any consideration whatever for the second phase.
It is as though one had before one a chapter from some
work in a foreign language—by Livy, for instance. The
first thing one wants to know is what Livy says in the
chapter; and it is only after this that the discussion
arises of whether what one has read is an historical
narrative or a legend or a digression on the part of the
author.

What conclusions can one draw from a correctly
translated dream? I have an impression that analytic
practice has not always avoided errors and over-esti-
mates on this point, partly owing to an exaggerated
respect for the 'mysterious unconscious'. It is only too
easy to forget that a dream is as a rule merely a thought
like any other, made possible by an easing-up of the
censorship and by unconscious intensification, and distorted by the operation of the censorship and by unconscious elaboration.

Let us take as an example the so-called dreams of
recovery. If a patient has had a dream of this kind, in
which he seems to abandon the restrictions of his
neurosis—if, for instance, he overcomes some phobia or
gives up some emotional attachment—we are inclined
to think that he has made a great step forward, that he

is ready to take his place in a new condition of life, that
he has begun to reckon upon his recovery, etc. This
may often be true, but quite as often such dreams of
recovery only have the value of dreams of convenience:
they signify a wish to be well at last, in order to avoid
another portion of the work of analysis which is felt to lie
ahead. In this sense, dreams of recovery very frequently
occur, for instance, when the patient is about to enter
upon a new and disagreeable phase of the transference.
He is behaving just like some neurotics who after a few
hours of analysis declare they have been cured—because they want to escape all the unpleasantness that
is bound to come up for discussion in the analysis.
Sufferers from war neuroses, too, who gave up their
symptoms because the therapy adopted by the army
doctors succeeded in making being ill even more uncom-
fortable than serving at the front—these sufferers, too,
were following the same economic laws, and in both
cases alike the cures have proved to be only temporary.

VI

It is by no means easy to arrive at general conclusions upon the value of correctly translated dreams.
If a conflict of ambivalence is taking place in a patient,
then the emergence in him of a hostile thought certainly
does not imply a permanent overcoming of his affectionate impulse, that is to say, a resolution of the conflict:
neither does any such implication follow from a *dream*
with a similarly hostile content. During a conflict of
ambivalence such as this, there are often two dreams
every night, each of them representing an opposite
attitude. In that case the progress lies in the fact that a
complete isolation of the two contrasted impulses has
been achieved and that each of them, with the help of
its unconscious intensifications, can be followed and
understood to its extreme limits. And if it sometimes
happens that one of the two ambivalent dreams has
been forgotten, one must not be deceived into assuming
that a decision has been made in favour of the one side.

The fact that one of the dreams has been forgotten shows, it is true, that for the moment one tendency is in the ascendant, but that is true only of the one day, and may be changed. The next night may perhaps bring the opposite expression into the foreground. The true state of the conflict can only be determined by taking into account all the other indications, including those of waking life.

VII

The question of the value to be assigned to dreams is intimately related to the other question of their susceptibility to influence from 'suggestion' by the physician. Analysts may at first be alarmed at the mention of this possibility. But on further reflection this alarm will give place to the realization that the influencing of the patient's dreams is no more a blunder on the part of the analyst or disgrace to him than the guiding of the patient's conscious thoughts.

The fact that the manifest content of dreams is influenced by the analytic treatment stands in no need of proof. It follows from our knowledge that dreams are dependent upon waking life and work over material derived from it. Occurrences during analytic treatment are of course among the impressions of waking life and soon become some of the most powerful of these. So it is not to be wondered at that patients should dream of things which the analyst has discussed with them and of which he has aroused expectations in them. At least it is no more to be wondered at than what is implied in the familiar fact of 'experimental' dreams.

And, from here, our interest proceeds to the question whether the latent dream-thoughts that have to be arrived at by interpretation can also be influenced or suggested by the analyst. And to this the answer must once more be that they obviously can be. For a portion of these latent dream-thoughts correspond to pre-conscious thought-formations, perfectly capable of being conscious, with which the dreamer might quite well have reacted to the physician's remarks in his waking state too—whether the patient's reactions were favourable to those remarks or in opposition to them. In fact, if we replace the dream by the dream-thoughts which it contains, the question of how far one can suggest dreams coincides with the more general question of how far a patient in analysis is accessible to suggestion.

On the mechanism of dream-formation itself, on the dream-work in the strict sense of the word, one never exercises any influence: of that one may be quite sure.

Besides that portion of the dream which we have already discussed—the preconscious dream-thoughts— every true dream contains indications of the repressed wishful impulses to which it owes the possibility of its formation. The doubter will reply that they appear in the dream because the dreamer knows that he ought to produce them—that they are expected by the analyst. The analyst himself will rightly think otherwise.

If a dream brings up situations that can be interpreted as referring to scenes from the dreamer's past, it seems especially important to ask whether the physician's influence can also play a part in such elements as those. And this question is most urgent of all in the case of what are called 'confirmatory' dreams, dreams which, as it were, lag after the analysis. With some patients these are the only dreams that one obtains. Such patients reproduce the forgotten experiences of their childhood only after one has constructed them from their symptoms, associations and other signs and has propounded these constructions to them. Then follow the confirmatory dreams, concerning which, however, the doubt arises whether they may not be entirely without evidential value, since they may have been imagined in compliance with the physician's words instead of having been brought to light from the dreamer's unconscious. This ambiguous position cannot be escaped in the analysis, since with these patients unless one interprets, constructs and propounds, one never obtains access to what is repressed in them.

The situation takes a favourable turn if the analysis of a confirmatory, lagging dream of this sort is immediately followed by feelings of remembering what has hitherto been forgotten. But even then the sceptic can fall back upon an assertion that the recollections are illusory. Moreover, such feelings are for the most part absent. The repressed material is only allowed through bit by bit; and every lack of completeness inhibits or delays the forming of a sense of conviction. Furthermore, what we are dealing with may not be the reproduction of a real and forgotten event but the emergence of an unconscious phantasy, about which no feeling of memory is ever to be expected, though the possibility may sometimes remain of a sense of subjective conviction.

Is it possible, then, that confirmatory dreams are really the result of suggestion, that they are compliant dreams? The patients who produce only confirmatory dreams are the same patients in whom doubt plays the principal part in resistance. One makes no attempt at shouting down this doubt by means of one's authority or at reducing it by arguments. It must persist until it is brought to an end in the further course of the analysis. The analyst, too, may himself retain a doubt of the same kind in some particular instances. What makes him certain in the end is precisely the complication of the problem before him, which is like the solution of a jig-saw puzzle. A coloured picture, pasted upon a thin sheet of wood and fitting exactly into a wooden frame, is cut into a large number of pieces of the most irregular and crooked shapes. If one succeeds in arranging the confused heap of fragments, each of which bears upon it an unintelligible piece of drawing, so that the picture acquires a meaning, so that there is no gap anywhere in the design and so that the whole fits into the frame—if all these conditions are fulfilled, then one knows that one has solved the puzzle and that there is no alternative solution.

An analogy of this kind can of course have no

meaning for a patient while the work of analysis is still uncompleted. At this point I recall a discussion which I was led into with a patient whose exceptionally ambivalent attitude was expressed in the most intense compulsive doubt. He did not dispute my interpretations of his dreams and was very much struck by their agreement with the hypotheses which I put forward. But he asked whether these confirmatory dreams might not be an expression of his compliance towards me. I pointed out that the dreams had also brought up a quantity of details of which I could have had no suspicion and that his behaviour in the treatment apart from this had not been precisely characterized by compliance. Whereupon he switched over to another theory and asked whether his narcissistic wish to be cured might not have caused him to produce these dreams, since, after all, I had held out to him a prospect of recovery if he were able to accept my constructions. I could only reply that I had not yet come across any such mechanism of dream-formation. But a decision was reached by another road. He recollected some dreams which he had had before starting analysis and indeed before he had known anything about it; and the analysis of these dreams, which were free from all suspicion of suggestion, led to the same interpretations as the later ones. It is true that his obsession for contradiction once more found a way out in the idea that the earlier dreams had been less clear than those that occurred during the treatment; but I was satisfied with their similarity. I think that in general it is a good plan occasionally to bear in mind the fact that people were in the habit of dreaming before there was such a thing as psycho-analysis.

VIII

It may well be that dreams during psycho-analysis succeed in bringing to light what is repressed to a greater extent than dreams outside that situation. But it cannot be proved, since the two situations are not comparable; the employment of dreams in analysis is something very remote from their original purpose. On the other hand, it cannot be doubted that within an analysis far more of the repressed is brought to light in connection with dreams than by any other method. In order to account for this, there must be some motive power, some unconscious force, which is better able to lend support to the purposes of analysis during the state of sleep than at other times. What is here in question cannot well be any factor other than the patient's compliance towards the analyst which is derived from his parental complex—in other words, the positive portion of what we call the transference; and in fact, in many dreams which recall what has been forgotten and repressed, it is impossible to discover any other unconscious wish to which the motive force for the formation of the dream can be attributed. So that if anyone wishes to maintain that most of the dreams that can be made use of in analysis are compliant dreams and owe their origin to suggestion, nothing can be said against that opinion from the point of view of analytical theory. I need only add a reference to what I have said in my *Introductory Lectures* [(1916–17) Lecture XXVIII], where I have dealt with the relation between transference and suggestion and shown how little the trustworthiness of our results is affected by a recognition of the operation of suggestion in our sense of the word.

In *Beyond the Pleasure Principle* [(1920), trans., 1922, 17ff.; new trans., 1950, 18ff.] I have dealt with the economic problem of how what are in every respect distressing experiences of the early infantile sexual period can succeed in forcing their way through to any kind of reproduction. I was obliged to ascribe to them an extraordinarily strong upward drive in the shape of the 'compulsion to repeat'—a force able to overcome the repression which, in the service of the pleasure principle, weighs down upon them—though not until 'the work of the treatment, operating in the same direction, has loosened the repression'. Here we may add that it is the positive transference that gives this assistance to the compulsion to repeat. Thus an alliance has been made between the treatment and the compulsion to repeat, an alliance which is directed in the first instance against the pleasure principle but of which the ultimate purpose is the establishment of the dominion of the reality principle. As I have shown in the passage to which I am referring, it happens only too often that the compulsion to repeat throws over its obligations under this alliance and is not content with the return of the repressed merely in the form of dream-pictures.

IX

So far as I can at present see, dreams that occur in a traumatic neurosis are the only *genuine* exceptions, and punishment dreams are the only *apparent* exceptions, to the rule that dreams are directed towards wish-fulfilment. In the latter class of dreams we are met by the remarkable fact that actually nothing belonging to the latent dream-thoughts is taken up into the manifest content of the dream. Something quite different appears instead, which must be described as a reaction-formation against the dream-thoughts, a rejection and complete contradiction of them. Such offensive action as this against the dream can only be ascribed to the critical function of the ego and it must therefore be assumed that the latter, provoked by the unconscious wish-fulfilment, has been temporarily re-established even during the sleeping state. It might have reacted to the undesirable content of the dream by waking up; but it has found a means, by the construction of the punishment dream, of avoiding an interruption of sleep.

For instance, in the case of the well-known dreams of the poet Rosegger which I have mentioned in *The Interpretation of Dreams* [English translation, revised ed. (1932), 438–440], we must suspect the existence of a suppressed version with an arrogant and boastful text, whereas the actual dream said to him: 'You are an incompetent journeyman-tailor.' It would, of course, be useless to look for a repressed wishful impulse as the motive power for a manifest dream such as this; one must be content with the fulfilment of the wish for self-criticism.

A dream-structure of this kind will excite less astonishment if one considers how frequently dream-distortion, acting in the service of the censorship, replaces a particular element by something that is in some sense or other its opposite or contrary. It is only a short step from there to the replacement of a characteristic portion of the content of the dream by a defensive denial, and one further step will lead to the whole objectionable dream-content being replaced by the punishment dream. I should like to give a couple of characteristic examples of the intermediate phase in the falsification of the manifest content.

Here is an extract from the dream of a girl with a strong fixation to her father, who had difficulty in talking during the analysis. She was sitting in a room with a girl friend, and dressed only in a kimono. A gentleman came in and she felt embarrassed. But the gentleman said: 'Why, this is the girl we once saw dressed so nicely!'—The gentleman stood for me, and, further back, for her father. But we can make nothing of the dream unless we make up our mind to replace the most important element in the gentleman's speech by its contrary: 'This is the girl I once saw *undressed* and who looked so nice then!' When she was a child of three or four she had for some time slept in the same room as her father and everything goes to suggest that she used then to throw back her clothes in her sleep in order to look pleasing to her father. The subsequent repression of her pleasure in exhibiting herself was the motive for her secretiveness in the treatment, her dislike of showing herself openly.

And here is another scene from the same dream. She was reading her own case history, which she had before her in print. In it was a statement that a young

man murdered his *fiancée*—cocoa—that comes under
anal erotism. This last phrase was a thought that she
had in the dream at the mention of cocoa.—The interpretation of this piece of the dream was even more
difficult than the former one. It emerged at last that
before going to sleep she had been reading my 'History
of an Infantile Neurosis' [(1918) *Collected Papers*, **3**, 473],
the central point of which is the real or imagined
observation by a patient of his parents copulating. She
had already once before related this case history to her
own, and this was not the only indication that in her
case as well there was a question of an observation of
the same kind. The young man murdering his *fiancée*
was a clear reference to a sadistic view of the scene of
copulation. But the next element, the cocoa, was very
remote from it. Her only association to cocoa was that
her mother used to say that cocoa gave one a headache,
and she maintained that she had heard the same thing
from other women. Moreover she had at one time
identified herself with her mother by means of headaches like hers. Now I could find no link between the
two elements of the dream except by supposing that
she wanted to make a diversion from the consequences
of the observation of coitus. No, she was saying, coitus
had nothing to do with the procreation of children; child-
dren came from something one ate (as they do in fairy
tales); and the mention of anal erotism, which looks like
an attempt in the dream at interpretation, supplemented the infantile theory which she had called to her
help, by adding anal birth to it.

X

Astonishment is sometimes expressed at the fact
that the dreamer's ego can appear two or more times in
the manifest dream, once as himself and again disguised
behind the figures of other people. During the course
of the construction of the dream, the secondary elaboration has evidently sought to obliterate this multiplicity
of the ego, which cannot fit in with any possible scenic

situation; but it is re-established by the work of interpretation. In itself this multiplicity is no more remarkable than the multiple appearance of the ego in a waking
thought, especially when the ego divides itself into subject and object, puts one part of itself as an observing
and critical agency in contrast to the other, or compares
its present nature with its recollected past, which was
also ego once; for instance, in such sentences as 'When *I*
think what *I*'ve done to this man' or 'When *I* think
that *I* too was a child once'. But I should reject as a
meaningless and unjustifiable piece of speculation the
notion that *all* figures that appear in a dream are to be
regarded as fragmentations and representatives of the
dreamer's own ego. It is enough that we should keep
firmly to the fact that the separation of the ego from an
observing, critical, punishing agency (an ego-ideal)
must be taken into account in the interpretation of
dreams.

XIII

SOME ADDITIONAL NOTES UPON DREAM-INTERPRETATION AS A WHOLE[1]

(1925)

(A) THE LIMITS TO THE POSSIBILITY OF INTERPRETATION

IT may be asked whether it is possible to give a complete and assured translation into the language of waking life (that is, an interpretation) of every product of dream-life. This question will not be treated here in the abstract but with reference to the conditions under which one works at interpreting dreams.

Our mental activities pursue either a useful aim or the immediate attainment of pleasure. In the former case what we are dealing with are intellectual judgements, preparations for action or the conveyance of information to other people. In the latter case we describe these activities as play or phantasy. What is useful is itself (as is well known) only a circuitous path to pleasurable satisfaction. Now, dreaming is an activity of the second kind, which is indeed, from the point of view of evolution, the earlier one. It is misleading to say that dreams are concerned with the tasks of life before us or seek to find a solution for the problems of our daily work. That is the business of preconscious thought. Useful work of this kind is as remote from dreams as is any intention of conveying information to another person. When a dream deals with a problem of actual life, it solves it in the manner of an irrational wish and not in the manner of a reasonable reflection. There is only one

[1] ['Einige Nachträge zum Ganzen der Traumdeutung' appeared for the first time in 1925 in *Ges. Schr.*, **3**, 172; reprinted *Ges. W.*, **1**. The three notes were evidently intended for inclusion in the eighth edition of *Traumdeutung* (1930). For some reason, however, they were omitted from it and were consequently also omitted from the Revised Edition of the English translation based upon it in 1932. Present translation, reprinted from *Int. J. Psycho-Anal.*, **24** (1943), 71, by James Strachey.]

useful task, only one function, that can be ascribed to a dream, and that is the guarding of sleep from interruption. A dream may be described as a piece of phantasy working on behalf of the maintenance of sleep.

It follows from this that it is on the whole a matter of indifference to the sleeping ego what may be dreamt during the night so long as the dream performs its task, and that those dreams best fulfil their function about which there is nothing to be said after waking. If it so often happens otherwise, if we remember dreams—even after years and decades—it always means that there has been an irruption of the repressed unconscious into the normal ego. Unless the repressed had been pacified in this way, it would not have consented to lend its help to the removal of the threat of disturbance to sleep. We know that it is the fact of this irruption that gives dreams their importance for psychopathology. If we can uncover a dream's motivating force, we shall obtain unsuspected information about the repressed impulses in the unconscious; and on the other hand, if we can undo its distortions, we shall overhear preconscious thought taking place in states of internal reflection which would not have attracted consciousness to themselves during the daytime.

No one can practice the interpretation of dreams as an isolated activity: it remains a part of the work of analysis. In analysis we direct our interest according to necessity, now to the preconscious content of the dream and now to the unconscious contribution to its formation; and we often neglect the one element in favour of the other. Nor would it be of any avail for anyone to endeavour to interpret dreams outside analysis. He would not succeed in escaping the conditions of the analytic situation; and if he worked at his own dreams, he would be undertaking a self-analysis. This comment would not apply to someone who did without the dreamer's collaboration and sought to interpret dreams by intuitive insight. But dream-interpretation of such a kind, without reference to the dreamer's associations, would in the most favourable case remain a piece of unscientific virtuosity of the most doubtful value.

If one practises dream-interpretation according to the sole justifiable technical procedure, one soon notices that success depends entirely upon the tension of resistance between the awakened ego and the repressed unconscious. Work under a 'high pressure of resistance' demands (as I have explained elsewhere [p. 137 above]) a different attitude on the part of the analyst from work under a low pressure. In analysis one has for long periods at a time to deal with strong resistances which are still unknown to one and which it will in any case be impossible to overcome so long as they remain unknown. It is therefore not to be wondered at that only a certain portion of a patient's dream-products can be translated and made use of, and even at that not completely. Even if, owing to one's own experience, one is in a position to understand many dreams to the interpretation of which the dreamer has contributed little, one must always remember that the certainty of such interpretations remains in doubt and one hesitates to press one's conjectures upon the patient.

Critical voices will now be raised. It will be objected that, since it is not possible to interpret every dream that is dealt with, one should cease asserting more than one can establish and should be content to say that *some* dreams can be shown by interpretation to have a meaning but that as to the rest we are in ignorance. But the very fact that success in interpretation depends upon the resistance absolves the analyst from the necessity for such modesty. He may have the experience of a dream which was at first unintelligible becoming clear during the very same hour after some fortunate piece of analytic work has got rid of one of the dreamer's resistances. A portion of the dream which he had hitherto forgotten may suddenly occur to him and may bring the key to the interpretation; or a new association may emerge which may throw light upon the darkness. It sometimes happens, too, that, after months or years of analytic labour, one returns to a dream which at the beginning of the treatment seemed meaningless and incomprehensible but which is now, in the light of knowledge obtained in the meantime, completely elucidated. And if one further takes into consideration the argument from the theory of dreams that the model dreams produced by children invariably have a clear meaning and are easy to interpret, then it will be justifiable to assert that dreams are quite generally mental structures that are capable of interpretation, though the situation may not always allow of an interpretation being reached.

When the interpretation of a dream has been discovered, it is not always easy to decide whether it is a 'complete' one—that is, whether further preconscious thoughts may not also have found expression in the same dream. In that case we must consider the meaning proved which is based upon the dreamer's associations and our estimate of the situation, without on that account feeling bound to reject the other meaning. It remains possible, though unproven: one must become accustomed to a dream being thus capable of having many meanings. Moreover, the blame for this is not always to be laid upon incompleteness of the work of interpretation; it may just as well be inherent in the latent dream-thoughts themselves. Indeed it may happen in waking life, quite apart from the situation of dream-interpretation, that one is uncertain whether some remark that one has heard or some piece of information that one has received justifies one in coming to such and such a conclusion or whether it is hinting at something else beyond its obvious meaning.

One interesting occurrence which has been insufficiently investigated is to be seen where the same manifest dream-content gives simultaneous expression to a set of concrete ideas and to an abstract line of thought based upon them. It is of course difficult for the dream-work to find a means for representing abstract thoughts.

(B) MORAL RESPONSIBILITY FOR THE CONTENT OF DREAMS

IN the introductory chapter of this book [*The Interpretation of Dreams*] (which deals with 'The Scientific Literature of Dream-Problems') I have shown the way in which writers have reacted to what is felt as the distressing fact that the unbridled content of dreams is so often at odds with the moral sense of the dreamer. (I deliberately avoid speaking of 'criminal' dreams, as such a description, which would overstep the limits of psychological interest, seems to me quite unnecessary.) The immoral character of dreams has naturally provided a fresh motive for denying them any psychological value: if dreams are the meaningless product of disordered mental activity, then there can be no ground for assuming responsibility for their apparent content.

The problem of responsibility for the manifest content of dreams has been fundamentally shifted and indeed disposed of by the explanations given in my *Interpretation of Dreams*.

We know now that the manifest content is an illusion, a *façade*. It is not worth while to submit it to an ethical examination or to take its breaches of morality any more seriously than its breaches of logic or mathematics. When the 'content' of the dream is spoken of, what must be referred to can only be the content of the preconscious thoughts and of the repressed wishful impulse which are revealed behind the *façade* of the dream by the work of interpretation. Nevertheless, this immoral *façade* has a question to put to us. We have heard that the latent dream-thoughts have to submit to a severe censorship before they are allowed access to the manifest content. How can it happen, then, that this censorship, which makes difficulties over more trivial things, breaks down so completely over these manifestly immoral dreams?

The answer is not easy to come by and may perhaps not seem completely satisfying. If, in the first place, one submits these dreams to interpretation, one finds that some of them have given no offence to the censorship because *au fond* they have no bad meaning. They are innocent boastings or identifications that put up a mask of pretence; they have not been censored because they do not tell the truth. But others of them—and, it must be admitted, the majority—really mean what they say and have undergone no distortion from the censorship. They are an expression of immoral, incestuous and perverse impulses or of murderous and sadistic lusts. The dreamer reacts to many of these dreams by waking up in a fright, in which case the situation is no longer obscure to us. The censorship has neglected its task, this has been noticed too late, and the development of anxiety is a substitute for the distortion that has been omitted. In still other instances of such dreams, even that expression of emotion is absent. The objectionable matter is carried along by the height of the sexual excitement that has been reached during the sleep, or it is viewed with the same tolerance with which even a waking person can regard a fit of rage, an angry mood or the indulgence in cruel phantasies.

But our interest in the genesis of these *manifestly* immoral dreams is greatly reduced when we find from analysis that the majority of dreams—innocent dreams, dreams without affect and anxiety dreams—are revealed, when the distortions of the censorship have been undone, as the fulfilments of immoral—egoistic, sadistic, perverse or incestuous—wishful impulses. As in the world of waking life, these masked criminals are far commoner than those with their vizors raised. The straightforward dream of sexual relations with one's mother, which Jocasta alludes to in the *Oedipus Rex*, is a rarity in comparison with all the multiplicity of dreams which psycho-analysis must interpret in the same sense.

I have dealt so exhaustively in these pages with this characteristic of dreams, which indeed provides the motive for their distortion, that I can pass at once from this topic to the problem that lies before us: Must one assume responsibility for the content of one's dreams? For the sake of completeness, it must, however, be added that dreams do not always offer immoral wish-fulfilments, but often energetic reactions against them in the form of 'punishment dreams'. In other words, the dream-censorship can not only express itself in distortions and the development of anxiety, but can go so far as to blot out the immoral subject-matter completely and replace it by something else that serves as an atonement, though it allows one to see what lies behind. But the problem of responsibility for the immoral content of dreams no longer exists for us as it formerly did for writers who knew nothing of latent dream-thoughts and the repressed part of our mental life. Obviously one must hold oneself responsible for the evil impulses of one's dreams. In what other way can one deal with them? Unless the content of the dream (rightly understood) is inspired by alien spirits, it is a part of my own being. If I seek to classify the impulses that are present in me according to social standards into good and bad, I must assume responsibility for both sorts; and if, in defence, I say that what is unknown, unconscious and repressed in me is not my 'ego', then I shall not be basing my position upon psycho-analysis, I shall not have accepted its conclusions and I shall perhaps be taught better by the criticisms of my fellow-men, by the disturbances in my actions and the confusion of my feelings. I shall perhaps learn that what I am repudiating not only 'is' in me but sometimes 'acts' from out of me as well.

It is true that in the metapsychological sense this bad repressed content does not belong to my 'ego'—that is, assuming that I am a morally blameless individual—but to an 'id' upon which my ego is seated. But this ego developed out of the id, it forms with it a single biological unit, it is only a specially modified peripheral portion of it, it is subject to the influences and obeys the

suggestions that arise from the id. For any vital purpose, a separation of the ego from the id would be a
hopeless undertaking.

Moreover, if I were to give way to my moral pride
and tried to decree that for purposes of moral valuation
I might disregard the evil in the id and need not make
my ego responsible for it, what use would that be to me?
Experience shows me that I nevertheless do take that
responsibility, that I am somehow compelled to do so.
Psycho-analysis has made us familiar with a pathological condition, the obsessional neurosis, in which the
poor ego feels itself responsible for all sorts of evil impulses of which it knows nothing, impulses which are
brought up against it in consciousness but which it is
unable to acknowledge. Something of this is present in
every normal person. It is a remarkable fact that the
more moral he is the more sensitive is his 'conscience'.
It is just as though we could say that the healthier a
man is, the more liable he is to contagions and to the
effects of injuries. This is no doubt because conscience
is itself a reaction-formation against the evil that is
perceived in the id. The more the latter is suppressed
the more active is the conscience.

The ethical narcissism of humanity should rest content with the knowledge that the fact of distortion in
dreams, as well as the existence of anxiety dreams and
punishment dreams, afford just as clear evidence of his
moral nature as dream-interpretation gives of the
existence and strength of his evil nature. If anyone is
dissatisfied with this and would like to be 'better' than
he was created, let him see whether he can attain more
in life than hypocrisy or inhibition.

The physician will leave it to the jurist to construct a
responsibility that is artificially limited to the metapsychological ego. It is notorious that the greatest
difficulties are encountered by attempts to derive from
such a construction any practical consequences not in
contradiction to human feelings.

(C) THE OCCULT SIGNIFICANCE OF DREAMS[1]

THERE seems to be no end to the problems of dream-life. But this can only be surprising if we forget that all the problems of mental life are repeated in dreams with the addition of a few new ones arising from the special nature of dreams. But many of the things that we study in dreams, because we meet with them there, have little or nothing to do with the psychological peculiarity of dreams. Thus, for instance, symbolism is not a dream-problem, but a topic connected with our archaic thinking—our 'root-language', as it was aptly called by the paranoic Schreber. [Cf. Freud (1911b), *Collected Papers*, **3**, 403.] It dominates myths and religious ritual no less than dreams, and dream-symbolism can scarcely even claim as a peculiarity the fact of its concealing more particularly what is important sexually. Again, it is not to be expected that the explanation of anxiety dreams will be found in the theory of dreams. Anxiety is a problem rather of neurosis, and all that remains to be discussed is how it comes about that anxiety can arise under dream conditions.

The position is just the same, I think, in the matter of the occult world. But, since dreams themselves have always been mysterious things, they have been brought into intimate connection with the other unknown mysteries. No doubt, too, they have a historic claim to that position, since in primaeval ages, when our mythology was being formed, dream-pictures may have played a part in the origin of ideas about spirits.

There would seem to be two categories of dreams with a claim to being reckoned as occult phenomena: prophetic dreams and telepathic ones. A countless

[1] [This subject and much of this actual material was dealt with by Freud at greater length in a posthumously published but hitherto untranslated paper 'Psychoanalyse und Telepathie' (1921), *Ges. W.*, **17**, 27; as well as in 'Dreams and Telepathy' (1922), *Collected Papers*, **4**, 408, and in Lecture XXX ('Dreams and the Occult') of his *New Introductory Lectures* (1932).]

multitude of witnesses speak in favour of both of them, while against both of them there is the obstinate aversion, or maybe prejudice, of science.

There can, indeed, be no doubt that there are such things as prophetic dreams, in the sense that their content gives some sort of picture of the future; the only question is whether these predictions coincide to any noticeable extent with what really happens subsequently. I must confess that upon this point my resolution in favour of impartiality deserts me. The notion that there is any mental power, apart from acute calculation, which can foresee future events in detail is on the one hand too much in contradiction to all the expectations and presumptions of science and on the other hand corresponds too closely to certain ancient and familiar human desires which criticism must reject as unjustifiable pretensions. I am therefore of opinion that after one has taken into account the untrustworthiness, credulity and unconvincingness of most of these reports, together with the possibility of falsifications of memory facilitated by emotional causes[1] and the inevitability of a few lucky shots, it may be anticipated that the spectre of prophetic dreams will disappear into nothing. Personally, I have never experienced anything or learnt of anything that could encourage a more favourable presumption.

It is otherwise with telepathic dreams. But at this point it must be made quite clear that no one has yet maintained that telepathic phenomena—the reception of a mental process by one person from another by means other than sensory perception—are exclusively related to dreams. Thus once again telepathy is not a dream-problem: our judgement upon whether it exists or not need not be based on a study of telepathic dreams.

If reports of telepathic occurrences (or, to speak less exactly, of thought-transference) are submitted to the same criticism as stories of other occult events, there remains a considerable amount of material which can-

[1] [Cf, above, page 70ff.]

not be so easily neglected. Further, it is much more possible to collect observations and experiences of one's own in this field which justify a favourable attitude to the problem of telepathy, even though they may not be enough to carry an assured conviction. One arrives at a provisional opinion that it may well be that telepathy really exists and that it provides the kernel of truth in many other hypotheses that would otherwise be incredible.

It is certainly right in what concerns telepathy, too, to adhere obstinately to a sceptical position and only to yield grudgingly to the force of evidence. I believe I have found a class of material which is exempt from the doubts which are otherwise justified—namely, unfulfilled prophecies of professional fortune-tellers. Unluckily, I have but few such observations at my disposal; but two among these have made a powerful impression on me. I am not in a position to describe them in such detail as would produce a similar effect upon other people, and I must restrict myself to bringing out a few essential points.

A prediction was made, then, to the people in question (at a strange place and by a strange fortune-teller, who at the same time went through some, presumably irrelevant, performances) that something would happen to them at a particular time, which in fact did *not* happen. The date at which the prophecy should have come true was long past. It was striking that those concerned told of their experience not with derision or disappointment but with obvious satisfaction. Included among what had been told them there were certain quite definite details which seemed capricious and unintelligible and would only have been justified if they had hit the mark. Thus, for instance, the palmist told a woman who was twenty-seven (though she looked much younger) and who had taken off her wedding-ring, that she would be married and have two children before she was thirty-two. The woman was forty-three when, now seriously ill, she told me the story in her analysis: she had remained childless. If one knew her private history (of which the 'Professor' in the lounge of the Paris hotel was certainly ignorant) one could understand the two numbers included in the prophecy. The girl had married after an unusually intense attachment to her father and had then had a passionate longing for children, so as to be able to put her husband in the place of her father. After years of disappointment, when she was on the brink of a neurosis, she obtained the prophecy, which promised her—the fate of her mother. For it was a fact that the latter had had two children by the time she was thirty-two. Thus it was only by the help of psycho-analysis that it was possible to give a significant interpretation of the peculiarities of this pretended message from without. But there was then no better explanation of the whole, unequivocally determined chain of events than to suppose that a strong wish on the part of the questioner—the strongest unconscious wish, in fact, of her whole emotional life and the motive force of her impending neurosis—had made itself manifest by being directly transferred to the fortune-teller, whose attention was distracted at the time by the performances he was going through.

I have often had an impression, in the course of experiments in my private circle, that strongly emotion-ally coloured recollections can be successfully trans-ferred without much difficulty. If one has the courage to submit to an analytical examination the associations of the person to whom the thoughts are supposed to be transferred, correspondences often come to light which would otherwise have remained undiscovered. On the basis of much experience I am inclined to draw the con-clusion that thought-transference of this kind comes about particularly easily at the moment at which an idea emerges from the unconscious, or, in theoretical terms, as it passes over from the 'primary process' to the 'secondary process'.

In spite of the caution which is prescribed by the importance, novelty and obscurity of the subject, I feel

F

that I should not be justified in holding back any longer these considerations upon the problem of telepathy. All of this has only this much to do with dreams: if there are such things as telepathic messages, the possibility cannot be dismissed of their reaching someone during sleep and coming to his knowledge in a dream. Indeed, on the analogy of other perceptual and intellectual material, the further possibility arises that telepathic messages received in the course of the day may only be dealt with during a dream of the following night. There would then be nothing contradictory in the material that had been telepathically communicated being modified and transformed in the dream like any other material. It would be satisfactory if with the help of psycho-analysis we could obtain further and better authenticated knowledge of telepathy.

XIV
THE RESISTANCES TO PSYCHO-ANALYSIS[1]
(1925)

A CHILD in his nurse's arms will turn away scream-ing at the sight of a strange face; a pious man will begin the new season with a prayer and he will also greet the first fruits of the year with a blessing; a peasant will refuse to buy a scythe unless it bears the trade-mark that was familiar to his parents. The distinction between these situations is obvious and would seem to justify one in looking for a different motive in each of them.

Nevertheless, it would be a mistake to overlook what they have in common. In each case we are dealing with unpleasure of the same kind. The child expresses it in an elementary fashion, the pious man lulls it by an artifice, while the peasant uses it as the motive for a decision. The source of this unpleasure is the demand made upon the mind by anything that is *new*, the psychical expenditure that it requires, the uncertainty, mounting up to anxious expectancy, which it brings along with it. It would be interesting to devote a whole study to mental reactions to novelty; for under certain, no longer primary, conditions we can observe behaviour of the contrary kind—a thirst for stimulation which flings itself upon anything that is new merely because it *is* new.

In scientific affairs there should be no place for re-coiling from novelty. Science, in her perpetual incom-pleteness and insufficiency, is driven to hope for her salvation in new discoveries and new ways of regarding things. She does well, in order not to be deceived, to arm herself with scepticism and to accept nothing new

[1] ['Die Widerstände gegen die Psychoanalyse' was first published in French in *La revue juive*, 1925. The original German appeared in *Imago*, **11** (1925), 1; reprinted *Ges. Schr.*, **11**, 224, and *Ges. W.*, **14**, 99. Translation by James Strachey.]

unless it has withstood the strictest examination. Sometimes, however, this scepticism shows two unexpected features; it may be sharply directed against what is new while it spares what is familiar and accepted, and it may be content to reject things before it has examined them. But in behaving thus it reveals itself as a prolongation of the primitive reaction against novelties and as a cloak for the retention of that reaction. It is a matter of common knowledge how often in the history of scientific research it has happened that innovations have met with intense and stubborn resistance, while subsequent events have shown that the resistance was unjustified and that the novelty was valuable and important. What provoked the resistance was, as a rule, certain factors in the subject-matter of the novelty, while, on the other side, several factors must have combined to make the irruption of the primitive reaction possible.

A particularly bad reception was accorded to psycho-analysis, which the present writer began to develop nearly thirty years ago from the discoveries of Josef Breuer (of Vienna) on the origin of neurotic symptoms. It cannot be disputed that it possessed the quality of novelty, even though it made use of plenty of material which was well-known from other sources (quite apart from Breuer's discoveries), such as the lessons from the teachings of Charcot, the great neuropathologist, and impressions derived from the sphere of hypnotic phenomena. Its original significance was purely therapeutic: it aimed at creating a new and efficient method for treating neurotic illnesses. But connections which could not be foreseen in the beginning caused psycho-analysis to reach out far beyond its original aim. It ended by claiming to have set our whole view of mental life upon a new basis and therefore to be of importance for every field of knowledge that is founded on psychology. After the years of complete neglect it suddenly became a subject of general interest—and let loose a storm of indignant opposition.

The *forms* in which the resistance to psycho-analysis

found expression need not now be considered. It is enough to say that the struggle over this innovation is by no means at an end, though it is already possible to see what direction it will take. Its opponents have not succeeded in suppressing the movement. Psycho-analysis, of which twenty years ago I was the only spokesman, has since attracted the support of numerous valuable and active workers, medical and non-medical, who make use of it as a procedure for the treatment of nervous diseases, as a method of psychological research and as an auxiliary instrument for scientific work in the most various departments of intellectual life. In the following pages our interest will be directed only to the *motives* of the resistance to psycho-analysis, with particular stress upon the composite character of that resistance and upon the differing amount of weight carried by its components.

From a clinical standpoint the neuroses must necessarily be put alongside the intoxications and such disorders as Graves' disease. These are conditions arising from an excess or a relative lack of certain highly active substances, whether produced inside the body or introduced into it from outside—in short, they are disturbances of the chemistry of the body, toxic conditions. If someone succeeded in isolating and demonstrating the hypothetical substance or substances concerned in neuroses, he would have no need to worry about opposition from the medical profession. For the present, however, no such avenue of approach to the problem is open. At the moment we can only start from the symptoms presented by a neurosis—symptoms which in the case of hysteria, for instance, consist of a combination of somatic and mental disturbances. Now Charcot's experiments as well as Breuer's clinical observations taught us that the *somatic* symptoms of hysteria are psychogenic too, that is, that they are precipitates of expired mental processes. By putting a subject into a state of hypnosis it was possible at will to produce the somatic symptoms of hysteria artificially.

Psycho-analysis took hold of this new realization and began to consider the problem of the nature of the psychical processes which led to these unusual consequences. But the direction taken by this enquiry was not to the liking of the contemporary generation of doctors. They had been brought up to respect only anatomical, physical and chemical factors. They were not prepared for taking psychical ones into account and therefore met them with indifference or antipathy. They obviously had doubts whether mental events allowed of any exact scientific treatment whatever. As an excessive reaction against an earlier phase during which medicine had been dominated by what was known as the 'philosophy of Nature',[1] they regarded abstractions, such as those with which psychology is obliged to work, as nebulous, fantastic and mystical; while they simply refused to believe in remarkable phenomena which might have been the starting-point of research. The symptoms of hysterical neuroses were looked upon as shamming and the phenomena of hypnotism as a hoax. Even the psychiatrists, upon whose attention the most unusual and astonishing mental phenomena were constantly being forced, showed no inclination to examine their details or enquire into their connections. They were content to classify the variegated array of symptoms and trace them back, so far as they could manage, to somatic, anatomical or chemical aetiological disturbances. During this materialistic or, rather, mechanistic period, medicine made splendid advances, but it also showed a short-sighted misunderstanding of the most prominent and most difficult problems of life.

It is easy to understand why doctors, with an attitude of this kind towards the mind, should have had no liking for psycho-analysis and should have demurred to its demand for learning many things afresh and for seeing many things in a different light. But as a compensa-

---

[1] [A pantheistic attitude, chiefly associated with the name of Schelling, which was very prevalent in Germany during the first part of the nineteenth century. Some details will be found in Bernfeld (1944).]

tion it might be supposed that the new theory would be all the more likely to meet with applause from philosophers. For philosophers were accustomed to putting abstract concepts (or, as unkind tongues would say, hazy words) in the forefront of their explanations of the universe, and it would be impossible that they should object to the extension of the sphere of psychology proposed by psycho-analysis. But here another obstacle arose. The philosophers' idea of what is mental was not that of psycho-analysis. The overwhelming majority of philosophers regard as mental only the phenomena of consciousness. For them the world of consciousness coincides with the sphere of what is mental. Everything else that may take place in the 'mind'—an entity so hard to grasp—is relegated by them to the organic determinants of mental processes or to processes parallel to mental ones. Or, more strictly speaking, the mind has no contents other than the phenomena of consciousness, and consequently psychology, the science of the mind, has no other subject-matter. And on this point the layman's view is the same.

What, then, can a philosopher say to a theory which, like psycho-analysis, asserts that on the contrary what is mental is in itself *unconscious* and that being conscious is only a *quality*, which may or may not accrue to a particular mental act and the withholding of which may perhaps alter that act in no other respect? He will naturally say that anything both unconscious and mental would be a monstrosity, a *contradictio in adjecto*, and he will fail to observe that in making this judgement he is merely repeating his own definition of what is mental, a definition which may perhaps be too narrow. It is easy for philosophers to feel this certainty, since they have no acquaintance with the material whose investigation has compelled analysts to believe in unconscious mental acts. Philosophers have never taken account of hypnosis, they have not concerned themselves with the interpreting of dreams—on the contrary, like doctors, they regard dreams as the meaning-

less products of reduced mental activity during sleep—
they are scarcely aware that there are such things as
obsessions and delusions and they would find themselves
in a most embarrassing situation if they were asked to
explain them on the basis of their own psychological
premises. Analysts, likewise, refuse to say what the
unconscious is, but they can indicate the domain of
phenomena whose observation has obliged them to
assume its existence. Philosophers, who know no kind
of observation other than self-observation, cannot follow them into that domain.

So it comes about that psycho-analysis derives
nothing but disadvantages from its middle position
between medicine and philosophy. Doctors regard it as
a speculative system and refuse to believe that, like
every other natural science, it is based upon a patient
and tireless elaboration of facts from the world of perception; philosophers, measuring it by the standard of
their own artificially constructed systems, find that it
starts from impossible premises and reproach it because
its most general concepts (which are only now in process
of evolution) lack clarity and precision.

This state of affairs is enough to account for the
reluctant and hesitant reception of analysis in scientific
quarters. But it does not explain the outbursts of
indignation, derision and scorn which, in disregard of
every standard of logic and good taste, have characterized the controversial methods of its opponents. A
reaction of such a kind suggests that resistances other
than purely intellectual ones were stirred up and that
powerful emotional forces were aroused. And there are
indeed plenty of things to be found in the theory of
psycho-analysis calculated to produce such an effect as
this upon the passions of men of every kind and not
upon scientists alone. Above all there is the very
important place in the mental life of human beings
which psycho-analysis assigns to what are known as the
sexual instincts. According to psycho-analytic theory
the symptoms of the neuroses are distorted substitutive

satisfactions of sexual instinctual forces, the direct satisfaction of which has been frustrated by internal resistances. Later on, when analysis had extended beyond its original field of work and began to be applied to normal mental life, it sought to show that these same sexual components, which could be diverted from their immediate aims and directed to other things, made the most important contributions to the cultural achievements of the individual and of society. These views were not entirely new. The incomparable significance of sexual life had been proclaimed by the philosopher Schopenhauer in an intensely impressive passage. Moreover, what psycho-analysis called sexuality was by no means identical with the impulsion towards a union of the two sexes or towards producing a pleasurable sensation in the genitals; it had far more resemblance to the all-inclusive and all-preserving Eros of Plato's *Symposium*.

But the opponents of psycho-analysis forgot its illustrious forerunners; they fell upon it as though it had made an assault upon the dignity of the human race. They accused it of 'pansexualism', though the psycho-analytic theory of the instincts had always been strictly dualistic and had at no time failed to recognize, alongside the sexual instincts, others to which it actually ascribed force enough to suppress the sexual instincts. (These mutually opposing forces were described to begin with as the sexual instincts and the ego instincts. A later theoretical development changed them into Eros and the instinct of death or destruction.) The suggestion that art, religion and social order originated in part in a contribution from the sexual instincts was represented by the opponents of analysis as a humiliation of the highest possessions of civilization. They emphatically declared that men have other interests besides this eternal one of sex, overlooking in their zeal the fact that animals too have other interests—indeed they are subject to sexuality, not permanently like men, but only in bouts occurring at specific periods—overlooking, too, the fact that the existence of these other interests in men had never been disputed and that nothing can be altered in the value of a cultural achievement by its being shown to have been derived from elementary animal instinctual sources.

Such a display of unfairness and lack of logic cries out for an explanation. Its origin is not hard to find. Human civilization rests upon two pillars, of which one is the control of natural forces and the other the restriction of our instincts. The ruler's throne rests upon fettered slaves. Among the instinctual components which are thus brought into service, the sexual instincts, in the narrower sense of the word, are conspicuous for their strength and savagery. Woe, if they should be set loose! The throne would be overturned and the ruler trampled under foot. Society is aware of this—and will not allow the subject to be mentioned.

But why not? What harm could the discussion do? Psycho-analysis has never said a word in favour of un-fettering instincts that would injure our community; on the contrary it has issued a warning and an exhortation to us to mend our ways. But society refuses to consent to the ventilation of the question because it has a bad conscience in more than one respect. In the first place it has set up a high ideal of morality—morality being restriction of the instincts—and insists that all its members shall fulfil that ideal without troubling itself with the possibility that obedience may bear heavily upon the individual. Nor is it sufficiently wealthy or well-organized to be able to compensate the individual for his expenditure in instinctual renunciation. It is consequently left to the individual to decide how he can obtain enough compensation for the sacrifice he has made to enable him to retain his mental balance. On the whole, however, he is obliged to live psychologically beyond his income, while the unsatisfied claims of his instincts make him feel the demands of civilization as a constant pressure upon him. Thus society maintains a condition of cultural hypocrisy, which is bound to be accompanied by a sense of insecurity and a necessity for guarding what is an undeniably precarious situation by forbidding criticism and discussion. This line of thought holds good for all the instinctual impulses, including, therefore, the egoistic ones. The question whether it applies to all possible forms of civilization, and not merely to those which have evolved hitherto, cannot be discussed here. As regards the sexual instincts in the narrower sense, there is the further point that in most people they are tamed insufficiently and in a manner which is psychologically wrong and are therefore readier than the rest to break loose.

Psycho-analysis has revealed the weaknesses of this system and has recommended that it should be altered. It proposes that there should be a reduction in the strictness with which instincts are repressed and that correspondingly more play should be given to truthfulness. Certain instinctual impulses, with whose suppression society has gone too far, should be permitted a greater amount of satisfaction; in the case of certain others the inefficient method of suppressing them by means of repression should be replaced by a better and securer procedure. As a result of these criticisms psycho-analysis is regarded as 'inimical to culture' and has been put under a ban as a 'social danger'. This resistance cannot last for ever. No human institution can in the long run escape the influence of fair criticism; but men's attitude to psycho-analysis is still dominated by this fear, which gives rein to their passions and diminishes their power of logical argument.

By its theory of the instincts psycho-analysis offended the feelings of individuals in so far as they regarded themselves as members of the social community; another branch of its theory was calculated to hurt every single person at the tenderest point of his own psychical development. Psycho-analysis disposed once and for all of the fairy tale of an asexual childhood. It demonstrated the fact that sexual interests and activities occur in small children from the beginning

of their lives. It showed what transformations those
activities pass through, how at about the age of five
they succumb to inhibition and how from puberty onwards they enter the service of the reproductive function. It recognized that early infantile sexual life
reaches its peak in what is known as the Oedipus complex (an emotional attachment by the child to the
parent of the opposite sex accompanied by an attitude
of rivalry to the parent of the same sex) and that at that
period of life these impulses still continue uninhibited as
straightforward sexual desires. This can be confirmed so
easily that only the greatest efforts could make it
possible to overlook it. Every individual has in fact
gone through this phase but has afterwards energetically repressed it and succeeded in forgetting it. A
horror of incest and an enormous sense of guilt are left
over from this prehistoric epoch of the individual's
existence. It may be that something quite similar
occurred in the prehistoric epoch of the human species
as a whole and that the beginnings of morality, religion
and social order were intimately connected with the
surmounting of that primaeval age. To adults their
prehistory seems so inglorious that they refuse to allow
themselves to be reminded of it: they were infuriated
when psycho-analysis tried to lift the veil of amnesia
from their years of childhood. There was only one way
out: what psycho-analysis asserted must be false and
what posed as a new science must be a tissue of fancies
and distortions.

Thus the strongest resistances to psycho-analysis
were not of an intellectual kind but arose from emotional
sources. This explained their passionate character as
well as their poverty in logic. The situation obeyed a
simple formula: men in the mass behaved to psycho-
analysis in precisely the same way as individual
neurotics under treatment for their disorders. It is
possible, however, by patient work to convince these
latter individuals that everything happened as we
maintained it did: we had not invented it ourselves but

had arrived at it from a study of other neurotics covering a period of twenty or thirty years. The position was
at once alarming and consoling: alarming because it was
no small thing to have the whole human race as one's
patient, and consoling because after all everything was
taking place as the premises laid down by psycho-
analysis declared that it was bound to.

If we cast our eyes once again over the various
resistances to psycho-analysis that have been enumer-
ated, it is evident that only a minority of them are of
the kind which habitually arise against most scientific innovations of any considerable importance. The majority
of them are due to the fact that powerful human feelings are hurt by the subject-matter of the theory.
Darwin's theory of descent met with the same fate,
since it tore down the barrier that had been arrogantly
set up between men and beasts. I drew attention to this
analogy in an earlier paper (1917), in which I showed
how the psycho-analytic view of the relation of the
conscious ego to an overpowering unconscious was a
severe blow to human self-love. I described this as the
psychological blow to men's narcissism, and compared it
with the *biological* blow delivered by the theory of
descent and the earlier *cosmological* blow aimed at it by
the discovery of Copernicus.

Purely external difficulties have also contributed to
the resistance to psycho-analysis. It is not easy to
arrive at an independent judgement upon matters to do
with analysis without having experienced it oneself or
practised it on someone else. Nor can one do the latter
without having acquired a specific and decidedly
delicate technique, while until recently there was no
easily accessible means of learning psycho-analysis and
its technique. This position has now been improved by
the foundation (in 1920) of the Berlin Psycho-Analytic
Clinic and Training Institute, and soon afterwards (in
1922) of an exactly similar institute in Vienna.

Finally, with all reserve, the question may be raised
whether the personality of the present writer as a Jew

who has never sought to disguise the fact that he is a Jew may not have had a share in provoking the antipathy of his environment to psycho-analysis. An argument of this kind is not often uttered aloud. But we have unfortunately grown so suspicious that we cannot avoid thinking that this factor may not have been quite without its effect. Nor is it perhaps entirely a matter of chance that the first advocate of psycho-analysis was a Jew. To profess belief in this new theory called for a certain degree of readiness to accept a position of solitary opposition—a position with which no one is more familiar than a Jew.

XV

A NOTE UPON THE 'MYSTIC WRITING-PAD'[1]

(1925)

IF I distrust my memory—neurotics, as we know, do so to a remarkable extent, but normal people have every reason for doing so as well—I am able to supplement and guarantee its working by making a note in writing. In that case the surface upon which this note is preserved, the pocket-book or sheet of paper, is as it were a materialized portion of my mnemic apparatus, the rest of which I carry about with me invisible. I have only to bear in mind the place where this 'memory' has been deposited and I can then 'reproduce' it at any time I like, with the certainty that it will have remained unaltered and so have escaped the possible distortions to which it might have been subjected in my actual memory.

If I want to make full use of this technique for improving my mnemic function, I find that there are two different procedures open to me. On the one hand, I can choose a writing-surface which will preserve intact any note made upon it for an indefinite length of time—for instance, a sheet of paper which I can write upon in ink. I am then in possession of a 'permanent memory-trace'. The disadvantage of this procedure is that the receptive capacity of the writing-surface is soon exhausted. The sheet is filled with writing, there is no room on it for any more notes, and I find myself obliged to bring another sheet into use, that has not been written on. Moreover, the advantage of this procedure, the fact that it provides a 'permanent trace', may lose its value for me if after a time the note ceases to interest me and I no longer want to 'retain it in my memory'. The alternative procedure avoids both of these dis-

---

[1] ['Notiz über den "Wunderblock".' First published simultaneously in *Int. Z. Psychoanal.*, **11** (1925), 1, and in *Ges. Schr.*, **6**, 415; reprinted *Ges. W.*, **14**,3. Translation, reprinted from *Int. J. Psycho-Anal.*, **21** (1940), 469, by James Strachey.]

advantages. If, for instance, I write with a piece of chalk upon a slate, I have a receptive surface which retains its receptive capacity for an unlimited time and the notes upon which can be destroyed as soon as they cease to interest me, without any need for throwing away the writing-surface itself. Here the disadvantage is that I cannot preserve a permanent trace. If I want to put some fresh notes upon the slate, I must first wipe out the ones which cover it. Thus an unlimited receptive capacity and a retention of permanent traces seem to be mutually exclusive properties in the apparatus which we use as substitutes for our memory: either the receptive surface must be renewed or the note must be destroyed.

All the forms of auxiliary apparatus which we have invented for the improvement or intensification of our sensory functions are built on the same model as the sense organs themselves or portions of them: for instance, spectacles, photographic cameras, ear-trumpets. Measured by this standard, devices to aid our memory seem particularly imperfect, since our mental apparatus accomplishes precisely what they cannot: it has an unlimited receptive capacity for new perceptions and nevertheless lays down permanent—even though not unalterable—memory-traces of them. As long ago as in 1900 I gave expression in *The Interpretation of Dreams*[1] to a suspicion that this unusual capacity was to be divided between two different systems (or organs of the mental apparatus). According to this view, we possess a system Pcpt.-Cs., which receives perceptions but retains no permanent trace of them, so that it can react like a clean sheet to every new perception; while the permanent traces of the excitations which have been

---

[1] [Cf. the English translation (Revised Edition, 1932), 497f. The translation of the decisive sentence, however, is misleading: 'for consciousness memory and quality are mutually exclusive in the ψ-systems' should read 'memory and the quality of being conscious are mutually exclusive in the ψ-systems'. As Freud mentions in *Beyond the Pleasure Principle* (1920; trans.,1922, 27n.; new trans., 1950, 28n.), this distinction had already been drawn by Breuer in his theoretical section of *Studien über Hysterie* (1895, 164, footnote).]

received are preserved in 'mnemic systems' lying behind the perceptual system. Later, in *Beyond the Pleasure Principle* (1920),[1] I added a remark to the effect that the inexplicable phenomenon of consciousness arises in the perceptual system *instead of* the permanent traces.

Some time ago there came upon the market, under the name of the Mystic Writing-Pad,[2] a small contrivance that promises to perform more than the sheet of paper or the slate. It claims to be nothing more than a writing-tablet from which notes can be erased by an easy movement of the hand. But if it is examined more closely it will be found that its construction shows a remarkable agreement with my hypothetical structure of our perceptual apparatus and that it can in fact provide both an ever-ready receptive surface and permanent traces of the notes that have been made upon it.

The Mystic Pad is a slab of dark brown resin or wax with a paper edging; over the slab is laid a thin transparent sheet, the top end of which is firmly secured to the slab while its bottom end rests upon it without being fixed to it. This transparent sheet is the more interesting part of the little device. It itself consists of two layers, which can be detached from each other except at their two ends. The upper layer is a transparent piece of celluloid; the lower layer is made of thin translucent waxed paper. When the apparatus is not in use, the lower surface of the waxed paper adheres lightly to the upper surface of the wax slab.

To make use of the Mystic Pad, one writes upon the celluloid portion of the covering-sheet which rests upon the wax slab. For this purpose no pencil or chalk is

[1] [English translation, 1922, 28, where, once more, the original meaning is unfortunately missed: 'consciousness arises *in the place of* the memory trace' should read '*instead of*'. (The mistake is corrected in the new translation, 1950, 29.) So too in *The Interpretation of Dreams* (Revised Edition, 1932, 49n.): 'consciousness occurs actually *in the locality* of the memory-trace', should read, once again, '*instead of* the memory-trace'.]

[2] [It is still obtainable as such in England, where, however, it is also known as 'Printator'.]

necessary, since the writing does not depend on material being deposited upon the receptive surface. It is a return to the ancient method of writing upon tablets of clay or wax: a pointed stilus scratches the surface, the depressions upon which constitute the 'writing'. In the case of the Mystic Pad this scratching is not effected directly, but through the medium of the covering-sheet. At the points which the stilus touches, it presses the lower surface of the waxed paper on to the wax slab, and the grooves are visible as dark writing upon the otherwise smooth whitish-grey surface of the celluloid. If one wishes to destroy what has been written, all that is necessary is to raise the double covering-sheet from the wax slab by a light pull, starting from the free lower end. The close contact between the waxed paper and the wax slab at the places which have been scratched (upon which the visibility of the writing depended) is thus brought to an end and it does not recur when the two surfaces come together once more. The Mystic Pad is now clear of writing and ready to receive fresh notes.

The small imperfections of the contrivance have, of course, no importance for us, since we are only concerned with its approximation to the structure of the perceptive apparatus of the mind.

If, while the Mystic Pad has writing upon it, we cautiously raise the celluloid from the waxed paper, we can see the writing just as clearly on the surface of the latter, and the question may arise why there should be any necessity for the celluloid portion of the cover. Experiment will then show that the thin paper would be very easily crumpled or torn if one were to write directly upon it with the stilus. The layer of celluloid thus acts as a protective sheath for the waxed paper, to keep off injurious effects from without. The celluloid is a 'protective shield against stimuli'; the layer which actually receives the stimuli is the paper. I may at this point recall that in *Beyond the Pleasure Principle* [trans., 1922, 22 ff.; new trans., 1950, 30 ff.]. I showed that the perceptive apparatus of our mind consists of two layers, of an external protective shield against stimuli whose task it is to diminish the strength of excitations coming in, and of a surface behind it which receives the stimuli, namely the system Pcpt.-Cs.

The analogy would not be of much value if it could not be pursued further than this. If we lift the entire covering-sheet—both the celluloid and the waxed paper —off the wax slab, the writing vanishes and, as I have already remarked, does not re-appear again. The surface of the Mystic Pad is clear of writing and once more capable of receiving impressions. But it is easy to discover that the permanent trace of what was written is retained upon the wax slab itself and is legible in suitable lights. Thus the Pad provides not only a receptive surface that can be used over and over again, like a slate, but also permanent traces of what has been written, like an ordinary paper pad: it solves the problem of combining the two functions *by dividing them between two separate but interrelated component parts or systems.* But this is precisely the way in which, according to the hypothesis which I mentioned just now, our mental apparatus performs its perceptual function. The layer which receives the stimuli—the system Pcpt.-Cs.— forms no permanent traces; the foundations of memory come about in other, adjoining, systems.

We need not be disturbed by the fact that in the Mystic Pad no use is made of the permanent traces of the notes that have been received; it is enough that they are present. There must come a point at which the analogy between an auxiliary apparatus of this kind and the organ which is its prototype will cease to apply. It is true, too, that, once the writing has been erased, the Mystic Pad cannot 'reproduce' it from within; it would be a mystic pad indeed if, like our memory, it could accomplish that. None the less, I do not think it is too far-fetched to compare the celluloid and waxed paper cover with the system Pcpt.-Cs. and its protective shield, the wax slab with the unconscious behind them, and the appearance and disappearance of the writing with the flickering-up and passing-away of consciousness in the process of perception.

But I must admit that I am inclined to press the comparison still further. On the Mystic Pad the writing vanishes every time the close contact is broken between the paper which receives the stimulus and the wax slab which preserves the impression. This agrees with a notion which I have long had about the method in which the perceptual apparatus of our mind functions, but which I have hitherto kept to myself.[1] My theory was that cathectic innervations are sent out and withdrawn in rapid periodic impulses from within into the completely pervious system Pcpt.-Cs. So long as that system is cathected in this manner, it receives perceptions (which are accompanied by consciousness) and passes the excitation on to the unconscious mnemic systems; but as soon as the cathexis is withdrawn, consciousness is extinguished and the functioning of the system comes to a standstill. It is as though the unconscious stretches out feelers, through the medium of the system Pcpt.-Cs., towards the external world and hastily withdraws them as soon as they have sampled the excitations coming from it. Thus the interruptions, which in the case of the Mystic Pad have an external origin, were attributed by my hypothesis to the discontinuity in the current of innervation; and the actual breaking of contact which occurs in the Mystic Pad was replaced in my theory by the periodic non-excitability of the perceptual system. I further had a suspicion that this discontinuous method of functioning of the system Pcpt.-Cs. lies at the bottom of the origin of the concept of time.

If we imagine one hand writing upon the surface of the Mystic Writing-Pad while another periodically raises its covering sheet from the wax slab, we shall have a concrete representation of the way in which I tried to picture the functioning of the perceptual apparatus of our mind.

---

[1] [It is hinted at in *Beyond the Pleasure Principle* (English translation, 1922, 32 ; new translation, 1950, 33).]

XVI

NEGATION[1]

(1925)

THE manner in which our patients bring forward their associations during the work of analysis gives us an opportunity for making some interesting observations. 'Now you'll think I mean to say something insulting, but really I've no such intention.' We see at once that this is a repudiation, by means of projection, of an association that has just emerged. Or again: 'You ask who this person in the dream can have been. It was *not* my mother.' We emend this: so it *was* his mother. In our interpretation we take the liberty of disregarding the negation and of simply picking out the subject-matter of the association. It is just as though the patient had said: 'It is true that I thought of my mother in connection with this person, but I don't feel at all inclined to allow the association to count.'

There is a most convenient method by which one can sometimes obtain a necessary light upon a piece of unconscious and repressed material. 'What', one asks, 'would you consider was about the most unlikely thing in the world in that situation? What do you think was furthest from your mind at the time?' If the patient falls into the trap and names what he thinks most incredible, he almost invariably in so doing makes the correct admission. A nice counterpart of this experiment is often met with in obsessional neurotics who have been initiated into the meaning of their symptoms. 'A new obsessive idea came over me; and it immediately occurred to me that it might mean so and so. But of course that can't be true, or it couldn't have occurred to me.' The explanation of the new obsessive idea,

[1] ['Die Verneinung.' First published *Imago*, 11 (1925), 217; reprinted *Ges. Schr.*, 11, 3, and *Ges. W.*, 14, 11. Translation, reprinted from *Int. J. Psycho-Anal.*, 6 (1925), 367, by Joan Riviere.]

which he rejects in this way upon grounds picked up from the treatment, is of course the right one.

Thus the subject-matter of a repressed image or thought can make its way into consciousness on condition that it is *denied*. Negation is a way of taking account of what is repressed; indeed, it is actually a removal of the repression, though not, of course, an acceptance of what is repressed. It is to be seen how the intellectual function is here distinct from the affective process. Negation only assists in undoing *one* of the consequences of repression—namely, the fact that the subject-matter of the image in question is unable to enter consciousness. The result is a kind of intellectual acceptance of what is repressed, though in all essentials the repression persists.[1] In the course of analytic work we often bring about a further very important and somewhat bewildering modification of the same situation. We succeed in defeating the negation too and in establishing a complete intellectual acceptance of what is repressed—but the repression itself is still not removed.

Since it is the business of the function of intellectual judgement to affirm or deny the subject-matter of thoughts, we have been led by the foregoing remarks to the psychological origin of that function. To deny something in one's judgement is at bottom the same thing as to say: 'That is something that I would rather repress.' A negative judgement is the intellectual substitute for repression; the 'No' in which it is expressed is the hall-mark of repression, a certificate of origin, as it were, like 'Made in Germany'. By the help of the symbol of negation, the thinking-process frees itself from the limitations of repression and enriches itself with the subject-matter without which it could not work efficiently.

[1] The same process is at the root of the familiar superstition that boasting is dangerous. 'How lovely that I've not had one of my headaches for such a long time!' But this is in fact the first announcement of a new attack, of whose approach the patient is already aware, though he is as yet unwilling to believe it.

judgement

The function of judgement is concerned ultimately with two sorts of decision. It may assert or deny that a thing has a particular property; or it may affirm or dispute that a particular image [*Vorstellung*] exists in reality. Originally the property to be decided about *1)* might be either 'good' or 'bad', 'useful' or 'harmful'. Expressed in the language of the oldest, that is, of the oral, instinctual impulses, the alternative runs thus: 'I should like to eat that, or I should like to spit it out'; or, carried a stage further: 'I should like to take this into me and keep that out of me.' That is to say: it is to be either *inside* me or *outside* me. As I have shown elsewhere, the original pleasure-ego tries to introject into itself everything that is good and to reject from itself everything that is bad. From its point of view what is bad, what is alien to the ego, and what is external are, to begin with, identical.[1]

The other sort of decision made by the function of *2)* judgement, namely, as to the real existence of something imagined, is a concern of the final reality-ego, which develops out of the previous pleasure-ego (a concern, that is, of the faculty that tests the reality of things). It is now no longer a question of whether something perceived (a thing) shall be taken into the ego or not, but of whether something which is present in the ego as an image can also be re-discovered in perception (that is, in reality). Once more, it will be seen, the question is one of *external* and *internal*. What is not real, what is merely imagined or subjective, is only *internal*; while on the other hand what is real is also present *externally*. When this stage is reached, the pleasure principle is no longer taken into account. Experience has taught that it is important not only whether a thing (an object from which satisfaction is sought) possesses the 'good' property, that is, whether it deserves to be taken into the ego, but also whether it is there in the external world, ready to be seized when it is

[1] Cf. 'Instincts and their Vicissitudes' (1915a), *Collected Papers*, **4** 60.

dev. of
thinking

wanted. In order to understand this step forward, we
must recollect that all images originate from perceptions
and are repetitions of them. So that originally the mere
existence of the image serves as a guarantee of the reality
of what is imagined. The contrast between what is subjective and what is objective does not exist from the
first. It only arises from the faculty which thought
possesses for reviving a thing that has once been perceived, by reproducing it as an image, without its being
necessary for the external object still to be present. Thus
the first and immediate aim of the process of testing
reality is not to discover an object in real perception
corresponding to what is imagined, but to *re-discover*
such an object, to convince oneself that it is still there.
The differentiation between what is subjective and what
is objective is further assisted by another faculty of the
power of thought. The reproduction of a perception as
an image is not always a faithful one; it can be modified
by omissions or by the fusion of a number of elements.
The process for testing the thing's reality must then
investigate the extent of these distortions. But it is
evident that an essential pre-condition for the institution of the function for testing reality is that objects
shall have been lost which have formerly afforded real
satisfaction.

Judging is the intellectual action which decides the
choice of motor action, which puts an end to the pro-
crastination of thinking, and which leads over from
thinking to acting. This procrastinating character of
thought, too, has been discussed by me elsewhere.[1]
Thought is to be regarded as an experimental action, a
kind of groping forward, involving only a small expenditure of energy in the way of discharge. Let us
consider where the ego can have made a previous use of
this kind of groping forward, where it can have learnt
the technique which it now employs in intellective processes. It was at the sensory end of the mental apparatus, in connection with sense perceptions. For upon our

[1] [Cf. Freud (1911a), *Collected Papers*, **4**, 16.]

hypothesis perception is not a merely passive process; *att'n cathexis* we believe rather that the ego periodically sends out small amounts of cathectic energy into the perceptual system and by their means samples the external stimuli, and after every such groping advance draws back again.[1]

The study of judgement affords us, perhaps for the first time, an insight into the derivation of an intellectual function from the interplay of the primary impulses. Judging has been systematically developed out of what was in the first instance introduction into the ego or expulsion from the ego carried out according to the pleasure principle. Its polarity appears to correspond to the opposition between the two groups of instincts which we have assumed to exist. Affirmation, as being a substitute for union, belongs to Eros; while negation, the derivative of expulsion, belongs to the instinct of destruction. The passion for universal negation, the 'negativism' displayed by many psychotics, is probably to be regarded as a sign of a 'defusion' of instincts due to the withdrawal of the libidinal components. The achievement of the function of judgement only becomes feasible, however, after the creation of the symbol of negation has endowed thought with a first degree of independence from the results of repression and at the same time from the sway of the pleasure principle.

This view of negation harmonizes very well with the fact that in analysis we never discover a 'No' in the unconscious, and that a recognition of the unconscious on the part of the ego is expressed in a negative formula. There is no stronger evidence that we have been successful in uncovering the unconscious than when the patient reacts with the words 'I didn't think that' or 'I never thought of that'.

[1] [See above, page 180.]

XVII

SOME PSYCHOLOGICAL CONSEQUENCES OF THE ANATOMICAL DISTINCTION BETWEEN THE SEXES[1]

(1925)

IN my own writings and in those of my followers more and more stress is laid upon the necessity for carrying the analyses of neurotics back into the remotest period of their childhood, the time of the early efflorescence of sexual life. It is only by examining the first manifestations of the patient's innate instinctual constitution and the effects of his earliest experiences that we can accurately gauge the motive forces that have led to his neurosis and can be secure against the errors into which we might be tempted by the degree to which they have become remodelled and overlaid in adult life. This requirement is not only of theoretical but also of practical importance, for it distinguishes our efforts from the work of those physicians whose interests are focussed exclusively upon therapeutic results and who employ analytic methods, but only up to a certain point. An analysis of early childhood such as we are considering is tedious and laborious and makes demands both upon the physician and upon the patient which cannot always be met. Moreover it leads us into dark regions where there are as yet no sign-posts. Indeed, analysts may feel reassured, I think, that there is no risk of their work becoming mechanical, and so of losing its interest, during the next few decades.

In the following pages I bring forward some findings of analytical research which would be of great importance if they could be proved to apply universally. Why do I not postpone publication of them until further

---

[1] ['Einige psychische Folgen des anatomischen Geschlechtsunterschieds.' First published *Int. Z. Psychoanal.*, **11** (1925), 401; reprinted *Ges. Schr.*, **11**, 8, and *Ges. W.*, **14**, 19. Translation, reprinted from *Int. J. Psycho-Anal.*, **8** (1927), 133, by James Strachey.]

experience has given me the necessary proof, if such proof is obtainable? Because the conditions under which I work have undergone a change, with implications which I cannot disguise. Formerly, I was never one of those who are unable to hold back what seems to be a new discovery until it has been either confirmed or corrected. My *Interpretation of Dreams* [1900] and my 'Fragment of an Analysis of a Case of Hysteria' [1905*c*] (the case of Dora) were suppressed by me—if not for the nine years enjoined by Horace—at all events for four or five years before I allowed them to be published. But in those days I had unlimited time before me and material poured in upon me in such quantities that fresh experiences were hardly to be escaped. Moreover, I was the only worker in a new field, so that my reticence involved no danger to myself and no risk of loss to others.

But now everything has changed. The time before me is limited. The whole of it is no longer spent in working, so that my opportunities for making fresh observations are not so numerous. If I think I see something new, I am uncertain whether I can wait for it to be confirmed. And further, everything that is to be seen upon the surface has already been exhausted; what remains has to be slowly and laboriously dragged up from the depths. Finally, I am no longer alone. An eager crowd of fellow-workers is ready to make use of what is unfinished or doubtful, and I can leave to them that part of the work which I should otherwise have done myself. On this occasion, therefore, I feel justified in publishing something which stands in urgent need of confirmation before its value or lack of value can be decided.

In examining the earliest mental shapes assumed by the sexual life of children we have been in the habit of taking as the subject of our investigations the male child, the little boy. With little girls, so we have supposed, things must be similar, though in some way or other they must nevertheless be different. The point in development at which this difference lay could not clearly be determined.

In boys the situation of the Oedipus complex is the first stage that can be recognized with certainty. It is easy to understand, because at that stage a child retains the same object which he previously cathected with his pregenital libido during the preceding period while he was being suckled and nursed. The further fact that in this situation he regards his father as a disturbing rival and would like to get rid of him and take his place is a straightforward consequence of the actual state of affairs. I have shown elsewhere (1924*b*) how the Oedipus attitude in little boys belongs to the phallic phase, and how it succumbs to the fear of castration, that is, to narcissistic interest in their own genitals. The matter is made more difficult to grasp by the complicating circumstance that even in boys the Oedipus complex has a double orientation, active and passive, in accordance with their bisexual constitution; a boy also wants to take his *mother's* place as the love-object of his *father*—a fact which we describe as the feminine attitude.

As regards the prehistory of the Oedipus complex in boys we are far from complete clarity. We know that that period includes an identification of an affectionate sort with the boy's father, an identification which is still free from any sense of rivalry in regard to his mother. Another element of that stage is invariably, I believe, a masturbatory stimulation of the genitals, the masturbation of early childhood, the more or less violent suppression of which by the persons in charge of the child sets the castration complex in action. It is to be assumed that this masturbation is attached to the Oedipus complex and serves as a discharge for the sexual excitation belonging to it. It is, however, uncertain whether the masturbation has this character from the first, or whether on the contrary it makes its first appearance spontaneously as an activity of a bodily organ and is only brought into relation with the Oedipus complex at some later date; this second possibility is by far the more probable. Another doubtful question is the part played by bed-wetting and by the breaking of that habit through the intervention of training measures. We are inclined to adopt the simple generalization that continued bed-wetting is a result of masturbation and that its suppression is regarded by boys as an inhibition of their genital activity, that is, as having the meaning of a threat of castration; but whether we are always right in supposing this remains to be seen. Finally, analysis shows us in a shadowy way how the fact of a child at a very early age listening to his parents copulating may set up his first sexual excitation, and how that event may, owing to its after-effects, act as a starting-point for the child's whole sexual development. Masturbation, as well as the two attitudes in the Oedipus complex, later on become attached to this early experience, the child having subsequently interpreted its meaning. It is impossible, however, to suppose that these observations of coitus are of universal occurrence, so that at this point we are faced with the problem of 'primal phantasies'. Thus the prehistory of the Oedipus complex, even in boys, raises all of these questions for sifting and explanation; and there is the further problem of whether we are to suppose that the process invariably follows the same course, or whether a great variety of different preliminary stages may not converge upon the same terminal situation.

In little girls the Oedipus complex raises one problem more than in boys. In both cases the mother is the original object; and there is no cause for surprise that boys retain that object in the Oedipus complex. But how does it happen that girls abandon it and instead take their father as an object? In pursuing this question I have been able to reach some conclusions which may throw light upon the prehistory of the Oedipus relation in girls.

Every analyst has come across certain women who

cling with especial intensity and tenacity to the bond
with their father and to the wish in which it culminates
of having a child by him. We have good reason to suppose that the same wishful phantasy was also the
motive force of their infantile masturbation, and it is
easy to form an impression that at this point we have
been brought up against an elementary and unanalysable fact of infantile sexual life. But a thorough analysis
of these very cases brings something different to light,
namely, that here the Oedipus complex has a long prehistory and is in some respects a secondary formation.

The old paediatrician Lindner [1879] once remarked
that a child discovers the genital zones (the penis or the
clitoris) as a source of pleasure while indulging in
sensual sucking (thumb-sucking)[1]: I shall leave it an
open question whether it is really true that the child
takes the newly found source of pleasure in exchange
for the recent loss of the mother's nipple—a possibility
to which later phantasies (fellatio) seem to point. Be
that as it may, the genital zone is discovered at some
time or other, and there seems no justification for
attributing any psychical content to its first stimulations. But the first step in the phallic phase which begins in this way is not the linking-up of the masturbation with the object-cathexes of the Oedipus situation,
but a momentous discovery which little girls are destined
to make. They notice the penis of a brother or playmate,
strikingly visible and of large proportions, at once
recognize it as the superior counterpart of their own
small and inconspicuous organ, and from that time
forward fall a victim to envy for the penis.

There is an interesting contrast between the behaviour of the two sexes. In the analogous situation,
when a little boy first catches sight of a girl's genital
region, he begins by showing irresolution and lack of
interest; he sees nothing or disowns what he has seen,
he softens it down or looks about for expedients for bring-

---

[1] Cf. *Three Essays on the Theory of Sexuality* (1905b. [English Translation. 1949, 58f.]).

ing it into line with his expectations. It is not until later, when some threat of castration has obtained a hold upon him, that the observation becomes important to him: if he then recollects or repeats it, it arouses a terrible storm of emotion in him and forces him to believe in the reality of the threat which he has hitherto laughed at. This combination of circumstances leads to two reactions, which may become fixed and will in that case, whether separately or together or in conjunction with other factors, permanently determine the boy's relations to women: horror of the mutilated creature or triumphant contempt for her. These developments, however, belong to the future, though not to a very remote one.

A little girl behaves differently. She makes her judgement and her decision in a flash. She has seen it and knows that she is without it and wants to have it.[1]

From this point there branches off what has been named the masculinity complex of women, which may put great difficulties in the way of their regular development towards femininity, if it cannot be got over soon enough. The hope of some day obtaining a penis in spite of everything and so of becoming like a man may persist to an incredibly late age and may become a motive for the strangest and otherwise unaccountable actions. Or again, a process may set in which might be described as a 'denial', a process which in the mental life of children seems neither uncommon nor very dangerous but which in an adult would mean the beginning of a psychosis. Thus a girl may refuse to accept the fact of being castrated, may harden herself in the conviction

---

[1] This is an opportunity for correcting a statement which I made many years ago. [Freud, 1905b (English Translation, 1949,72).] I believed that the sexual interest of children, unlike that of pubescents, was aroused, not by the difference between the sexes, but by the problem of where babies come from. We now see that, at all events with girls, this is certainly not the case. With boys it may no doubt happen sometimes one way and sometimes the other; or with both sexes chance experiences may determine the event.

that she *does* possess a penis and may subsequently be compelled to behave as though she were a man.

The psychical consequences of penis-envy, in so far as it does not become absorbed in the reaction-formation of the masculinity complex, are various and far-reaching. After a woman has become aware of the wound to her narcissism, she develops, like a scar, a sense of inferiority. When she has passed beyond her first attempt at explaining her lack of a penis as being a punishment personal to herself and has realized that that sexual character is a universal one, she begins to share the contempt felt by men for a sex which is the lesser in so important a respect, and, at least in the holding of that opinion, insists upon being like a man.[1]

Even after penis-envy has abandoned its true object, it continues to exist: by an easy displacement it persists in the character-trait of *jealousy*. Of course, jealousy is not limited to one sex and has a wider foundation than this, but I am of opinion that it plays a far larger part in the mental life of women than of men and that that is because it is enormously reinforced from the direction of displaced penis-envy. While I was still unaware of this source of jealousy and was considering the phantasy 'A Child is Being Beaten' (1919), which occurs so commonly in girls, I constructed a first phase

[1] In my first critical account of the 'History of the Psycho-Analytic Movement', written in 1914 (*Collected Papers*, 1, 287), I recognized that this fact represents the core of truth contained in Adler's theory. That theory has no hesitation in explaining the whole world by this single point ('organ inferiority', 'the masculine protest', breaking away from 'the feminine line') and prides itself upon having in this way robbed sexuality of its importance and put the desire for power in its place. Thus the only organ which could claim to be called 'inferior' without any ambiguity would be the clitoris. On the other hand, one hears of analysts who boast that, though they have worked for dozens of years, they have never found a sign of the existence of a castration complex. We must bow our heads in recognition of the greatness of this achievement, even though it is only a negative one, a piece of virtuosity in the art of over-looking and mistaking. The two theories form an interesting pair of opposites: in one of them not a trace of a castration complex, in the other nothing at all but its effects.

for it in which its meaning was that another child, a rival of whom the subject was jealous, was to be beaten. This phantasy seems to be a relic of the phallic period in girls. The peculiar rigidity which struck me so much in the monotonous formula 'a child is being beaten' can probably be interpreted in a special way. The child which is being beaten (or caressed) may at bottom be nothing more nor less than the clitoris itself, so that at its very lowest level the statement will contain a confession of masturbation, which has remained attached to the content of the formula from its beginning in the phallic phase up to the present time.

A third consequence of penis-envy seems to be a loosening of the girl's relation with her mother as a love-object. The situation as a whole is not very clear, but it can be seen that in the end the girl's mother, who sent her into the world so insufficiently equipped, is almost always held responsible for her lack of a penis. The way in which this comes about historically is often that soon after the girl has discovered that her genitals are unsatisfactory she begins to show jealousy of another child on the ground that her mother is fonder of it than of her, which serves as a reason for her giving up her affectionate relation to her mother. It will fit in with this if the child which has been preferred by her mother is made into the first object of the beating-phantasy which ends in masturbation.

There is yet another surprising effect of penis-envy, or of the discovery of the inferiority of the clitoris, which is undoubtedly the most important of all. In the past I had often formed an impression that in general women tolerate masturbation worse than men, that they more frequently fight against it and that they are unable to make use of it in circumstances in which a man would seize upon it as a way of escape without any hesitation. Experience would no doubt elicit innumerable exceptions to this statement, if we attempted to turn it into a rule. The reactions of human individuals of both sexes are of course made up of masculine and

G

feminine traits. But it appeared to me nevertheless as though masturbation were further removed from the nature of women than of men, and the solution of the problem could be assisted by the reflection that masturbation, at all events of the clitoris, is a masculine activity and that the elimination of clitoridal sexuality is a necessary pre-condition for the development of femininity. Analyses of the remote phallic period have now taught me that in girls, soon after the first signs of penis-envy, an intense current of feeling against masturbation makes its appearance, which cannot be attributed exclusively to the educational influence of those in charge of the child. This impulse is clearly a forerunner of the wave of repression which at puberty will do away with a large amount of the girl's masculine sexuality in order to make room for the development of her femininity. It may happen that this first opposition to auto-erotic stimulation fails to attain its end. And this was in fact the case in the instances which I analysed. The conflict continued, and both then and later the girl did everything she could to free herself from the compulsion to masturbate. Many of the later manifestations of sexual life in women remain unintelligible unless this powerful motive is recognized.

I cannot explain the opposition which is raised in this way by little girls to phallic masturbation except by supposing that there is some concurrent factor which turns her violently against that pleasurable activity. Such a factor lies close at hand in the narcissistic sense of humiliation which is bound up with penis-envy, the girl's reflection that after all this is a point on which she cannot compete with boys and that it would therefore be best for her to give up the idea of doing so. Thus the little girl's recognition of the anatomical distinction between the sexes forces her away from masculinity and masculine masturbation on to new lines which lead to the development of femininity.

So far there has been no question of the Oedipus complex, nor has it up to this point played any part.

But now the girl's libido slips into a new position by means—there is no other way of putting it—of the equation 'penis = child'. She gives up her wish for a penis and puts in place of it a wish for a child: and *with this purpose in view* she takes her father as a love-object. Her mother becomes the object of her jealousy. The girl has turned into a little woman. If I am to credit a single exaggerated analytic instance, this new situation can give rise to physical sensations which would have to be regarded as a premature awakening of the female genital apparatus. If the girl's attachment to her father comes to grief later on and has to be abandoned, it may give place to an identification with him and the girl may thus return to her masculinity complex and perhaps remain fixated in it.

I have now said the essence of what I had to say: I will stop, therefore, and cast an eye over our findings. We have gained some insight into the prehistory of the Oedipus complex in girls. The corresponding period in boys is more or less unknown. In girls the Oedipus complex is a secondary formation. The operations of the castration complex precede it and prepare for it. As regards the relation between the Oedipus and castration complexes there is a fundamental contrast between the two sexes. *Whereas in boys the Oedipus complex succumbs to the castration complex,*[1] *in girls it is made possible and led up to by the castration complex.* This contradiction is cleared up if we reflect that the castration complex always operates in the sense dictated by its subject-matter: it inhibits and limits masculinity and encourages femininity. The difference between the sexual development of males and females at the stage we have been considering is an intelligible consequence of the anatomical distinction between their genitals and of the psychical situation involved in it; it corresponds to the difference between a castration that has been carried out and one that has merely been threatened. In their

[1] Cf. 'The Passing of the Oedipus Complex' (1924*b*).

essentials, therefore, our findings are self-evident and it should have been possible to foresee them.

The Oedipus complex, however, is such an important thing that the manner in which one enters and leaves it cannot be without its effects. In boys (as I have shown at length in the paper to which I have just referred and to which all of my present remarks are closely related) the complex is not simply repressed, it is literally smashed to pieces by the shock of threatened castration. Its libidinal cathexes are abandoned, desexualized and in part sublimated; its objects are incorporated into the ego, where they form the nucleus of the super-ego and give that new structure its characteristic qualities. In normal, or rather in ideal cases, the Oedipus complex exists no longer, even in the unconscious; the super-ego has become its heir. Since the penis (to follow Ferenczi) owes its extraordinarily high narcissistic cathexis to its organic significance for the propagation of the species, the catastrophe of the Oedipus complex (the abandonment of incest and the institution of conscience and morality) may be regarded as a victory of the race over the individual. This is an interesting point of view when one considers that neurosis is based upon a struggle of the ego against the demands of the sexual function. But to leave the standpoint of individual psychology is not likely to be of any immediate help in clarifying this complicated situation.

In girls the motive for the destruction of the Oedipus complex is lacking. Castration has already had its effect, which was to force the child into the situation of the Oedipus complex. Thus the Oedipus complex escapes the fate which it meets with in boys: it may either be slowly abandoned or got rid of by repression, or its effects may persist far into women's normal mental life. I cannot escape the notion (though I hesitate to give it expression) that for women the level of what is ethically normal is different from what it is in men. Their super-ego is never so inexorable, so impersonal, so independent of its emotional origins as we require it to be in men.

Character-traits which critics of every epoch have brought up against women—that they show less sense of justice than men, that they are less ready to submit to the great necessities of life, that they are more often influenced in their judgements by feelings of affection or hostility—all these would be amply accounted for by the modification in the formation of their super-ego which we have already inferred. We must not allow ourselves to be deflected from such conclusions by the denials of the feminists, who are anxious to force us to regard the two sexes as completely equal in position and worth; but we shall, of course, willingly agree that the majority of men are also far behind the masculine ideal and that all human individuals, as a result of their bi-sexual disposition and of cross-inheritance, combine in themselves both masculine and feminine characteristics, so that pure masculinity and femininity remain theoretical constructions of uncertain content.

I am inclined to set some value on the considerations I have brought forward upon the psychological consequences of the anatomical distinction between the sexes. I am aware, however, that this opinion can only be maintained if my findings, which are based on a handful of cases, turn out to have general validity and to be typical. If not, they would remain no more than a contribution to our knowledge of the different paths along which sexual life develops.

In the valuable and comprehensive studies upon the masculinity and castration complex in women by Abraham (1921), Horney (1923) and Helene Deutsch (1925) there is much that touches closely upon what I have written but nothing that coincides with it completely, so that here again I feel justified in publishing this paper.[1]

---

[1] [Freud returned to this subject in a later work (1931), page 252 of his volume.]

XVIII

FETISHISM[1]

(1927)

IN the last few years I have had an opportunity of studying analytically a number of men whose object-choice was ruled by a fetish. One need not suppose that these persons had sought analysis on account of a fetish; the devotees of fetishes regard them as abnormalities, it is true, but only rarely as symptoms of illness; usually they are quite content with them or even extol the advantages they offer for erotic gratification. As a rule, therefore, the fetish made its appearance in analysis as a subsidiary finding.

For obvious reasons I cannot go into the details of these cases in a published paper; nor can I show how the selection of individual fetishes is in part conditioned by accidental circumstances. The case of a young man who had exalted a certain kind of 'shine on the nose' into a fetishistic condition seemed most extraordinary. The very surprising explanation of this was that the patient had been first brought up in an English nursery and had later gone to Germany, where he almost completely forgot his mother-tongue. The fetish, which derived from his earliest childhood, had to be deciphered into English, not German; the *Glanz auf der Nase* [*shine* on the nose] was really 'a *glance* at the nose'; the nose was thus the fetish, which, by the way, he endowed when he wished with the necessary special brilliance, which other people could not perceive.

In all the cases the meaning and purpose of the fetish turned out under analysis to be the same. It revealed itself so unequivocally and seemed to me so categorical that I should expect the same solution in all

---

[1] ['Fetischismus.' First published *Int. Z. Psychoanal.*, **13** (1927), 373; reprinted *Ges. Schr.*, **11**, 395, and *Ges. W.*, **14**, 311. Translation, reprinted from *Int. J. Psycho-Anal.*, **9** (1928), 161, by Joan Riviere.]

cases of fetishism. When I now disclose that the fetish is a penis-substitute I shall certainly arouse disappointment; so I hasten to add that it is not a substitute for any chance penis, but for a particular quite special penis that had been extremely important in early childhood but was afterwards lost. That is to say: it should normally have been given up, but the purpose of the fetish precisely is to preserve it from being lost. To put it plainly: the fetish is a substitute for the woman's (mother's) phallus which the little boy once believed in and does not wish to forego—we know why.[1]

What had happened, therefore, was that the boy had refused to take cognizance of the fact perceived by him that a woman has no penis. No, that cannot be true, for if a woman can be castrated then his own penis is in danger; and against that there rebels part of his narcissism which Nature has providentially attached to this particular organ. In later life grown men may experience a similar panic, perhaps when the cry goes up that throne and altar are in danger, and similar illogical consequences will also follow then. If I am not mistaken, Laforgue would say in this case that the boy 'scotomizes' the perception of the woman's lack of a penis.[2] Now a new term is justified when it describes a new fact or brings it into prominence. There is nothing of that kind here; the oldest word in our psychoanalytical terminology, 'repression', already refers to this pathological process. If we wish to differentiate between what happens to the *idea* as distinct from the *affect*, we can restrict 'repression' to relate to the affect;

[1] This interpretation was mentioned in 1910, without any reasons being given for it, in my study on Leonardo da Vinci (1910).

[2] I correct myself here, however, by adding that I have the best reasons for knowing that Laforgue would not say this at all. It is clear from his own remarks that 'scotomization' is a term deriving from a description of dementia praecox, not arising through the application of psycho-analytical conceptions to the psychoses, and cannot be applied to the processes of development and formation of neurosis. In the text I have been at pains to demonstrate this incompatibility. [Cf. Laforgue (1926).]

the correct word for what happens to the idea is then
'denial'.[1] 'Scotomization' seems to me particularly unsuitable, for it suggests that the perception is promptly
obliterated, so that the result is the same as when a
visual impression falls on the blind spot on the retina.
In the case we are discussing, on the contrary, we see
that the perception has persisted and that a very
energetic action has been exerted to keep up the denial
of it. It is not true that the child emerges from his experience of seeing the female parts with an unchanged
belief in the woman having a phallus. He retains this
belief but he also gives it up; during the conflict between
the deadweight of the unwelcome perception and the
force of the opposite wish, a compromise is constructed
such as is only possible in the realm of unconscious
modes of thought—by the primary processes. In the
world of psychical reality the woman still has a penis in
spite of all, but this penis is no longer the same as it once
was. Something else has taken its place, has been
appointed its successor, so to speak, and now absorbs
all the interest which formerly belonged to the penis.
But this interest undergoes yet another very strong
reinforcement, because the horror of castration sets up a
sort of permanent memorial to itself by creating this
substitute. Aversion from the real female genitals,
which is never lacking in any fetishist, also remains as
an indelible stigma of the repression that has taken
place. One can now see what the fetish achieves and
how it is enabled to persist. It remains a token of
triumph over the threat of castration and a safeguard
against it; it also saves the fetishist from being a homosexual by endowing women with the attribute which
makes them acceptable as sexual objects. In later life the
fetishist sees other advantages in his substitute for
the genital. The significance of fetishes is not known to
the world at large and therefore not prohibited; they are
easily obtainable and sexual gratification by their means
is thus very convenient. The fetishist has no trouble in

[1] [Cf. Freud's paper on 'Repression' (1915b), *Collected Papers*, **4,** 91.]

getting what other men have to woo and exert them-selves to obtain.

Probably no male human being is spared the terrifying shock of threatened castration at the sight of the female genitals. We cannot explain why it is that some of them become homosexual in consequence of this experience, others ward it off by creating a fetish, and the great majority overcome it. It is possible that we do not yet know, among all the many factors operating, those which determine the more rare pathological results; we must be satisfied when we can explain what has happened, and may for the present leave on one side the task of explaining why something has *not* happened.

One would expect that the organs or objects selected as substitutes for the penis whose presence is missed in the woman would be such as act as symbols for the penis in other respects. This may happen occasionally but is certainly not the determining factor. It seems rather that when the fetish comes to life, so to speak, some process has been suddenly interrupted—it reminds one of the abrupt halt made by memory in traumatic amnesias. In the case of the fetish, too, interest is held up at a certain point—what is possibly the last im-pression received before the uncanny traumatic one is preserved as a fetish. Thus the foot or shoe owes its attraction as a fetish, or part of it, to the circumstance that the inquisitive boy used to peer up the woman's legs towards her genitals. Velvet and fur reproduce—as has long been suspected—the sight of the pubic hair which ought to have revealed the longed-for penis; the underlinen so often adopted as a fetish reproduces the scene of undressing, the last moment in which the woman could still be regarded as phallic. But I do not maintain that it is always possible to ascertain the determination of every fetish.

Investigations into fetishism are to be recommended to all who still doubt the existence of the castration complex or who can still believe that the horror of the

G2

female genitals has some other foundation: for instance, that it derives from a supposed memory of the trauma of birth.

For me there was another point of interest in the explanation of fetishism. Not long ago in quite a speculative way I formulated the proposition that the essential difference between neurosis and psychosis consists in this: that in neurosis the ego suppresses part of the id out of allegiance to reality, whereas in psychosis it lets itself be carried away by the id and detached from a part of reality.[1] But soon after this I had cause to regret that I had been so daring. In the analyses of two young men I learnt that each of them—one in his second and the other in his tenth year—had refused to acknowledge the death of his father—had 'scotomized' it—and yet neither of them had developed a psychosis. A very important piece of reality had thus been denied by the ego, in the same way as the fetishist denies the unwelcome fact of the woman's castrated condition. I also began to suspect that similar occurrences are by no means rare in childhood, and thought I had made a mistake in my differentiation between neurosis and psychosis. It is true, there was one way out of the difficulty: it might be that my formula held good only when a higher degree of differentiation existed in the mental apparatus; reactions might be possible in a child which would cause severe injury in an adult.

But further research led to another solution of the contradiction. It turned out, that is, as follows: the two young men had no more 'scotomized' the death of their fathers than a fetishist scotomizes the castration of women. It was only one current of their mental processes that had not acknowledged the father's death; there was another which was fully aware of the fact; the one which was consistent with reality stood alongside the one which accorded with a wish. One of these two cases of mine had derived an obsessional neurosis of

[1] 'Neurosis and Psychosis' (1924a) and 'The Loss of Reality in Neurosis and Psychosis' (1924c).

some severity from this dissociation; in every situation in life he oscillated between two assumptions—on the one his father was still alive and hindered him from action, on the other his father was dead and he had the right to regard himself as his successor. In a psychosis the true idea which accorded with reality would have been *really* absent.

To return to my description of fetishism, I have to add that there are numerous and very weighty proofs of the double attitude of fetishists to the question of the castration of women. In very subtle cases the fetish itself has become the vehicle both of denying and of asseverating the fact of castration. This was exemplified in the case of a man whose fetish was a suspensory belt which can also be worn as bathing drawers; this piece of clothing covers the genitals and altogether conceals the difference between them. The analysis showed that it could mean that a woman is castrated, or that she is not castrated, and it even allows of a supposition that a man may be castrated, for all these possibilities could be equally well hidden beneath the belt; its forerunner in childhood had been the fig-leaf seen on a statue. Naturally, a fetish of this kind constructed out of two opposing ideas is capable of great tenacity. Sometimes the double attitude shows itself in what the fetishist— either actually or in phantasy—does with the fetish. It is not the whole story to say that he worships it; very often he treats it in a way which is plainly equivalent to castrating it. This happens particularly when a strong father-identification has been developed, since the child ascribed the original castration of the woman to the father. Tender and hostile treatment of fetishes is mixed in unequal degrees—like the denial and the recognition of castration—in different cases, so that the one or the other is more evident. Here one gets a sort of glimpse of comprehension, as from a distance, of the behaviour of people who cut off women's plaits of hair; in them the impulse to execute the castration which they deny is what comes to the fore. The action contains within it two incompatible propositions: the woman has still got a penis and the father has castrated the woman. Another variety of this, which might be regarded as a race-psychological parallel to fetishism, is the Chinese custom of first mutilating a woman's foot and then revering it. The Chinese man seems to want to thank the woman for having submitted to castration.

The normal prototype of all fetishes is the penis of the man, just as the normal prototype of an organ felt to be inferior is the real little penis of the woman, the clitoris.[1]

[1][Freud reverted to the subject of fetishism later. Cf. 1938a (below, page 373) and 1938b, 73 ff.]

XIX

POSTSCRIPT TO A DISCUSSION ON LAY ANALYSIS[1]

(1927)

THE immediate occasion of my writing the little book which was the starting-point of the present discussion was a charge of quackery brought against a non-medical member of our Society, Dr. Theodor Reik, in the Vienna Courts. It is generally known, I think, that after all the preliminary proceedings had been completed and a number of expert opinions had been received, the charge was dismissed. I do not believe that this was a result of my book. No doubt the prosecution's case was too weak, and the person who brought the charge as an aggrieved party proved an untrustworthy witness. So that the dismissal of the proceedings against Dr. Reik is probably not to be regarded as a considered judgement of the Vienna Courts on the general question of lay analysis. When I drew the figure of the 'impartial' protagonist in my tract, I had before my mind one of our high officials. This was a man with a friendly attitude and a mind of unusual integrity, to whom I had myself talked about Reik's case and for whom I had, at his request, written a confidential opinion on the subject. I knew I had not succeeded in converting him to my views, and that was why the impartial inquirer in my dialogue remained unconvinced as well.

Nor did I expect that I should succeed in bringing about unanimity in the attitude of *analysts* towards the

---

[1]['Nachwort zur "Frage der Laienanalyse".' In 1926 Freud published a small volume, *The Question of Lay Analysis*. This was made an opportunity for an exhaustive discussion of the subject, in which many psycho-analysts from all parts of the world took part, and which was published in German in the *Int. Z. Psychoanal.*, **13** (1927), and in English in the *Int. J. Psycho-Anal.*, **8** (1927). The discussion was wound up by this further contribution from Freud. Present translation by James Strachey.]

problem of lay analysis. Anyone who compares the views expressed by the Hungarian Society in this discussion with those of the New York group will perhaps conclude that my book has produced no effect whatever and that everyone persists in his former opinion. But I do not believe this either. I think that many of my colleagues have modified their extreme *parti pris* and that the majority have accepted my view that the problem of lay analysis ought not to be decided along the lines of traditional usage but that it arises from a novel situation and therefore demands a fresh judgement.

Again, the turn which I gave to the whole discussion seems to have met with approval. My main thesis was that the important question is not whether an analyst possesses a medical degree but whether he has had the special training necessary for the practice of analysis. This served as the starting-point for a discussion, which was eagerly embarked upon, as to what is the training most suitable for an analyst. My own view was and still remains that it is not the training prescribed by the University for future physicians. What is known as medical education appears to me to be an arduous and circuitous way of approaching the profession of analysis. No doubt it offers an analyst much that is indispensable to him. But it burdens him with too much else of which he can never make use, and there is a danger of its diverting his interest and his whole mode of thought from the understanding of mental phenomena. A scheme of training for analysts has still to be created. It must include elements from the mental sciences, from psychology, the history of civilization and sociology, as well as from anatomy, biology and the study of evolution. There is so much to be taught in all this that it is justifiable to omit from the curriculum anything which has no direct bearing upon the practice of analysis and only serves indirectly (like any other study) as a training for the intellect and for the powers of observation. It is easy to meet this suggestion by objecting that analytic colleges of this kind do not exist except as an ideal scheme. An ideal, no doubt. But an ideal which can and must be realized. And in our training institutes, despite all their youthful insufficiencies, that realization has already begun.

It will not have escaped my readers that in what I have said I have assumed as axiomatic something that is still violently disputed in the discussion. I have assumed, that is to say, that psycho-analysis is not a specialized branch of medicine. I cannot see how it is possible to dispute this. Psycho-analysis falls under the head of psychology; not of medical psychology in the old sense, nor of the psychology of morbid processes, but simply of psychology. It is certainly not the whole of psychology, but its substructure and perhaps even its entire foundation. The possibility of its application to medical purposes must not lead us astray. Electricity and radiology also have their medical application, but the science to which they both belong is none the less physics. Nor can their situation be affected by historical arguments. The whole theory of electricity had its origin in an observation of a nerve-muscle preparation; yet no one would dream to-day of regarding it as a part of physiology. It is argued that psycho-analysis was after all discovered by a physician in the course of his efforts to assist his patients. But that is clearly neither here nor there. On the other hand, the historical argument is double-edged. We might pursue the story and recall the unfriendliness and indeed the animosity with which the medical profession treated analysis from the very first. That would seem to imply that it can have no claims over analysis to-day. And though I do not accept that implication, I still feel some doubts as to whether the present wooing of psycho-analysis by the doctors is based, from the point of view of the libido theory, upon the first or upon the second of Abraham's sub-stages[1]—whether they wish to take possession of their object for the purpose of destroying or of preserving it.

[1] [Cf. Abraham (1924), English translation, 1927, 450 f.]

I should like to consider the historical argument a moment longer. Since it is with me personally that we are concerned, I can throw a little light, for anyone who may be interested, on my own motives. After forty-one years of medical activity, my self-knowledge tells me that I have never really been a doctor in the proper sense. I became a doctor through being compelled to deviate from my original purpose; and the triumph of my life lies in my having, after a long and roundabout journey, found my way back to my earliest path. I have no knowledge of having had any craving in my early childhood to succour suffering humanity. My innate sadistic disposition was not a very strong one, so that I had no need to develop this one of its derivatives. Nor did I ever play the 'doctor game'; my infantile curiosity evidently chose other paths. In my youth I felt an overpowering need to understand something of the riddles of the world in which we live and perhaps even to contribute something to their solution. The most hopeful means of achieving this end seemed to be to enrol myself in the medical faculty; but even then I experimented—unsuccessfully—with zoology and chemistry, till at last, under the influence of Brücke, which carried more weight with me than any other in my whole life, I settled down to physiology, though in those days it was too narrowly restricted to histology. By that time I had already passed all my medical examinations; but I took no interest in anything to do with medicine till the teacher whom I so deeply respected warned me that in view of my restricted material circumstances I could not possibly take up a theoretical career. Thus I passed from the histology of the nervous system to neuropathology and then, prompted by fresh influences, I began to be concerned with the neuroses. I scarcely think, however, that my lack of a genuine medical temperament has done much damage to my patients. For it is not greatly to the advantage of patients if their physician's therapeutic interest has too marked an emotional emphasis. They are best helped if he carries out his task coolly and, so far as possible, with precision.

No doubt what I have just said throws little light on the problem of lay analysis; but it was only intended to exhibit my personal credentials as being myself a supporter of the value of psycho-analysis *per se* and independently of its application to medicine. But it will be objected at this point that whether psycho-analysis, regarded as a science, is a subdivision of medicine or of psychology is a purely academic question and of no practical interest. The real point at issue, it will be said, is a different one, namely the application of analysis to the treatment of patients; in so far as it claims to do this it must be content, the argument will run, to be accepted as a specialized branch of medicine, like radiology, for instance, and to submit to the rules laid down for all therapeutic methods. I recognize that that is so; I admit it. I only want to feel assured that the therapy will not destroy the science. Unluckily analogies only carry one a short distance; a point is soon reached at which the subjects of comparison take divergent paths. The case of analysis differs from that of radiology. A physicist does not require to have a patient in order to study the laws that govern X-rays. But the only subject-matter of psycho-analysis is the mental processes of human beings and it is only in human beings that it can be studied. For reasons which can easily be understood, neurotic human beings offer far more instructive and accessible material than normal ones, and to withhold that material from anyone who wishes to study and apply analysis is to remove a good half of his training possibilities. I have, of course, no intention of asking that the interest of neurotic patients should be sacrificed to that of instruction and scientific research. The aim of my little book on the question of lay analysis was precisely to show that, if certain precautions are observed, the two interests can quite easily be brought into harmony and that the medical interest, as rightly understood, will not be the last to profit by such a solution.

I myself brought forward all the necessary precautions and I can safely say that the discussion added nothing on this point. But I should like to remark that the emphasis was often placed in a manner which disregarded the facts. What was said about the difficulties of differential diagnosis and the uncertainty in many cases in deciding about somatic symptoms—situations, that is, in which medical knowledge and medical intervention are necessary—this is all of it perfectly true. Nevertheless, the number of cases in which doubts of this kind never arise at all and in which a doctor is *not* required is surely incomparably greater. These cases may be quite uninteresting scientifically, but they play an important enough part in life to justify the activity of lay analysts, who are perfectly competent to deal with them. Some time ago I analysed a colleague who had developed a particularly strong dislike of the idea of anyone being allowed to engage in a medical activity who was not himself a medical man. I was in a position to say to him: 'We have now been working for more than three months. At what point in our analysis have I had occasion to make use of my medical knowledge?' He admitted that I had had no such occasion.

Again, I attach no great importance to the argument that a lay analyst, because he must be prepared to consult a physician, will have no authority in the eyes of his patients and will be treated with no more respect than such people as bone-setters or masseurs. Once again, the analogy is an imperfect one—quite apart from the fact that what governs patients in their recognition of authority is usually their emotional transference and that the possession of a medical degree does not impress them nearly so much as physicians believe. A professional lay analyst will have no difficulty in winning as much respect as is due to a secular spiritual guide. Indeed, these words, 'a secular spiritual guide', might well serve as a general formula for describing the function which the analyst, whether he is a doctor or a layman, has to perform in his relation to the public. Our friends among the protestant clergy, and more recently among the catholic clergy as well, are often able to relieve their parishioners of the inhibitions of their daily life by confirming their faith—after having first offered them a little analytic information about the nature of their conflicts. Our opponents, the Adlerian 'individual psychologists', endeavour to produce a similar result in people who have become unstable and inefficient by arousing their interest in the social community—after having first thrown some light upon a single corner of their mental life by showing them the part played in their illness by their egoistic and distrustful impulses. Both of these procedures, which derive their power from being based on analysis, have their place in psychotherapy. We who are analysts set before us as our aim the most complete and profoundest possible analysis of whoever may be our patient. We do not seek to bring him relief by receiving him into the catholic, protestant or socialist community. We seek rather to enrich him from his own internal sources, by putting at the disposal of his ego those energies which, owing to repression, are inaccessibly confined in his unconscious, as well as those which his ego is obliged to squander in the fruitless task of maintaining these repressions. Such work as this is spiritual guidance in the best sense of the words. Have we set ourselves too high an aim? Are the majority of our patients worth the pains that this work requires of us? Would it not be more economical to prop up their weaknesses from without rather than to rebuild them from within? I cannot say; but there is something else that I *do* know. Psycho-analysis has from the very first maintained an inseparable bond between cure and research. Knowledge brought therapeutic success. It was impossible to treat a patient without learning something new; it was impossible to gain fresh insight without perceiving its beneficent results. Our analytic procedure is the only one in which this precious conjunction is assured. It is only by carrying on our analytic spiritual guidance that we can deepen our dawning comprehension of the human mind. This prospect of scientific gain has been the rarest and proudest feature of analytic work. Are we to sacrifice it for the sake of considerations of a practical sort?

Some remarks that have been made in the course of this discussion have led me to suspect that, in spite of everything, my book on lay analysis has been misunderstood in one respect. The doctors have been defended against me, as though I had declared that they were in general incompetent to practise analysis and as though I had given it out as a pass-word for our training institutes that medical reinforcements were to be rejected. That was far from my intention. The idea probably arose from my having been led to declare in the course of my observations (which had a controversial end in view) that untrained medical analysts were more dangerous than laymen. I might make my true opinion on this question clear by echoing a cynical remark about women that once appeared in *Simplicissimus*. One man was complaining to another about the weaknesses and troublesome nature of the fair sex. 'All the same', replied his companion, 'women are the best thing we have in that line.' I am bound to admit that, so long as schools such as we desire for the training of analysts are not yet in existence, persons who have had a preliminary education in medicine are the best material for future analysts. We have a right to demand, however, that they should not mistake their preliminary education for a complete training, that they should overcome the onesidedness that is fostered by instruction in medical schools and that they should resist the temptation to flirt with endocrinology and the autonomic nervous system, when what is needed is an apprehension of psychological facts with the help of a framework of psychological concepts. I also share the view that all those problems which relate to the connection between psychical phenomena and their organic, anatomical and chemical foundations can be approached only by those who have studied both, that is, by medical analysts. It should not be forgotten, however, that this is not the whole of psycho-analysis, and that for its other aspect we can never do without the co-operation of persons who have had a preliminary education in the *mental* sciences. For practical reasons we have been in the habit—and this is true, incidentally, of our publications as well—of distinguishing between medical and applied analysis. But that is not a correct distinction. The true line of division is between *scientific* analysis and its *applications* alike in medical and in non-medical fields.

In these discussions the bluntest rejection of lay analysis has been expressed by our American colleagues. A few words to them in reply will therefore not be out of place. I can scarcely be accused of making a misuse of analysis for controversial purposes if I express an opinion that their resistance is derived wholly from practical factors. They see how in their own country lay analysts put analysis to all kinds of mischievous and illegitimate purposes and in consequence cause injury both to their patients and to the good name of analysis. It is therefore not to be wondered at if in their indignation they turn their backs on such unscrupulous mischief-makers and try to prevent their having any share in analysis. But these facts are already enough to diminish the significance of the American position; for the question of lay analysis must not be decided on practical considerations alone, and local conditions in America cannot be the sole determining influence on our views.

The resolution passed by our American colleagues against lay analysts, based as it essentially is upon practical reasons, appears to me nevertheless to be unpractical; for it cannot affect one of the factors which govern the situation. It amounts more or less to an attempt at repression. If it is impossible to prevent the lay analysts from pursuing their activities and if the public does not support the campaign against them, would it not be more expedient to recognize the fact of their existence by offering them opportunities for training? Might it not be possible in this way to gain some influence over them? And, if they were offered as an inducement the possibility of receiving the approval of the medical profession and of being invited to cooperate, might they not have some interest in raising their own ethical and intellectual level?

XX

HUMOUR[1]

(1928)

I N my work on *Wit and its Relation to the Unconscious* (1905a) I considered humour really from the economic point of view alone. My object was to discover the source of the pleasure derived from humour, and I think I was able to show that that pleasure proceeds from a saving in expenditure of affect.

There are two ways in which the process at work in humour may take place. Either one person may himself adopt a humorous attitude, while a second person acts as spectator, and derives enjoyment from the attitude of the first; or there may be two people concerned, one of whom does not himself take any active share in producing the humorous effect, but is regarded by the other in a humorous light. To take a very crude example: when a criminal who is being led to the gallows on a Monday observes, 'Well, this is a good beginning to the week', he himself is creating the humour; the process works itself out in relation to himself and evidently it affords him a certain satisfaction. I am merely a listener who has not assisted in this functioning of his sense of humour, but I feel its effect, as it were from a distance. I detect in myself a certain humorous satisfaction, possibly much as he does.

We have an instance of the second type of humour when a writer or a narrator depicts the behaviour of real or imaginary people in a humorous fashion. There is no need for the people described to display any humour; the humorous attitude only concerns the person who makes them the object of it, and the reader or hearer shares his enjoyment of the humour, as in the former instance. To sum up, then, we may say that the

---

[1] ['Der Humor.' First published *Imago*, **14** (1928), 1; reprinted *Ges. Schr.*, **11**, 402, and *Ges. W.*, **14**, 383. Translation, reprinted from *Int. J. Psycho-Anal.*, **9** (1928), 1, by Joan Riviere.]

humorous attitude—in whatever it consists—may have reference to the subject's self or to other people; further, we may assume that it is a source of enjoyment to the person who adopts it, and, finally, a similar pleasure is experienced by observers who take no actual part in it.

We shall best understand the origin of the pleasure derived from humour if we consider the process which takes place in the mind of anyone listening to another man's jest. He sees this other person in a situation which leads him to anticipate that the victim will show signs of some affect; he will get angry, complain, manifest pain, fear, horror, possibly even despair. The person who is watching or listening is prepared to follow his lead, and to call up the same emotions. But his anticipations are deceived; the other man does not display any affect—he makes a joke. It is from the saving of expenditure in feeling that the hearer derives the humorous satisfaction.

It is easy to get so far, but we soon say to ourselves that it is the process in the other man, the 'humorist', which calls for the greater attention. There is no doubt that the essence of humour is that one spares oneself the affects to which the situation would naturally give rise and overrides with a jest the possibility of such an emotional display. Thus far, the process must be the same in the humorist and his hearer. Or, to put it more accurately, the hearer must have copied the process in the mind of the humorist. But how does the latter arrive at that mental attitude, which makes the discharge of affect superfluous? What is the dynamic process underlying the 'humorous attitude'? Clearly, the solution of this problem is to be found in the humorist himself; in the listener we may suppose there is only an echo, a copy of this unknown process.

It is now time to acquaint ourselves with some of the characteristics of humour. Like wit and the comic, humour has in it a *liberating* element. But it has also something fine and elevating, which is lacking in the other two ways of deriving pleasure from intellectual activity. Obviously, what is fine about it is the triumph of narcissism, the ego's victorious assertion of its own invulnerability. It refuses to be hurt by the arrows of reality or to be compelled to suffer. It insists that it is impervious to wounds dealt by the outside world, in fact, that these are merely occasions for affording it pleasure. This last trait is a fundamental characteristic of humour. Suppose the criminal being led to execution on a Monday had said: 'It doesn't worry me. What does it matter, after all, if a fellow like me is hanged? The world won't come to an end.' We should have to admit that this speech of his displays the same magnificent rising superior to the real situation; what he says is wise and true, but it does not betray a trace of humour. Indeed, it is based on an appraisal of reality which runs directly counter to that of humour. Humour is not resigned; it is rebellious. It signifies the triumph not only of the ego, but also of the pleasure principle, which is strong enough to assert itself here in the face of the adverse real circumstances.

These last two characteristics, the denial of the claim of reality and the triumph of the pleasure principle, cause humour to approximate to the regressive or reactionary processes which engage our attention so largely in psychopathology. By its repudiation of the possibility of suffering, it takes its place in the great series of methods devised by the mind of man for evading the compulsion to suffer—a series which begins with neurosis and culminates in delusions, and includes intoxication, self-induced states of abstraction and ecstasy. Owing to this connection, humour possesses a dignity which is wholly lacking, for instance, in wit, for the aim of wit is either simply to afford gratification, or, in so doing, to provide an outlet for aggressive tendencies. Now in what does this humorous attitude consist, by means of which one refuses to undergo suffering, asseverates the invincibility of one's ego against the real world and victoriously upholds the pleasure principle, yet all without quitting the ground of mental sanity, as happens when other means to the same end are adopted? Surely it seems impossible to reconcile the two achievements.

If we turn to consider the situation in which one person adopts a humorous attitude towards others, one view which I have already tentatively suggested in my book on wit will seem very evident. It is this: that the one is adopting towards the other the attitude of an adult towards a child, recognizing and smiling at the triviality of the interests and sufferings which seem to the child so big. Thus the humorist acquires his superiority by assuming the role of the grown-up, identifying himself to some extent with the father, while he reduces the other people to the position of children. This supposition is probably true to fact, but it does not seem to take us very far. We ask ourselves what makes the humorist arrogate to himself this role?

Here we must recall the other, perhaps the original and more important, situation in humour, in which a man adopts a humorous attitude towards himself in order to ward off possible suffering. Is there any sense in saying that someone is treating himself like a child and is at the same time playing the part of the superior adult in relation to this child?

This idea does not seem very plausible, but I think that if we consider what we have learnt from pathological observations of the structure of our ego, we shall find a strong confirmation of it. This ego is not a simple entity; it harbours within it, as its innermost core, a special agency: the super-ego. Sometimes it is amalgamated with this, so that we cannot distinguish the one from the other, while in other circumstances the two can be sharply differentiated. Genetically the super-ego inherits the parental function; it often holds the ego in strict subordination, and still actually treats it as the parents (or the father) treated the child in his early years. We obtain a dynamic explanation of the humorous attitude, therefore, if we conclude that it consists in the subject's removing the accent from his own ego and transferring it on to his super-ego. To the super-ego, thus inflated, the ego can appear tiny and all its interests trivial, and with this fresh distribution of energy it may be an easy matter for it to suppress the potential reactions of the ego.

To preserve our customary phraseology, let us not speak of transferring the accent, but rather of displacing large quantities of cathexis. We shall then ask whether we are justified in imagining such extensive displacements from one agency in the mental apparatus to another. It looks like a new hypothesis, conceived *ad hoc*; yet we may recollect that repeatedly, even if not often enough, we have taken such a factor into account when endeavouring to form some metapsychological conception of the mental processes. For instance, we assumed that the difference between ordinary erotic object-cathexis and the state of being in love was that in the latter case incomparably more cathexis passes over to the object, the ego as it were emptying itself into the object. The study of some cases of paranoia proved to me that ideas of persecution are formed early, and exist for a long time without any perceptible effect, until as the result of some definite occasion they receive a sufficient amount of cathexis to cause them to become dominant. The cure of paranoiac attacks of this sort, too, would lie not so much in resolving and correcting the delusional ideas as in withdrawing from them the cathexis they have attracted. The alternation between melancholia and mania, between a cruel suppressing of the ego by the super-ego and the liberation of the ego after this oppression, suggests some such shifting of cathexis; and this conception would, moreover, explain a number of phenomena in normal mental life. If, hitherto, we have but seldom had recourse to this explanation, it has been on account of our customary caution, which is surely rather praiseworthy than otherwise. The ground on which we feel ourselves secure is that of mental pathology; it is here that we make our observations and win our convictions. For the present we commit ourselves to an opinion concerning the normal only in so far as we detect it amongst the isolated and distorted features of the morbid. When once this hesitation is overcome, we shall recognize how greatly the static conditions as well as the dynamic alteration in the quantity of the energic cathexis contribute to our understanding of mental processes.

I think, therefore, that the possibility I have suggested, namely, that in a given situation the subject suddenly effects a hyper-cathexis of the super-ego, which in its turn alters the reactions of the ego, is one which deserves to be retained. Moreover, we find a striking analogy to this hypothesis of mine about humour in the kindred field of wit. I was led to assume that wit originates in the momentary abandoning of a conscious thought to unconscious elaboration, wit being therefore the contribution of the unconscious to the comic. In just the same way humour would be a contribution to the comic made through the agency of the super-ego.

In other respects we know that the super-ego is a stern master. It may be said that it accords ill with its character that it should wink at affording the ego a little gratification. It is true that the pleasure derived from humour is never so intense as that produced by the comic or by wit and never finds a vent in hearty laughter. It is also true that, in bringing about the humorous attitude, the super-ego is in fact repudiating reality and serving an illusion. But (without quite knowing why) we attribute to this less intensive pleasure a high value: we feel it to have a peculiarly liberating and elevating effect. Besides, the jest made in humour is not the essential; it has only the value of a demonstration. The principal thing is the intention which humour fulfils, whether it concerns the subject's self or other people. Its meaning is: 'Look here! This is all that this seemingly dangerous world amounts to. Child's play— the very thing to jest about!'

If it is really the super-ego which, in humour, speaks

such kindly words of comfort to the intimidated ego, this teaches us that we have still very much to learn about the nature of that agency. Further, we note that it is not everyone who is capable of the humorous attitude: it is a rare and precious gift, and there are many people who have not even the capacity for deriving pleasure from humour when it is presented to them by others. Finally, if the super-ego does try to comfort the ego by humour and to protect it from suffering, this does not conflict with its derivation from the parental function.

XXI
DOSTOEVSKY AND PARRICIDE[1]
(1928)

FOUR facets may be distinguished in the rich personality of Dostoevsky: the creative artist, the
neurotic, the moralist and the sinner. How is one
to find one's way in this bewildering complexity?

The creative artist is the least doubtful: Dostoevsky's
place is not far behind Shakespeare. *The Brothers
Karamazov* is the most magnificent novel ever written;
the episode of the Grand Inquisitor, one of the peaks in
the literature of the world, can hardly be valued too
highly. Before the problem of the creative artist analysis
must, alas, lay down its arms.

The moralist in Dostoevsky is the most readily
assailable. If we seek to rank him high as a moralist on
the plea that only a man who has gone through the
depths of sin can reach the highest summit of morality,
we are neglecting a doubt that arises. A moral man is
one who reacts to temptation as soon as he feels it in his
heart, without yielding to it. A man who alternately
sins and then in his remorse erects high moral standards
lays himself open to the reproach that he has made
things too easy for himself. He has not achieved the
essence of morality, renunciation, for the moral conduct
of life is a practical human interest. He reminds one of
the barbarians of the great migrations, who murdered
and did penance for it, till penance became an actual
technique for enabling murder to be done. Ivan the
Terrible behaved in exactly this way; indeed, this com-

---

[1] ['Dostojewski und die Vatertötung' was first published as a preface
to *Die Urgestalt der Brüder Karamasoff* (1928), edited by Fülöp-Miller
and Eckstein as one of the supplementary volumes to the complete German edition of Dostoevsky's works. Reprinted *Ges. Schr.*, 12, 7, and
Ges. W., 14, 399. The present translation by D. F. Tait was published in
The Realist (London, Macmillan), 1 (1929), No. 4, 18. It was reprinted,
extensively revised by James Strachey, *Int. J. Psycho-Anal.*, 26 (1945),
1.]

promise with morality is a characteristic Russian trait. Nor was the final outcome of Dostoevsky's moral strivings anything very glorious. After the most violent struggles to reconcile the instinctual demands of the individual with the claims of the community, he landed in the retrograde position of submission both to temporal and spiritual authority, of veneration both for the Tsar and for the God of the Christians, and of a narrow Russian nationalism—a position which lesser minds have reached with smaller effort. This is the weak point in that great personality. Dostoevsky threw away the chance of becoming a teacher and liberator of humanity and made himself one with their gaolers. The future of human civilization will have little to thank him for. It seems probable that he was condemned to this failure by his neurosis. The greatness of his intelligence and the strength of his love for humanity might have opened to him another, an apostolic, way of life.

To consider Dostoevsky as a sinner or a criminal rouses violent opposition, which need not be based upon a philistine assessment of crime. The real motive for this opposition soon becomes apparent. Two traits are essential in a criminal: boundless egoism and a strong destructive impulse. Common to both of these, and a necessary condition for their expression, is absence of love, lack of an emotional appreciation of (human) objects. One at once recalls the contrast to this presented by Dostoevsky—his great need of love and his enormous capacity for love, which is to be seen in manifestations of exaggerated kindness and caused him to love and to help where he had a right to hatred and revenge, as, for example, in his relations with his first wife and her lover. That being so, it must be asked why there is any temptation to reckon Dostoevsky among the criminals. The answer is that it comes from his choice of material, which singles out from all others violent, murderous and egoistic characters, thus pointing to the existence of similar tendencies in his own soul, and also from certain facts in his life, like his passion for gambling and his possible admission of a sexual assault upon a young girl.[1] The contradiction is resolved by the realization that Dostoevsky's very strong destructive instinct, which might easily have made him a criminal, was in his actual life directed mainly against his own person (inward instead of outward) and thus found expression as masochism and a sense of guilt. Nevertheless, his personality retained sadistic traits in plenty, which show themselves in his irritability, his love of tormenting and his intolerance even towards people he loved, and which appear also in the way in which, as an author, he treats his readers. Thus in little things he was a sadist towards others, and in bigger things a sadist towards himself, in fact a masochist, that is to say the mildest, kindliest, most helpful person possible.

We have selected three factors from Dostoevsky's complex personality, one quantitative and two qualitative: the extraordinary intensity of his emotional life, his perverse instinctual predisposition, which inevitably marked him out to be a sado-masochist or a criminal, and his unanalysable artistic endowment. This combination might very well exist without neurosis; there are people who are complete masochists without being neurotic. Nevertheless, the balance of forces between his instinctual demands and the inhibitions opposing them (plus the available methods of sublimation) would even so make it necessary to classify Dostoevsky as what is known as an 'instinctual character'. But the position is obscured by the simultaneous presence of neurosis, which, as we have said, was not in the circumstances inevitable, but which comes into being the more readily, the richer the complication which has to

[1] See the discussion on this point in Fülöp-Miller and Eckstein (1926). Stefan Zweig (1920) writes: 'He was not halted by the barriers of bourgeois morality; and no one can say exactly how far he transgressed the bounds of law in his own life or how much of the criminal instincts of his heroes was realized in himself.' For the intimate connection between Dostoevsky's characters and his own experiences, see René Fülöp-Miller's remarks in the introductory section of Fülöp-Miller and Eckstein (1925), which are based upon Nikolai Strakhov.

be mastered by the ego. For neurosis is after all only a sign that the ego has not succeeded in making a synthesis, that in attempting to do so it has forfeited its unity.

How then, strictly speaking, does his neurosis show itself? Dostoevsky called himself an epileptic, and was regarded as such by other people, on account of his severe seizures, which were accompanied by loss of consciousness, muscular convulsions and subsequent depression. Now it is highly probable that this so-called epilepsy was only a symptom of his neurosis and must accordingly be classified as hystero-epilepsy, that is, as severe hysteria. We cannot be completely certain on this point for two reasons, first, because the anamnestic data on Dostoevsky's alleged epilepsy are defective and untrustworthy, and secondly, because our understanding of pathological states combined with epileptiform seizures is imperfect.

To take the second point first. It is unnecessary here to reproduce the whole pathology of epilepsy, for it would throw no decisive light on the problem. But this may be said. The old *morbus sacer* is still in evidence as an ostensible clinical entity, the uncanny disease with its incalculable, apparently unprovoked convulsive seizures, its changing of the character into irritability and aggressiveness, and its progressive lowering of all the mental faculties. But the outlines of this picture are quite lacking in precision. The seizures, so savage in their onset, accompanied by biting of the tongue and incontinence of urine and working up to the dangerous *status epilepticus* with its risk of severe self-injuries, may, nevertheless, be reduced to brief periods of absence, or rapidly passing attacks of vertigo or may be replaced by short spaces of time during which the patient does something out of character, as though he were under the control of his unconscious. These seizures, though as a rule determined, in a way we do not understand, by purely physical causes, may nevertheless owe their first appearance to some purely mental

H

cause (a fright, for instance) or may react in other respects to mental excitations. However characteristic intellectual impairment may be in the overwhelming majority of cases, at least *one* case is known to us (that of Helmholtz) in which the affliction did not interfere with the highest intellectual achievement. (Other cases of which the same assertion has been made are either disputable or open to the same doubts as the case of Dostoevsky himself.) People who are victims of epilepsy may give an impression of dullness and arrested development, just as the disease often accompanies the most palpable idiocy and the grossest cerebral defects, even though not as a necessary component of the clinical picture. But these seizures with all their variations, also occur in other people who display complete mental development and, if anything, an excessive and as a rule insufficiently controlled emotional life. It is no wonder in these circumstances that it has been found impossible to maintain that 'epilepsy' is a single clinical entity. The similarity that we find in the manifest symptoms seems to call for a functional view of them. It is as though a mechanism for abnormal instinctual discharge had been laid down organically, which could be made use of in quite different circumstances—both in the case of disturbances of cerebral activity due to severe histolytic or toxic affections, and also in the case of inadequate control over the mental economy and at times when the activity of the energy operating in the mind reaches crisis-pitch. Behind this dichotomy we have a glimpse of the identity of the underlying mechanism of instinctual discharge. Nor can that mechanism stand remote from the sexual processes, which are fundamentally of toxic origin: the earliest physicians described copulation as a minor epilepsy, and thus recognized in the sexual act a mitigation and adaptation of the epileptic method of discharging stimuli.

The 'epileptic reaction', as this common element may be called, is also undoubtedly at the disposal of the neurosis whose essence it is to get rid by somatic means of quantities of excitation which it cannot deal with psychically. Thus the epileptic seizure becomes a symptom of hysteria and is adapted and modified by it just as it is by the normal sexual process of discharge. It is therefore quite right to distinguish between an organic and an 'affective' epilepsy. The practical significance of this is that a person who suffers from the first kind has a disease of the brain, while a person who suffers from the second kind is a neurotic. In the first case his mental life is subjected to an alien disturbance from without, in the second case the disturbance is an expression of his mental life itself.

It is extremely probable that Dostoevsky's epilepsy was of the second kind. This cannot, strictly speaking, be proved. To do so we should have to be in a position to insert the first appearance of the seizures and their subsequent fluctuations into the thread of his mental life; and for that we know too little. The descriptions of the seizures themselves teach us nothing and our information about the relations between the seizures and Dostoevsky's experiences is defective and often contradictory. The most probable assumption is that the seizures went back far into his childhood, that their place was taken to begin with by milder symptoms and that they did not assume an epileptic form until after the shocking experience of his eighteenth year—the murder of his father.[1] It would be very much to the

---

[1] See René Fülöp-Miller (1924). [Cf. also the account given by Aimée Dostoyevsky (1921) in her life of her father.] Of especial interest is the information that in the novelist's childhood 'something terrible, unforgettable and agonizing' happened, to which the first signs of his illness were to be traced (from an article by Suvorin in the newspaper *Novoe Vremya*, 1881, quoted in the introduction to Fülöp-Miller and Eckstein, 1925, xlv). See also Orest Miller (1882), 140: 'There is, however, another special piece of evidence about Feodor Mikhailovich's illness, which relates to his earliest youth and brings the illness into connection with a tragic event in the family life of his parents. But, although this piece of evidence was given to me orally by one who was a close friend of Feodor Mikhailovich, I cannot bring myself to reproduce it fully and precisely since I have had no confirmation of this rumour from any other quarter.' Biographers and scientific research workers cannot feel grateful for this discretion.

point if it could be established that they ceased completely during his exile in Siberia, but other accounts
contradict this.[1]

The unmistakable connection between the murder
of the father in *The Brothers Karamazov* and the fate of
Dostoevsky's own father has struck more than one of
his biographers, and has led them to refer to 'a certain modern school of psychology'. From the standpoint of psycho-analysis (for that is what is meant), we
are tempted to see in that event the severest trauma and
to regard Dostoevsky's reaction to it as the turning-point
of his neurosis. But if I undertake to substantiate this
view psycho-analytically, I am bound to risk the danger of
being unintelligible to all those readers who are unfamiliar
with the language and theories of psycho-analysis.

We have one certain starting-point. We know the
meaning of the first attacks from which Dostoevsky
suffered in his early years, long before the incidence of
the 'epilepsy'. These attacks had the significance of
death: they were heralded by a fear of death and consisted of lethargic, somnolent states. The illness first
came over him, while he was still a boy, in the form of a
sudden, groundless melancholy, a feeling, as he later
told his friend Soloviev, as though he were going to die
on the spot. And there in fact followed a state exactly
similar to real death. His brother Andrei tells us that
even when he was quite young Feodor used to leave
little notes about before he went to sleep, saying that
he was afraid he might fall into this death-like sleep
during the night and therefore begged that his burial
should be postponed for five days. (Fülöp-Miller and
Eckstein, 1925, lx.)

---

[1] Most of the accounts, including Dostoevsky's own, assert on the
contrary that the illness only assumed its final, epileptic character during
the Siberian exile. Unfortunately there is reason to distrust the auto-
biographical statements of neurotics. Experience shows that their
memories introduce falsifications, which are designed to interrupt disagreeable causal connections. Nevertheless, it appears certain that
Dostoevsky's detention in the Siberian prison markedly altered his
pathological condition. Cf. Fülöp-Miller (1924, 1186.)

We know the meaning and intention of such death-like seizures. They signify an identification with a dead person, either with someone who is really dead or with someone who is still alive and whom the subject wishes dead. The latter case is the more significant. The attack then has the value of a punishment. One has wished another person dead, and now one *is* this other person and is dead oneself. At this point psycho-analytical theory brings in the assertion that for a boy this other person is usually his father and that the attack (which is termed hysterical) is thus a self-punishment for a death-wish against a hated father.

Parricide, according to a well-known view, is the principal and primal crime of humanity as well as of the individual. (See my essays on *Totem and Taboo*, 1912–13.) It is in any case the main source of the sense of guilt, though we do not know if it is the only one: researches have not yet been able to establish with certainty the mental origin of guilt and the need for expiation. But it is not necessary for it to be the only one. The psychological situation is complicated and requires elucidation. The relation of a boy to his father is, as we say, an 'ambivalent' one. In addition to the hate which seeks to get rid of the father as a rival, a measure of tenderness for him is also habitually present. The two attitudes of mind combine to produce identification with the father; the boy wants to be in his father's place because he admires him and wants to be like him, and also because he wants to put him out of the way. This whole development now comes up against a powerful obstacle. At a certain moment the child comes to understand that an attempt to remove his father as a rival would be punished by him with castration. So from fear of castration, that is, in the interests of preserving his masculinity, he gives up his wish to possess his mother and get rid of his father. In so far as this wish remains in the unconscious it forms the basis of the sense of guilt. We believe that what we have here been describing are the normal processes, the normal fate of the so-called 'Oedipus complex'; never-theless it requires an important amplification.

A further complication arises when the constitutional factor we call bisexuality is comparatively strongly developed in the child. For then, under the threat to the boy's masculinity by castration, his inclination becomes strengthened to deflect in the direction of femininity, to put himself instead in his mother's place and take over her role as object of his father's love. But the fear of castration makes *this* solution impossible as well. The boy understands that he must also submit to castration if he wants to be loved by his father as a woman. Thus both impulses, hatred of the father and being in love with the father, undergo repression. There is a certain psychological distinction in the fact that the hatred of the father is given up on account of fear of an *external* danger (castration), while the being in love with the father is treated as an *internal* instinctual danger, though fundamentally it goes back to the same external danger.

What makes hatred of the father unacceptable is *fear* of the father; castration is terrible, whether as a punishment or as the price of love. Of the two factors which repress hatred of the father, the first, the direct fear of punishment and castration, may be called the normal one; its pathogenic intensification seems to come only with the addition of the second factor, the fear of the feminine attitude. Thus a strong bisexual pre-disposition becomes one of the pre-conditions or re-inforcements of neurosis. Such a predisposition must certainly be assumed in Dostoevsky, and it shows itself in a viable form (as latent homosexuality) in the im-portant part played by male friendships in his life, in his strangely tender attitude towards rivals in love and in his remarkable understanding of situations which are explicable only by repressed homosexuality, as many examples from his novels show.

I am sorry, though I cannot alter the facts, if this exposition of the attitudes of hatred and love towards the father and their transformations under the influence of the threat of castration seems to readers unfamiliar with psycho-analysis unsavoury and incredible. I should myself expect that it is precisely the castration complex that would be bound to arouse the most universal repugnance. But I can only insist that psycho-analytic experience has put these relations in particular beyond the reach of doubt and has taught us to recognize in them the key to every neurosis. This key, then, we must apply to our author's so-called epilepsy. So alien to our consciousness are the things by which our unconscious mental life is governed!

But what has been said so far does not exhaust the consequences of the repression of the hatred of the father in the Oedipus complex. There is something fresh to be added: namely that in spite of everything the identification with the father finally makes a permanent place for itself in the ego. It is received into the ego, but establishes itself there as a separate agency in contrast to the rest of the content of the ego. We then give it the name of super-ego and ascribe to it, the inheritor of the parental influence, the most important functions. If the father was hard, violent and cruel, the super-ego takes over those attributes from him and, in the relations between the ego and it, the passivity which was supposed to have been repressed is re-established. The super-ego has become sadistic, and the ego becomes masochistic, that is to say, at bottom passive in a feminine way. A great need for punishment develops in the ego, which in part offers itself as a victim to fate, and in part finds satisfaction in ill-treatment by the super-ego (that is, in the sense of guilt). For every punishment is ultimately castration and, as such, a fulfilment of the old passive attitude towards the father. Even fate is, in the last resort, only a later father-projection.

The normal processes in the formation of conscience must be similar to the abnormal ones described here. We have not yet succeeded in fixing the boundary line

between them. It will be observed that here the largest
share in the event is ascribed to the passive component
of repressed femininity. Moreover, it must be of importance as an accidental factor whether the father, who is
feared in any case, is also especially violent in reality.
This was true in Dostoevsky's case, and we can trace
back the fact of his extraordinary sense of guilt and of
his masochistic conduct of life to a specially strong
feminine component. Thus the formula for Dostoevsky
is as follows: a person of specially strong bisexual predisposition, who can defend himself with special intensity against dependence on a specially severe father.
This characteristic of bisexuality comes as an addition
to the components of his nature that we have already
recognized. His early symptom of death-like seizures
can thus be understood as a father-identification on the
part of his ego, permitted by his super-ego as a punishment. 'You wanted to kill your father in order to be
your father yourself. Now you *are* your father, but a
dead father'—the regular mechanism of hysterical
symptoms. And further: 'Now your father is killing
you.' For the ego the death symptom is a satisfaction in
phantasy of the masculine wish and at the same time a
masochistic satisfaction; for the super-ego it is a punishment satisfaction, that is, a sadistic satisfaction. Both
of them, the ego and the super-ego, carry on the role of
father.

To sum up, the relation between the subject and his
father-object, while retaining its content, has been
transformed into a relation between the ego and the
super-ego—a new setting on a fresh stage. Infantile
reactions from the Oedipus complex such as these may
disappear if reality gives them no further nourishment.
But the characteristics of the father remain the same,
or rather, they deteriorate with the years, and so too
Dostoevsky's hatred for his father and his death-wish
against that wicked father were maintained. Now it is a
dangerous thing if reality fulfils such repressed wishes.
The phantasy has become reality and all defensive

measures are thereupon reinforced. Dostoevsky's attacks now assumed an epileptic character; they still undoubtedly signified an identification with his father as a punishment, but they had become terrible, like his father's frightful death itself. What further content they had absorbed, particularly what sexual content, escapes conjecture.

One thing is remarkable: in the aura of the epileptic attack, one moment of supreme bliss is experienced. This may very well be a record of the triumph and sense of liberation felt on hearing the news of the death, to be followed immediately by an all the more cruel punishment. We have divined just such a sequence of triumph and mourning, of festive joy and mourning, in the brothers of the primal horde who murdered their father, and we find it repeated in the ceremony of the totem meal. If it proved to be the case that Dostoevsky was free from his seizures in Siberia, that would merely substantiate the view that his seizures were his punishment. He did not need them any longer when he was being punished in another way. But that cannot be proved. Rather does this necessity for punishment on the part of Dostoevsky's mental economy explain the fact that he passed unbroken through these years of misery and humiliation. Dostoevsky's condemnation as a political prisoner was unjust and he must have known it, but he accepted the undeserved punishment at the hands of the Little Father, the Tsar, as a substitute for the punishment he deserved for his sin against his real father. Instead of punishing himself, he got himself punished by his father's deputy. Here we have a glimpse of the psychological justification of the punishments inflicted by society. It is a fact that large groups of criminals long for punishment. Their super-ego demands it and so saves itself the necessity for inflicting the punishment itself.

Everyone who is familiar with the complicated transformation of meaning undergone by hysterical symptoms will understand that no attempt can be made here to follow out the meaning of Dostoevsky's attacks beyond this beginning.[1] It is enough that we may assume that their original meaning remained unchanged behind all later accretions. We can safely say that Dostoevsky never got free from the feelings of guilt arising from his intention of murdering his father. They also determined his attitude in the two other spheres in which the father-relation is the decisive factor, his attitude towards the authority of the State and towards belief in God. In the first of these he ended up with complete submission to his Little Father, the Tsar, who had once performed with him in *reality* the comedy of killing which his seizures had so often represented in *play*. Here penitence gained the upper hand. In the religious sphere he retained more freedom: according to apparently trustworthy reports he wavered, up to the last moment of his life, between faith and atheism. His great intellect made it impossible for him to overlook any of the intellectual difficulties to which faith leads. By an individual recapitulation of a development in world-history he hoped to find a way out and a liberation from guilt in the Christ ideal, and even to make use of his sufferings as a claim to be playing a Christ-like role. If on the whole he did not achieve freedom and became a reactionary, that was because the filial guilt, which is present in human beings generally and on which religious feeling is built, had in him attained a super-individual intensity and remained insurmountable even to his great intelligence. In writing this we are laying ourselves open to the charge of having abandoned the impartiality of analysis and of subjecting Dostoevsky to judgements that can only be

---

[1] See *Totem and Taboo* (1912–13). The best account of the meaning and content of his seizures was given by Dostoevsky himself, when he told his friend Strakhov that his irritability and depression after an epileptic attack were due to the fact that he seemed to himself a criminal and could not get rid of the feeling that he had a burden of unknown guilt upon him, that he had committed some great misdeed, which oppressed him. (Fülöp-Miller, 1924, 1188.) In self-accusations like these psychoanalysis sees signs of a recognition of 'psychical reality', and it endeavours to make the unknown guilt known to consciousness.

justified from the partisan standpoint of a particular philosophy of life. A conservative would take the side of the Grand Inquisitor and would judge Dostoevsky differently. The objection is just; and one can only say in extenuation that Dostoevsky's decision has every appearance of having been determined by an intellectual inhibition due to his neurosis.

It can scarcely be owing to chance that three of the masterpieces of the literature of all time—the *Oedipus Rex* of Sophocles, Shakespeare's *Hamlet* and Dostoevsky's *The Brothers Karamazov*—should all deal with the same subject, parricide. In all three, moreover, the motive for the deed, sexual rivalry for a woman, is laid bare.

The most straightforward is certainly the representation in the drama derived from the Greek legend. In this it is still the hero himself who commits the crime. But poetic treatment is impossible without softening and disguise. The naked admission of an intention to commit parricide, as we arrive at it in analysis, seems intolerable without analytical preparation. The Greek drama, while retaining the crime, introduces the indispensable toning-down in a masterly fashion by projecting the hero's unconscious motive into reality in the form of a compulsion by a destiny which is alien to him. The hero commits the deed unintentionally and apparently uninfluenced by the woman; this latter element is however taken into account in the circumstance that the hero can only obtain possession of the queen mother after he has repeated his deed upon the monster who symbolizes the father. After his guilt has been revealed and made conscious, the hero makes no attempt to exculpate himself by appealing to the artificial expedient of the compulsion of destiny. His crime is acknowledged and punished as though it were fully conscious—which is bound to appear unjust to our reason, but which psychologically is perfectly correct.

In the English play the presentation is more indirect; the hero does not commit the crime himself; it is carried out by someone else, for whom it is not parricide. The forbidden motive of sexual rivalry for the woman does not need, therefore, to be disguised. Moreover, we see the hero's Oedipus complex, as it were, in a reflected light, by learning the effect upon him of the other's crime. He ought to avenge the crime, but finds himself, strangely enough, incapable of doing so. We know that it is his sense of guilt that is paralysing him; but, in a manner entirely in keeping with neurotic processes, the sense of guilt is displaced on to the perception of his inadequacy for fulfilling his task. There are signs that the hero feels this guilt as a super-individual one. He despises others no less than himself: 'Use every man after his desert, and who should 'scape whipping?'

The Russian novel goes a step further in the same direction. There also the murder is committed by some-one else. This other person, however, stands to the murdered man in the same filial relation as the hero, Dmitri; in this other person's case the motive of sexual rivalry is openly admitted; he is a brother of the hero's, and it is a remarkable fact that Dostoevsky has attri-buted to him his own illness, the alleged epilepsy, as though he were seeking to confess that the epileptic, the neurotic, in himself was a parricide. Then, again, in the speech for the defence at the trial, there is the famous joke at the expense of psychology—it is a 'knife that cuts both ways': a splendid piece of disguise, for we have only to reverse it in order to discover the deepest mean-ing of Dostoevsky's view of things. It is not psychology that deserves to be laughed at, but the procedure of judicial enquiry. It is a matter of indifference who actually committed the crime; psychology is only con-cerned to know who desired it emotionally and who welcomed it when it was done. And for that reason all of the brothers, except the contrasted figure of Alyosha, are equally guilty, the impulsive sensualist, the sceptical cynic and the epileptic criminal. In *The Brothers Kara-mazov* there is one particularly revealing scene. In the course of his talk with Dmitri, Father Zossima recognizes that Dmitri is prepared to commit parricide, and he bows down at his feet. It is impossible that this can be meant as an expression of admiration; it must mean that the holy man is rejecting the temptation to despise or detest the murderer and for that reason humbles himself before him. Dostoevsky's sympathy for the criminal is, in fact, boundless; it goes far beyond the pity which the unhappy wretch might claim, and reminds us of the 'holy awe' with which epileptics and lunatics were regarded in the past. A criminal is to him almost a Redeemer, who has taken on himself the guilt which must else have been borne by others. There is no longer any need for one to murder, since *he* has already murdered; and one must be grateful to him, for, except for him, one would have been obliged oneself to murder. That is not just kindly pity, it is identification on the basis of a similar murderous impulse—in fact, a slightly displaced narcissism. (In saying this, we are not disputing the ethical value of this kindliness.) This may perhaps be quite generally the mechanism of kindly sympathy with other people, a mechanism which one can discern with especial ease in the extreme case of the guilt-ridden novelist. There is no doubt that this sympathy by identification was a decisive factor in determining Dostoevsky's choice of material. He dealt first with the common criminal (whose motives are egotistical) and the political and religious criminal; and not until the end of his life did he come back to the primal criminal, the parricide, and use him, in a work of art, for making his confession.

The publication of Dostoevsky's posthumous papers and of his wife's diaries has thrown a glaring light on one episode in his life, namely the period in Germany when he was obsessed with a mania for gambling (cf. Fülöp-Miller and Eckstein, 1925), which no one could regard as anything but an unmistakable fit of pathological passion. There was no lack of rationalizations for this remarkable and unworthy behaviour. As often happens with neurotics, Dostoevsky's burden of guilt had taken a tangible shape as a burden of debt, and he was able to take refuge behind the pretext that he was trying by his winnings at the tables to make it possible for him to return to Russia without being arrested by his creditors. But this was no more than a pretext; and Dostoevsky was acute enough to recognize the fact and honest enough to admit it. He knew that the chief thing was gambling for its own sake—*le jeu pour le jeu*.[1] All the details of his impulsively irrational conduct show this and something more besides. He never rested until he had lost everything. For him gambling was another method of self-punishment. Time after time he gave his young wife his promise or his word of honour not to play any more or not to play any more on that particular day; and, as she says, he almost always broke it. When his losses had reduced himself and her to the direst need, he derived a second pathological satisfaction from that. He could then scold and humiliate himself before her, invite her to despise him and to feel sorry that she had married such an old sinner; and when he had thus unburdened his conscience, the whole business would begin again next day. His young wife accustomed herself to this cycle, for she had noticed that the one thing which offered any real hope of salvation—his literary production—never went better than when they had lost everything and pawned their last possessions. Naturally she did not understand the connection. When his sense of guilt was satisfied by the punishments he had inflicted on himself, the inhibitions upon his work became less severe and he allowed himself to take a few steps along the way to success.[2]

What part of a gambler's long-buried childhood is it

---

[1] 'The main thing is the play itself,' he writes in one of his letters. 'I swear that greed for money has nothing to do with it, although Heaven knows I am sorely in need of money.'

[2] 'He always remained at the gaming tables till he had lost everything and was totally ruined. It was only when the damage was quite complete that the demon at last retired from his soul and made way for the creative genius.' (Fülöp-Miller and Eckstein, 1925, lxxxvi.)

that forces its way to repetition in his obsession for play? The answer may be divined without difficulty from a story by one of our younger writers. Stefan Zweig, who has incidentally devoted a study to Dostoevsky himself (1920), has included in his collection of three stories *Die Verwirrung der Gefühle* (1927) one which he calls 'Vierundzwanzig Stunden aus dem Leben einer Frau' ['Four-and-Twenty Hours in a Woman's Life']. This little masterpiece ostensibly sets out only to show what an irresponsible creature woman is, and to what excesses, surprising even to herself, an unexpected experience may drive her. But the story tells far more than this. If it is subjected to an analytical interpretation, it will be found to represent (without any apologetic intent) something quite different, something universally human, or rather something masculine. And such an interpretation is so extremely obvious that it cannot be resisted. It is characteristic of the nature of artistic creation that the author, who is a personal friend of mine, was able to assure me, when I asked him, that the interpretation which I put to him had been completely strange to his knowledge and intention, although some of the details woven into the narrative seemed expressly designed to give a clue to the hidden secret.

In this story, an elderly lady of distinction tells the author of an experience she has had more than twenty years earlier. She has been left a widow when still young and is the mother of two sons, who no longer need her. In her forty-second year, expecting nothing further of life, she happens, on one of her aimless journeyings, to visit the Rooms at Monte Carlo. There, among all the remarkable impressions which the place produces, she is soon fascinated by the sight of a pair of hands which seem to betray all the feelings of the unlucky gambler with terrifying sincerity and intensity. These hands belong to a handsome young man—the author, as though unintentionally, makes him of the same age as the narrator's elder son—who, after losing everything, leaves the Rooms in the depth of despair, with the evident intention of ending his hopeless life in the Casino gardens. An inexplicable feeling of sympathy compels her to follow him and make every effort to save him. He takes her for one of the importunate women so common there and tries to shake her off; but she stays with him and finds herself obliged, in the most natural way possible, to join him in his apartment at the hotel, and finally to share his bed. After this improvised night of love, she exacts a most solemn vow from the young man, who has now apparently calmed down, that he will never play again, provides him with money for his journey home and promises to meet him at the station before the departure of his train. Now, however, she begins to feel a great tenderness for him, is ready to sacrifice all she has in order to keep him and makes up her mind to go with him instead of saying goodbye. Various mischances delay her, so that she misses the train. In her longing for the lost one she returns once more to the Rooms and there, to her horror, sees once more the hands which had first excited her sympathy: the faithless youth had gone back to his play. She reminds him of his promise, but, obsessed by his passion, he calls her a spoil-sport, tells her to go and flings back the money with which she has tried to rescue him. She hurries away in deep mortification and learns later that she has not succeeded in saving him from suicide.

The brilliantly told, faultlessly motivated story is of course complete in itself and is certain to make a deep effect upon the reader. But analysis shows us that its invention is based fundamentally upon a wishful phantasy belonging to the period of puberty, which a number of people actually remember consciously. The phantasy embodies a boy's wish that his mother should herself initiate him into sexual life in order to save him from the dreaded injuries caused by masturbation. (The numerous creative works that deal with the theme of redemption have the same origin.) The 'vice' of masturbation is replaced by the mania for gambling; and the emphasis laid upon the passionate activity of the hands betrays this derivation. The passion for play is an equivalent of the old compulsion to masturbate; 'playing' is the actual word used in the nursery to describe the activity of the hands upon the genitals. The irresistible nature of the temptation, the solemn resolutions, which are nevertheless invariably broken, never to do it again, the numbing pleasure and the bad conscience which tells the subject that he is ruining himself (committing suicide)—all these elements remain unaltered in the process of substitution. It is true that Zweig's story is told by the mother, not by the son. It must flatter the son to think: 'if my mother only knew what dangers masturbation involves me in, she would certainly save me from them by allowing me to lavish all my tenderness on her own body.' The equation of the mother with a prostitute, which is made by the young man in the story, is linked up with the same phantasy. It brings the unattainable within easy reach. The bad conscience which accompanies the phantasy brings about the unhappy ending of the story. It is also interesting to notice how the *façade* given to the story by its author seeks to disguise its analytic meaning. For it is extremely questionable whether the erotic life of women is dominated by sudden and mysterious impulses. On the contrary, analysis reveals an adequate motivation for the surprising behaviour of this woman who had hitherto turned away from love. Faithful to the memory of her dead husband, she had armed herself against all similar attractions; but—and here the son's phantasy is right—she did not, as a mother, escape her quite unconscious transference of love on to her son, and fate was able to catch her at this undefended spot.

If the mania for gambling, with the unsuccessful struggles to break the habit and the opportunities it affords for self-punishment, is a repetition of the compulsion to masturbate, we shall not be surprised to find that it occupied such a large space in Dostoevsky's life.

After all, we find no cases of severe neurosis in which the autoerotic satisfaction of early childhood and of puberty has not played a part; and the relation between efforts to suppress it and fear of the father are too well known to need more than a mention.[1]

[1] Most of the views which are here expressed are also contained in an excellent book by Jolan Neufeld (1923).

XXII
A RELIGIOUS EXPERIENCE[1]
(1928)

IN the autumn of 1927, G. S. Viereck, a German-American journalist who had paid me a welcome visit, published an account of a conversation with me, in the course of which he mentioned my lack of religious faith and my indifference on the subject of survival after death. This 'interview', as it was called, was widely read and brought me, among others, the following letter from an American physician:

'. . . What struck me most was your answer to the question whether you believe in a survival of personality after death. You are reported as having said, "I give no thought to the matter."

'I am writing now to tell you of an experience that I had in the year I graduated at the University of X. One afternoon while I was passing through the dissecting-room my attention was attracted to a sweet-faced dear old woman who was being carried to a dissecting-table. This sweet-faced woman made such an impression on me that a thought flashed up in my mind, "There is no God: if there were a God he would not have allowed this dear old woman to be brought into the dissecting-room."

'When I got home that afternoon the feeling I had had at the sight in the dissecting-room had determined me to discontinue going to church. The doctrines of Christianity had before this been the subject of doubts in my mind.

'While I was meditating on this matter a voice spoke to my soul that "I should consider the step I was about to take". My spirit replied to this inner voice by saying, "If I knew of a certainty that

[1] ['Ein religiöses Erlebnis.' First published *Imago*, **14** (1928), 7; reprinted *Ges. Schr.*, **11**, 467, and *Ges. W.*, **14**, 393. First translated *Int. J. Psycho-Anal.*, **10** (1929), 1. Present translation by James Strachey.]

Christianity was truth and the Bible was the Word of God, then I would accept it.''

'In the course of the next few days God made it clear to my soul that the Bible was his Word, that the teachings about Jesus Christ were true, and that Jesus was our only hope. After such a clear revelation I accepted the Bible as God's Word and Jesus Christ as my personal Saviour. Since then God has revealed himself to me by many infallible proofs.

'I beg you as a brother physician to give thought to this most important matter, and I can assure you, if you look into this subject with an open mind, God will reveal the *truth* to your soul, the same as he did to me and to multitudes of others. . . .'

I sent a polite answer, saying that I was glad to hear that this experience had enabled him to retain his faith. As for myself, God had not done so much for me. He had never allowed me to hear an inner voice; and if, in view of my age, he did not make haste, it would not be my fault if I remained to the end of my life what I now was—'an infidel Jew'.

In the course of a friendly reply, my colleague gave me an assurance that being a Jew was not an obstacle in the pathway to true faith and proved this by several instances. His letter culminated in the information that prayers were being earnestly addressed to God that he might grant me 'faith to believe'.

I am still awaiting the outcome of this intercession. In the meantime, my colleague's religious experience provides food for thought. It seems to me to demand some attempt at an interpretation based upon emotional motives; for his experience is puzzling in itself and is based on particularly bad logic. God, as we know, allows horrors to take place of a kind very different from the removal to a dissecting-room of the dead body of a pleasant-looking old woman. This has been true at all times, and it must have been so while my American colleague was pursuing his studies. Nor, as a medical student, can he have been so sheltered from the world as to have known nothing of such evils. Why was it then, that his indignation against God broke out precisely when he received this particular impression in the dissecting-room?

For anyone who is accustomed to regard men's internal experiences and actions analytically the explanation is very obvious—so obvious that it actually crept into my recollection of the facts themselves. Once when I was referring to my pious colleague's letter in the course of a discussion, I spoke of his having written that the dead woman's face had reminded him of his own mother. In fact these words were not in his letter, and a moment's reflection will show that they could not possibly have been. But that is the explanation irresistibly forced on us by his affectionately phrased description of the 'sweet-faced dear old woman'. Thus the weakness of judgement displayed by the young doctor is to be accounted for by the emotion roused in him by the memory of his mother. It is difficult to escape from the bad psycho-analytic habit of bringing forward as evidence details which also allow of more superficial explanations—and I am tempted to recall the fact that my colleague addressed me later as a 'brother physician'.

We may suppose, therefore, that this was the way in which things happened. The sight of a woman's dead body, naked or on the point of being stripped, reminded the young man of his mother. It roused in him a longing for his mother which sprang from his Oedipus complex, and this was immediately completed by a feeling of indignation against his father. His ideas of 'father' and 'God' had not yet become widely separated; so that his desire to destroy his father could become conscious as doubt in the existence of God and could seek to justify itself in the eyes of reason as indignation about the ill-treatment of a mother-object. It is of course typical for a child to regard what his father does to his mother in sexual intercourse as ill-treatment. The new impulse, which was displaced into the sphere of religion, was only a repetition of the Oedipus situation and consequently soon met with a similar fate. It succumbed to a powerful opposing current. During the actual conflict the level of displacement was not maintained: there is no mention of arguments in justification of God, nor are we told what the infallible signs were by which God proved his existence to the doubter. The conflict seems to have been unfolded in the form of an hallucinatory psychosis: inner voices were heard which uttered warnings against resistance to God. But the outcome of the struggle was displayed once again in the sphere of religion and it was of a kind pre-determined by the fate of the Oedipus complex: complete submission to the will of God the Father. The young man became a believer and accepted everything he had been taught since his childhood about God and Jesus Christ. He had had a religious experience and had undergone a conversion.

All of this is so simple and straightforward that we cannot but ask ourselves whether by understanding this case we have thrown any light on the psychology of conversion in general. I may refer the reader to an admirable volume on the subject by Sante de Sancatis (1924), which incidentally takes all the findings of psycho-analysis into account. Study of this work confirms our expectation that by no means every case of conversion can be understood so easily as this one. In no respect, however, does our case contradict the views arrived at on the subject by modern research. The point which our present observation throws into relief is the manner in which the conversion was attached to a particular determining event, which caused the subject's scepticism to flare up for a last time before being finally extinguished.

XXIII

LIBIDINAL TYPES[1]

(1931)

OBSERVATION teaches us that in individual human beings the general features of humanity are embodied in almost infinite variety. If we follow the promptings of a legitimate desire to distinguish particular types in this multiplicity, we must begin by selecting the characteristics to look for and the points of view to bear in mind in making our differentiation. For this purpose physical qualities will be no less useful than mental; it will be most valuable of all if we can make our classification on the basis of a regularly occurring combination of physical and mental characteristics.

It is doubtful whether we are as yet able to discover types of this order, although we shall certainly be able to do so sometime on a basis of which we are still ignorant. If we confine our efforts to defining certain purely psychological types, the libidinal situation will have the first claim to serve as the basis of our classification. It may fairly be demanded that this classification should not merely be deduced from our knowledge or our conjectures about the libido, but that it should be easily verified in actual experience and should help to clarify the mass of our observations and enable us to grasp their meaning. Let it be admitted at once that there is no need to suppose that, even in the psychical sphere, these libidinal types are the only possible ones; if we take other characteristics as our basis of classification we might be able to distinguish a whole series of other psychological types. But there is one rule which must apply to all such types: they must not coincide

---

[1] ['Über libidinöse Typen.' First published *Int. Z. Psychoanal.*, **17** (1931), 313; reprinted *Ges. Schr.*, **12**, 115, and *Ges. W.*, **14**, 509. Translation, reprinted from *Int. J. Psycho-Anal.*, **13** (1932), 277, by Joan Riviere.]

with specific clinical pictures. On the contrary, they should embrace all the variations which according to our practical standards fall within the category of the normal. In their extreme developments, however, they may well approximate to clinical pictures and so help to bridge the gulf which is assumed to exist between the normal and the pathological.

Now we can distinguish three main libidinal types, according as the subject's libido is mainly allocated to one or another region of the mental apparatus. To name these types is not very easy; following the lines of our depth-psychology, I should be inclined to call them the *erotic*, the *narcissistic* and the *obsessional* type.

The *erotic* type is easily characterized. Erotics are persons whose main interest—the relatively largest amount of their libido—is focused on love. Loving, but above all being loved, is for them the most important thing in life. They are governed by the dread of loss of love, and this makes them peculiarly dependent on those who may withhold their love from them. Even in its pure form this type is a very common one. Variations occur according as it is blended with another type and as the element of aggression in it is strong or weak. From the social and cultural standpoint this type represents the elementary instinctual claims of the id, to which the other psychical agencies have become docile.

The second type is that which I have termed the *obsessional*—a name which may at first seem rather strange; its distinctive characteristic is the supremacy exercised by the super-ego, which is segregated from the ego with great accompanying tension. Persons of this type are governed by anxiety of conscience instead of by the dread of losing love; they exhibit, we might say, an inner instead of an outer dependence; they develop a high degree of self-reliance, and from the social standpoint they are the true upholders of civilization, for the most part in a conservative spirit.

The characteristics of the third type, justly called the *narcissistic*, are in the main negatively described.

There is no tension between ego and super-ego—indeed, starting from this type one would hardly have arrived at the notion of a super-ego; there is no preponderance of erotic needs; the main interest is focused on self-preservation; the type is independent and not easily overawed. The ego has a considerable amount of aggression available, one manifestation of this being a proneness to activity; where love is in question, loving is preferred to being loved. People of this type impress others as being 'personalities'; it is on them that their fellow-men are specially likely to lean; they readily assume the role of leader, give a fresh stimulus to cultural development or break down existing conditions.

These pure types will hardly escape the suspicion of being deduced from the theory of the libido. But we feel that we are on the firm ground of experience when we turn to the mixed types which are to be found so much more frequently than the unmixed. These new types: the *erotic-obsessional,* the *erotic-narcissistic* and the *narcissistic-obsessional* do really seem to provide a good grouping of the individual psychical structures revealed in analysis. If we study these mixed types we find in them pictures of characters with which we have long been familiar. In the *erotic-obsessional* type the preponderance of the instincts is restricted by the influence of the super-ego: dependence on persons who are *contemporary* objects and, at the same time, on the residues of *former* objects—parents, educators and ideal figures—is carried by this type to the furthest point. The *erotic-narcissistic* type is perhaps the most common of all. It combines contrasting characteristics which are thus able to moderate one another; studying this type in comparison with the other two erotic types, we can see how aggressiveness and activity go with a predominance of narcissism. Finally, the *narcissistic-obsessional* type represents the variation most valuable from the cultural standpoint, for it combines independence of external factors and regard for the requirements of conscience with the capacity for energetic action, and it reinforces the ego against the super-ego.

It might be asked in jest why no mention has been made of another mixed type which is theoretically possible: the *erotic-obsessional-narcissistic*. But the answer to this jest is serious: such a type would no longer be a type at all, but the absolute norm, the ideal harmony. We thereupon realize that the phenomenon of different *types* arises just in so far as one or two of the three main modes of expending the libido in the mental economy have been favoured at the cost of the others.

Another question that may be asked is what is the relation of these libidinal types to pathology, whether some of them have a special disposition to pass over into neurosis and, if so, which types lead to which forms of neurosis. The answer is that the hypothesis of these libidinal types throws no fresh light on the genesis of the neuroses. Experience testifies that persons of all these types can live free from neurosis. The pure types marked by the undisputed predominance of a single psychical agency seem to have a better prospect of manifesting themselves as pure character-formations, while we might expect that the mixed types would provide a more fruitful soil for the conditioning factors of neurosis. But I do not think that we should make up our mind on these points until they have been carefully submitted to appropriate tests.

It seems easy to infer that when persons of the erotic type fall ill they will develop hysteria, just as those of the obsessional type will develop obsessional neurosis; but even this conclusion partakes of the uncertainty to which I have just alluded. People of the narcissistic type, who, being otherwise independent, are exposed to frustration from the external world, are peculiarly disposed to psychosis; and their mental composition also contains some of the essential conditioning factors which make for criminality.

We know that we have not as yet exact certainty

about the aetiological conditions of neurosis. The precipitating occasions are frustrations and inner conflicts: conflicts between the three great psychical agencies, conflicts arising in the libidinal economy by reason of our bisexual disposition, conflicts between the erotic and the aggressive instinctual components. It is the endeavour of the psychology of the neuroses to discover what imparts a pathogenic character to these processes, which are a part of the normal course of mental life.

XXIV

FEMALE SEXUALITY[1]

(1931)

I

IN that phase of children's libidinal development which is characterized by the normal Oedipus complex we find that they are tenderly attached to the parent of the opposite sex, while their relation to the other parent is predominantly hostile. In the case of boys the explanation is simple. A boy's mother was his first love-object; she remains so, and, as his feelings for her become more passionate and he understands more of the relation between father and mother, the former inevitably appears as a rival. With little girls it is otherwise. For them, too, the mother was the first love-object; how then does a little girl find her way to her father? How, when and why does she detach herself from her mother? We have long realized that in women the development of sexuality is complicated by the task of renouncing that genital zone which was originally the principal one, namely, the clitoris, in favour of a new zone—the vagina. But there is a second change which appears to us no less characteristic and important for feminine development: the original mother-object has to be exchanged for the father. We cannot as yet see clearly how these two tasks are linked up.

We know that women with a strong father-attachment are numerous and need not by any means be neurotic. In studying this type I have made some observations which I propose to communicate here and which have led me to a certain view of female sexuality. I have been struck, above all, by two facts. First,

---

[1] ['Uber die weibliche Sexualität.' First published *Int. Z. Psychoanal.*, **17** (1931), 317; reprinted *Ges. Schr.*, **12**, 120, and *Ges. W.*, **14**, 517. Translation, reprinted from *Int. J. Psycho-Anal.*, **13** (1932), 281, by Joan Riviere.]

analysis has shown that where the attachment to the
father was peculiarly strong it had been preceded by a
phase of equally strong and passionate attachment
exclusively to the mother. Except for the change in the
object, the love-life had acquired hardly a single new
feature in the second phase. The primary mother-
relation had developed in a very rich and many-sided
way.

Secondly, I learnt that the duration of this attachment to the mother had been greatly underestimated.
In a number of cases it persisted well into the fourth
and, in one, into the fifth year, so that it comprised by
far the longer period of the early sexual efflorescence.
Indeed, one had to give due weight to the possibility
that many a woman may remain arrested at the original
mother-attachment and never properly achieve the
change-over to men.

These facts show that the pre-Oedipus phase in
women is more important than we have hitherto supposed.

Since there is time during this phase for all the
fixations and repressions which we regard as the source
of the neuroses, it seems that we shall have to retract
the universality of the dictum that the Oedipus complex
is the nucleus of neurosis. But if anyone feels reluctant
to adopt this correction, he need not do so. For, on the
one hand, we can extend the content of the Oedipus
complex to include all the child's relations to both
parents or, on the other, we can give due recognition to
our new findings by saying that women reach the
normal, positive Oedipus situation only after surmounting a first phase dominated by the negative complex.
Actually, during this phase, to a little girl, her father is
not very different from a troublesome rival even though
her hostility towards him never reaches such a pitch as
does the boy's. We have, after all, long given up any
expectation of a neat parallelism between male and
female sexual development.

Our insight into this early, pre-Oedipus phase in the

little girl's development comes to us as a surprise, comparable in another field with the effect of the discovery of the Minoan-Mycenaean civilization behind that of Greece.

Everything connected with this first mother-attachment has in analysis seemed to me so elusive, lost in a past so dim and shadowy, so hard to resuscitate, that it seemed as if it had undergone some specially inexorable repression. But possibly I have received this impression because, when I have analysed women, they have been able to cling on to that very father-attachment in which they took refuge from the early phase of which I am speaking. It would in fact appear that women-analysts —for instance, Jeanne Lampl - de Groot and Helene Deutsch—had been able to apprehend the facts with greater ease and clearness because they had the advantage of being suitable mother-substitutes in the transference-situation with the patients whom they were studying. I have not indeed succeeded in completely unravelling any of the cases in point and will therefore confine myself to communicating my most general conclusions and giving only a few examples of the new ideas which have suggested themselves to me. Amongst these is my conjecture that this phase of mother-attachment is specially closely connected with the aetiology of hysteria (this is indeed by no means surprising when we reflect that both the phase and the neurosis in question are characteristically feminine); further, that in this dependence on the mother we have the germ of later paranoia in women.[1] For it appears that this germ is the surprising, yet regular, dread of being killed (? devoured) by the mother. It would seem plausible to conjecture that this anxiety corresponds to the hostility which the child develops towards her mother because of the manifold restrictions imposed by the latter in the process of training and physical care,

[1] In the well-known case [of delusional jealousy] reported by Ruth Mack Brunswick (1928a) the direct source of the disorder was the patient's pre-Oedipus fixation (to her sister).

and that the immaturity of the child's psychical organization favours the mechanism of projection.

II

I have begun by stating the two facts which have struck me as new: first, that the great dependence on the father in women merely takes over the heritage of an equally great attachment to the mother and, secondly, that this earlier phase lasts longer than we should have anticipated. I must now go back a little in order to insert these new conclusions in their proper place in the picture of female sexual development with which we are already familiar. A certain amount of repetition is here inevitable. It will help our exposition if, as we go along, we compare the course of female development with that of the male.

First of all, there can be no doubt that the bisexual disposition which we maintain to be characteristic of human beings manifests itself much more plainly in the female than in the male. The latter has only one principal sexual zone—only one sexual organ—whereas the former has two: the vagina, the true female organ, and the clitoris, which is analogous to the male organ. We believe that we may justly assume that for many years the vagina is virtually non-existent and possibly remains without sensation until puberty. It is true, however, that recently an increasing number of observers have been inclined to think that vaginal stirrings are present even in those early years. In any case female genitality must, in childhood, centre principally in the clitoris. The sexual life of the woman is regularly split up into two phases, the first of which is of a masculine character, whilst only the second is specifically feminine. Thus in female development there is a process of transition from the one phase to the other, to which there is nothing analogous in males. A further complication arises from the fact that the clitoris, with its masculine character, continues to function in later female sexual life in a very variable manner, which we certainly do not as yet fully understand. Of course, we do not know what are the biological roots of these specific characteristics of the woman, and we are still less able to assign to them any teleological purpose.

Parallel with this first great difference there is another, which concerns the love-object. The first love-object of the male is the mother, because it is she who feeds and tends him, and she remains his principal love-object until she is replaced by another which resembles her or is derived from her. With the female too the mother must be the first object, for the primary conditions of object-choice are the same for all children. But at the end of the girl's development it is the man— the father—who must come to be the new love-object; *i.e.* as she changes in sex, so must the sex of her love-object change. What we now have to discover is how this transformation takes place, how radical or how incomplete it is, and all the different things that may happen in this process of development.

We have already observed that there is yet another difference between the sexes in their relation to the Oedipus complex. We have the impression that what we have said about that complex applies in all strictness only to male children, and that we are right in rejecting the term 'Electra complex' which seeks to insist that the situation of the two sexes is analogous. It is only in male children that there occurs the fateful simultaneous conjunction of love for the one parent and hatred of the other as rival. It is thereupon the discovery of the possibility of castration, as evidenced by the sight of the female genital which necessitates the transformation of the boy's Oedipus complex, leads to the creation of the super-ego and thus initiates all the processes that culminate in enrolling the individual in civilized society. After the paternal function has been internalized so as to form the super-ego, the next task is to detach the latter from those persons of whom it was originally the psychical representative. In this remarkable course of development the agent employed to restrain infantile sexuality is precisely that narcissistic genital interest which centres in the preservation of the penis.

One residue of the castration complex in the man is a measure of disparagement in his attitude towards women, whom he regards as having been castrated. In extreme cases this inhibits his object-choice, and, if reinforced by organic factors, it may result in exclusive homosexuality. Very different is the effect of the castration complex on the girl. She acknowledges the fact of her castration, the consequent superiority of the male and her own inferiority, but she also rebels against these unpleasant facts. So divided in her mind, she may follow one of three lines of development. The first leads to her turning her back on sexuality altogether. The budding woman, frightened by the comparison of herself with boys, becomes dissatisfied with her clitoris and gives up her phallic activity and therewith her sexuality in general and a considerable part of her masculine proclivities in other fields. If she pursues the second line, she clings in obstinate self-assertion to her threatened masculinity; the hope of getting a penis sometime is cherished to an incredibly late age and becomes the aim of her life, whilst the phantasy of really being a man, in spite of everything, often dominates long periods of her life. This 'masculinity complex' may also result in a manifestly homosexual object-choice. Only if her development follows the third, very circuitous path does she arrive at the ultimate normal feminine attitude in which she takes her father as love-object, and thus arrives at the Oedipus complex in its feminine form. Thus, in women, that complex represents the final result of a lengthy process of development; castration does not destroy but rather creates it, and it escapes the strong hostile influences which, in men, tend to its destruction—in fact, only too often a woman never surmounts it at all. Hence too the cultural effects of the break-up of this complex are slighter and less important in women than in men. We should probably not err in saying that it is this difference in the inter-relation of the Oedipus and the castration-complexes which gives its special stamp to the character of woman as a member of society.[1]

We see then that the phase of exclusive attachment to the mother, which may be called the *pre-Oedipus* phase, is far more important in women than it can claim to be in men. Many phenomena of feminine sexual life which were difficult to understand before can be fully explained by reference to this phase. For example, we had noted long ago that many a woman who takes her father as the model for her choice of a husband, or assigns her father's place to him, yet in her married life repeats with her husband her bad relations with her mother. He should have succeeded to her relation with her father, but in reality he takes over her relation to her mother. This is easily explained as an obvious case of regression. The mother-relation was the original one, upon which the father-relation was built up; in married life the original basis emerges from repression. For her development to womanhood consisted mainly in trans-ferring affective ties from the mother to the father-object.

With many women we have the impression that the period of their maturity is entirely taken up with con-flicts with their husbands, just as they spent their youth in conflicts with their mothers. In the light of what I have now said we shall conclude that the hostile attitude to the mother is not a consequence of the rivalry

---

[1] It is to be anticipated that male analysts with feminist sympathies, and our women analysts also, will disagree with what I have said here. They will hardly fail to object that such notions have their origin in the man's 'masculinity complex', and are meant to justify theoretically his innate propensity to disparage and suppress women. But this sort of psycho-analytic argument reminds us here, as it so often does, of Dostoevsky's famous 'knife that cuts both ways'. The opponents of those who reason thus will for their part think it quite comprehensible that members of the female sex should refuse to accept a notion that appears to gainsay their eagerly coveted equality with men. The use of analysis as a weapon of controversy obviously leads to no decision.

implicit in the Oedipus complex, but rather originates in the preceding phase and has simply found in the Oedipus situation reinforcement and an opportunity for asserting itself. Direct analytic investigation confirms this view. Our interest must be directed to the mechanisms at work in the turning away from the mother-object, originally so vehemently and exclusively loved. We are prepared to find not one solitary factor but a whole number of these contributing to the same end.

Σ p262-3

Amongst these factors are some which are conditioned by the circumstances of infantile sexuality in general and so hold good equally for the love-relations of boys. First and foremost we must mention jealousy of other persons—brothers and sisters and rivals, amongst whom is also the father. Childish love knows no bounds, it demands exclusive possession, is satisfied with nothing less than all. But it has a second characteristic: it has no real aim; it is incapable of complete satisfaction and this is the principal reason why it is doomed to end in disappointment and to give place to a hostile attitude. Later on in life, the lack of ultimate gratification may conduce to a different result. This very factor may ensure the undisturbed continuance of the libidinal cathexis, as is the case in love-relations inhibited in their aim. But in the stress of the processes of development it regularly happens that the libido abandons its unsatisfactory position in order to find a new one.

There is another, far more specific motive for the turning away from the mother, arising out of the effect of the castration-complex on the little creature without a penis. Some time or other the little girl makes the discovery of her organic inferiority, of course earlier and more easily if she has brothers or other boy companions. We have already noted the three paths which diverge from this point: (*a*) that which leads to the suspension of the whole sexual life, (*b*) that which leads to the defiant over-emphasis of her own masculinity, and (*c*) the first steps towards definitive femininity. It is not easy to say precisely when these processes occur or to lay down their typical course. Even the point of time when the discovery of castration is made varies and many other factors seem to be inconstant and to depend on chance. The condition of the girl's own phallic activity plays a part, as also whether it is discovered or not, and how far it is hindered after the discovery.

The little girl generally finds out spontaneously her mode of phallic activity—masturbation of the clitoris—and in the first instance it is no doubt unaccompanied by phantasies. The way in which the tending of the child's body influences the awakening of this activity is reflected in the very common phantasy of seduction by her mother, her wet-nurse or nursemaid. Whether little girls practise masturbation more rarely and from the beginning less energetically than little boys is a point which we must leave undecided: quite possibly this is the case. Actual seduction is likewise common enough, either at the hands of other children or of nurses who want to soothe the child, send her to sleep or make her dependent on them. Where seduction intervenes, it invariably disturbs the natural course of development and often has profound and lasting consequences.

The prohibition of masturbation may, as we have seen, act as an incentive for giving the habit up, but it may also operate as a motive for rebellion against the person who forbids, *i.e.* the mother, or the mother-substitute who later regularly merges into the mother. The defiant persistence in masturbation would appear to open the way to masculinity. Even when the child does not succeed in mastering her habit, the effect of the apparently unavailing prohibition is seen in her later efforts to free herself at all costs from a gratification which has been made distasteful to her. When the girl reaches maturity her object-choice may still be influenced by this firmly maintained purpose. Resentment at being prevented from free sexual activity has much to do with her detachment from her mother. The same motive recurs after puberty when the mother takes up the duty of protecting her daughter's chastity. Of course, we must remember here that the mother opposes masturbation in the boy in the same way, thus providing him also with a powerful motive for rebellion.

When a little girl has sight of a male genital organ and so discovers her own deficiency, she does not accept the unwelcome knowledge without hesitation and reluctance. As we have seen, she clings obstinately to the expectation of acquiring a similar organ sometime, and the desire for it survives long after the hope is extinguished. Invariably the child regards castration in the first instance as a misfortune peculiar to herself; only later does she realize that it extends to certain other children and at length to certain adults. When the universality of this negative character of her sex dawns upon her, womanhood, and with it also her mother, suffers a heavy loss of credit in her eyes.

Very possibly this account of the little girl's reaction to her impression of castration and the prohibition of masturbation will strike the reader as confused and contradictory. That is not altogether the writer's fault. A description which fits every case is in fact almost impossible. In different individuals we find the most various reactions; even in the same individual contrary attitudes exist side by side. With the first intervention of the prohibition there begins a conflict which from that moment will accompany the development of the sexual function. It is particularly difficult to get a clear insight into what takes place because it is so hard to distinguish the mental processes of this first phase from the later ones by which they become overlaid and distorted in memory. For example, the fact of castration is sometimes construed later as a punishment for masturbation, and its infliction is ascribed to the father; of course, neither of these ideas can be the original one. With boys also it is regularly the father from whom castration is dreaded, although in their case, as in the little girl's, it is mostly the mother who utters the threat.

However this may be, at the end of this first phase of attachment to the mother there emerges, as the strongest motive for turning away from her, the child's reproach that her mother has not given her a proper genital, *i.e.* that she was born a woman. A second reproach, not going quite so far back, comes as rather a surprise: it is that the mother gave the child too little milk and did not suckle her long enough. Under the conditions of modern civilization this may very often be quite true, but certainly not so often as is maintained in analysis. It would seem rather that this complaint expresses the general dissatisfaction of children who under our monogamous civilization are weaned at the age of from six to nine months, whereas the primitive mother devotes herself exclusively to her child for two or three years. It is as if our children remained for ever unappeased, as if they had never been suckled long enough. But I am not sure whether, if one analysed children who had been suckled as long as those of primitive races, one would not encounter the same complaint. So great is the greed of the childish libido! If we survey the whole range of motives brought to light by analysis for turning away from the mother: that she neglected to provide the little girl with the only proper genital organ, that she did not feed her enough, compelled her to share her mother's love with others, never fulfilled all the expectations of the child's love and, finally, that she first excited and then forbade her daughter's own sexual activity—all these seem inadequate as a justification of the hostility finally felt. Some of these reproaches follow inevitably from the nature of infantile sexuality; others look like rationalizations devised later to explain the uncomprehended change in feeling. Perhaps the real fact is that the attachment to the mother must inevitably perish just because it is the first and the most intense, similarly to what we so often find in the first marriages of young women, entered into when they were most passionately in love. In both cases the love-relation probably comes to grief by reason of the unavoidable disappointments and an accumulation of occasions for aggression. As a rule second marriages turn out much better.

We cannot go so far as to assert that the ambivalence of emotional cathexes is a universally valid psychological law, that it is quite impossible to feel great love for a person without the accompaniment of a hatred perhaps as great, and vice versa. Normal adults do, undoubtedly, succeed in separating these two attitudes, and do not find themselves compelled to hate their love-objects and love as well as hate their enemies. But this seems to be the result of later development. In the first phases of the love-life ambivalence is evidently the rule. Many people retain this archaic trait throughout life; it is characteristic of obsessional neurotics that in their object-relations love and hate counterbalance one another. In members of primitive races also we may say that ambivalence predominates. We shall conclude, then, that the little girl's vehement attachment to her mother is strongly ambivalent and that, reinforced as it is by the above other factors, it is precisely this ambivalence which determines the child's turning away from her. That is to say, it is the consequence once more of one of the universal characteristics of infantile sexuality.

An objection immediately presents itself to the explanation I have suggested: 'How is it that boys succeed in keeping intact their attachment to the mother, which is certainly no less strong than the girl's?' An instant answer is: 'Because boys are able to deal with their ambivalent feelings towards her by transferring all their hostility to the father.' But, in the first place, we should be chary of asserting this until we have exhaustively studied the pre-Oedipus phase in boys and, secondly, it would probably be more prudent altogether to admit that we have not yet got to the bottom of processes which, after all, we have only just come to know of.

III

Another question is this: 'What exactly is it that the little girl demands of her mother? What is the nature of her sexual aims during the period of exclusive attachment to her mother?' The answer which we gather from the analytic material is just what we should expect. The little girl's sexual aims in relation to her mother are both active and passive and are determined by the different libidinal phases through which the child passes. Here the relation of activity to passivity is specially interesting. It is easy to observe how, in every field of psychical experience and not merely in that of sexuality, an impression passively received evokes in children a tendency to an active response. They try to do themselves what has just been done to them. This is part of their task of mastering the outside world, and may even lead to their endeavouring to repeat impressions which they would have good reason to avoid because of their disagreeable content. Children's play, too, is made to serve this purpose of completing and thus, as it were, annulling a passive experience by active behaviour. When, in spite of resistance, a physician has opened a child's mouth to examine his throat, the same child will, after he has gone, play at being 'the doctor' and will repeat the same forcible procedure on a little brother or sister, as defenceless against him as he was against the physician. We cannot fail to recognize here a revolt against passivity and a preference for the active role. This swing-over from passivity to activity does not take place with the same regularity and vigour in all children: in some it may not occur at all. From their behaviour in this respect we can draw some conclusion as to the relative strength of the masculine and the feminine tendencies which will be revealed in their sexual life.

The first sexual or sexually tinged experiences of a child in its relation to the mother are naturally passive in character. It is she who suckles, feeds, cleans and dresses it, and instructs it in the performance of all its physical functions. Part of the child's libido goes on clinging to these experiences and enjoys the various gratifications associated with them, while another part strives to convert them into activity. First, the process of being suckled at the mother's breast gives place to active sucking. In its other relations with its mother the child either contents itself with independence (*i.e.* with successfully performing itself what was previously done to it) or with actively repeating in play its passive experiences, or else it does really make the mother the object in relation to which it assumes the role of the active subject. This last reaction, which comes into play in the form of real activity, I long held to be incredible, until experience removed all my doubts on the subject.

We seldom hear of a little girl's wanting to wash or dress her mother or tell her to perform her bodily functions. Sometimes she says: 'Now let's play that I am mother and you are child'; but generally she fulfils these active wishes indirectly in playing with her doll, she herself representing the mother and the doll the child. The fact that girls are fonder of playing with dolls than are boys is commonly interpreted as an early sign of awakened femininity. That is quite true, only we must not overlook the fact that it is the *active* side of femininity which finds expression here and that the little girl's preference for dolls probably testifies to the exclusiveness of her attachment to her mother, accompanied by total neglect of the father-object.

The very surprising sexual activity of the little girl in relation to her mother manifests itself in chronological succession in oral, sadistic and finally even phallic impulses directed upon her. It is difficult to give a detailed account of these, because often they are dim impulses which it was impossible for the child to grasp psychically at the time and which were only interpreted later, and express themselves in analysis in forms that are certainly not the original ones. Sometimes we find them transferred to the later father-object, where they do not belong and badly interfere with our understanding of the situation. We find aggressive oral and sadistic wishes in a form forced on them by early repression, *i.e.* in the dread of being killed by the mother—a dread which on its side justifies the death-wish against her, if this enters consciousness. It is impossible to say how often this dread of the mother draws countenance from an unconscious hostility on her part, which the child divines. (The dread of being *eaten* I have so far found only in men; it is referred to the father, but is probably the result of the transformation of oral aggressive tendencies directed upon the mother. The person the child wants to devour is the mother who nourished him: in the case of the father there is no such obvious occasion for the wish.)

The women patients characterized by a strong attachment to the mother, in whom I have been able to study the pre-Oedipus phase, have all told me that when their mother gave them enemas or rectal douches they used to offer the strongest possible resistance and react with fear and screams of rage. This is probably very usual or even universal with children. I only came to understand the reasons for this specially passionate struggle through a remark by Ruth Mack Brunswick, who was studying these problems at the same time as I was. She said that she would compare the outbreak of fury after an enema with the orgasm following on genital excitation. The accompanying anxiety should be construed as a transformation of the desire for aggression which had been stirred up. I believe that this is actually the case and that, on the anal-sadistic level, the intense passive excitation of the intestinal zone evokes an outbreak of desire for aggression, manifesting itself either directly in the form of rage or, as a consequence of suppression, as anxiety. In later years this reaction seems to die away.

In considering the passive impulses of the phallic phase we are struck by the fact that girls regularly charge their mothers with seducing them, because their first or at any rate strongest genital sensations came to them when they were being cleansed and tended by their mothers (or the nurses representing them). Mothers have often told me that they have observed that their little daughters of two or three years old enjoy these sensations and try to get their mother to heighten them by repeated touching and rubbing of the parts. I believe that the fact that the mother so unavoidably initiates the child into the phallic phase is the reason why in the phantasies of later years the father so regularly appears as the sexual seducer. When the girl turns away from the mother she transfers to the father at the same time the responsibility for having introduced her to sexual life.

Finally in the phallic phase strong active wishes towards the mother also make their appearance. The sexual activity of this period culminates in clitoridal masturbation; probably the child accompanies this with images of her mother, but whether she really imagines a sexual aim and what that aim is my experience does not make clear. It is only when all her interests have received a fresh impetus through the arrival of a baby brother or sister that we can clearly recognize any such aim. The little girl, just like the boy, wants to believe that she has given her mother this new child, and her reaction to the event and her behaviour towards the child are the same as his. I know this sounds quite absurd, but perhaps only because the idea is such an unfamiliar one to us.

The turning-away from the mother is a most important step in the little girl's development: it is more than a mere change of object. We have already described what takes place and what a number of motives are alleged for it; we must now add that we observe, hand in hand with it, a marked diminution in the active and an augmentation of the passive sexual impulses. It is true that the active impulses have suffered more severely from frustration: they have proved totally impracticable and therefore the libido has more readily abandoned them. But the passive trends also have not escaped disappointment. Frequently, with the turning-away from the mother there is cessation of clitoridal masturbation, and very often when the little girl represses her previous masculinity a considerable part of her general sexual life is permanently injured. The transition to the father-object is accomplished with the assistance of the passive tendencies so far as these have escaped overthrow. The way to the development of femininity then lies open to the girl, except in so far as she is hampered by remains of the pre-Oedipus mother-attachment which she has passed through.

If we survey the phases of feminine sexual development I have described, there is a definite conclusion about femininity as a whole which we cannot resist: the same libidinal forces, we have found, are at work in female and in male children, and we have been able to convince ourselves that for a certain period these forces take the same course and produce the same results.

Subsequently, biological factors deflect them from their original aims and conduct even active and in every sense masculine strivings into feminine channels. Since we cannot dismiss the notion that sexual excitation is derived from the operation of certain chemical substances, it would at first seem natural to expect that some day biochemistry will reveal two distinct substances, the presence of which produces male and female sexual excitation respectively. But this hope is surely no less naïve than that other one which has happily been abandoned nowadays, namely, that it would be possible to isolate under the microscope the different causative factors of hysteria, obsessional neurosis, melancholia, etc.

In sexual chemistry, too, the processes must be rather more complicated. For psychology, however, it is a matter of indifference whether there is in the body a single sexually stimulating substance, or two, or an endless number. Psycho-analysis teaches us to manage with a single libido, though its aims, *i.e.* its modes of gratification, are both active and passive. In this antithesis, above all in the existence of libidinal impulses whose aims are passive, the rest of our problem is contained.

IV

A study of the analytical literature on this subject makes evident that it already contains everything that I have said here. This paper would be superfluous were it not that in so obscure a field of research every account of any worker's direct experience and the conclusions to which he personally is led may be of value. I have, moreover, I think, defined certain points more precisely and shown them in stricter isolation than has hitherto been done. Some of the other writings on the subject are confusing because they deal at the same time with the problems of the super-ego and the sense of guilt. This I have avoided, and also, in describing the various outcomes of this phase of development, I have refrained from touching on the complications which arise when a child, disappointed in her relation with her father, returns to the abandoned mother-attachment, or in the course of her life repeatedly shifts over from the one attitude to the other. But just because this article is only one contribution amongst others I may be dispensed from an exhaustive survey of the literature on the subject and will confine myself to indicating the more important points on which I agree with some or differ from other writers.[1]

Abraham's (1921) description of the manifestations of the female castration complex is still unsurpassed, but one would have liked it to include the factor of the original exclusive attachment to the mother. With the principal points in Jeanne Lampl - de Groot's[2] (1927)

[1] [Freud does not mention his own earlier paper on the subject (1925b), page 186 of this volume.]

[2] In the *Zeitschrift* the author's name was given as 'A. Lampl de Groot', and I make this correction at her request.

important work I am in agreement. She recognizes that the pre-Oedipus phase is completely identical in boys and in girls, and she affirms (and proves from her own observations) that the little girl's attitude towards the mother includes sexual (phallic) activity. The turning-away from the mother is traced by this writer to the influence of the child's perception of castration, which forces her to abandon her sexual object and often at the same time the practice of masturbation. The whole development is described in the following formula: the little girl has to pass through a phase of the 'negative' Oedipus complex before arriving at the positive. There is one point in which I find her account inadequate: she represents the turning-away from the mother as merely a change of object and does not show that it is accompanied by the plainest manifestations of hostility. To this factor complete justice is done in Helene Deutsch's latest paper on the subject (1930), in which she also recognizes the little girl's phallic activity and the strength of her attachment to her mother. Helene Deutsch states, further, that in turning to the father the little girl follows her passive tendencies (already awakened in her relation with her mother). In her earlier book (1925) this author was still influenced by the endeavour to apply the Oedipus scheme to the pre-Oedipus phase and for this reason she interpreted the little girl's phallic activity as an identification with the father.

Fenichel (1930) rightly emphasizes the difficulty of recognizing in the material produced in analysis what represents the unchanged content of the pre-Oedipus phase and what has been distorted in the course of regression (or some other process). He does not accept Jeanne Lampl - de Groot's view of the little girl's phallic activity and he protests against Melanie Klein's (1928) 'displacement backwards' of the Oedipus complex, whose beginnings she assigns to the commencement of the second year of life. This view of the date of origin of the complex, in addition to its necessitating a modi-

fication of our view of all the rest of the child's development, is in fact not in accordance with what we learn
from the analyses of adults and is especially incompatible with my findings as to the long duration of the
girl's pre-Oedipus attachment to her mother. This
contradiction may be softened by the reflection that
we are not as yet able to distinguish in this field between
what is rigidly fixed by biological laws and what is
subject to change or shifting under the influence of
accidental experience. We have long recognized that
seduction may have the effect of hastening and stimulating to maturity the sexual development of children,
and it is quite possible that other factors operate in the
same way; such, for instance, as the child's age when
brothers or sisters are born or when it discovers the
difference between the sexes, or, again, its direct observation of sexual intercourse, its parents' behaviour in
evoking or repelling its love, and so forth.

Some authors are inclined to disparage the importance of the child's first, most primal libidinal
impulses, laying stress rather on later developmental
processes, so that—putting this view in its extreme
form—all that the former can be said to do is to indicate
certain trends, while the amounts of energy[*Intensitäten*]
with which these trends are pursued are drawn from
later regressions and reaction-formations. Thus, for
example, K. Horney (1926) is of opinion that we greatly
over-estimate the girl's primary penis-envy and that the
strength of her subsequent striving towards masculinity
is to be attributed to a *secondary* penis-envy, which is
used to ward off her feminine impulses, especially those
connected with her attachment to her father. This does
not agree with the impressions that I myself have
formed. Certain as it is that the earliest libidinal
tendencies are reinforced later by regression and
reaction-formation and difficult as it is to estimate the
relative strength of the various confluent libidinal
components, I still think that we must not overlook the
fact that those first impulses have an intensity of their

own which is greater than anything that comes later and may indeed be said to be incommensurable with any other force. It is certainly true that there is an antithesis between the attachment to the father and the masculinity-complex—this is the universal antithesis between activity and passivity, masculinity and femininity—but we have no right to assume that only the one is primary, while the other owes its strength merely to the process of defence. And if the defence against femininity is so vigorous, from what other source can it derive its strength than from that striving for masculinity which found its earliest expression in the child's penis-envy and might well take its name from this?

A similar objection applies to Jones's view (1927) that the phallic phase in girls represents a secondary, protective reaction rather than a genuine stage of development. This does not correspond to either the dynamic or the chronological conditions.

XXV

WHY WAR?[1]

(1932)

VIENNA, *September*, 1932.

DEAR PROFESSOR EINSTEIN,

When I heard that you intended to invite me to
an exchange of views on some subject that interested
you and that seemed to deserve the interest of others
besides yourself, I readily agreed. I expected you to
choose a problem on the frontiers of what is knowable
to-day, a problem to which each of us, a physicist and a
psychologist, might have our own particular angle of
approach and where we might come together from
different directions upon the same ground. You have
taken me by surprise, however, by posing the question
of what can be done to protect mankind from the curse
of war. I was scared at first by the thought of my—I
had almost written 'our'—incapacity for dealing with
what seemed to be a practical problem, a concern for
statesmen. But I then realized that you had raised the
question not as a natural scientist and physicist but as a
philanthropist: you were following the promptings of
the League of Nations just as Fridtjof Nansen, the polar
explorer, took on the work of bringing help to the
starving and homeless victims of the World War. I
reflected, moreover, that I was not being asked to make
practical proposals but only to set out the problem of
avoiding war as it appears to a psychological observer.
Here again you yourself have said almost all there is to

[1] [*Warum Krieg?* was the title of an interchange of open letters between Professor Albert Einstein and Freud. This formed one of a series
of similar interchanges arranged by the International Institute of
Intellectual Co-operation under the auspices of the League of Nations,
and was first published simultaneously in German, French and English
in Paris in 1933. Freud's letter was reprinted *Ges. Schr.*, **12**, 347, and
Ges. W., **16**. Professor Einstein's, which preceded it, was a short one
setting out the problems to be discussed. Present translation by James
Strachey.]

say on the subject. But though you have taken the wind out of my sails I shall be glad to follow in your wake and content myself with confirming all you have said by amplifying it to the best of my knowledge—or conjecture.

You begin with the relation between Right and Might.[1] There can be no doubt that that is the correct starting-point for our investigation. But may I replace the word 'might' by the balder and harsher word 'violence'? To-day right and violence appear to us as antitheses. It can easily be shown, however, that the one has developed out of the other; and if we go back to the earliest beginnings and see how that first came about, the problem is easily solved. You must forgive me if in what follows I go over familiar and commonly accepted ground as though it were new, but the thread of my argument requires it.

It is a general principle, then, that conflicts of interest between men are settled by the use of violence. This is true of the whole animal kingdom, from which men have no business to exclude themselves. In the case of men, no doubt, conflicts of *opinion* occur as well which may reach the highest pitch of abstraction and which seem to demand some other technique for their settlement. That, however, is a later complication. To begin with, in a small human horde,[2] it was superior muscular strength which decided who owned things or whose will should prevail. Muscular strength was soon supplemented and replaced by the use of tools: the winner was the one who had the better weapons or who used them the more skilfully. From the moment at which weapons were introduced, intellectual superiority already began to replace brute muscular strength; but the final purpose of the fight remained the same—one

---

[1] [In the original the words '*Recht*' and '*Macht*' are used throughout the essay. It has unfortunately been necessary to sacrifice this stylistic unity in the translation. '*Recht*' has been rendered indifferently by 'right', 'law' and 'justice'; and '*Macht*' by 'might', 'force' and 'power'.]

[2] [Freud uses the word 'horde' to denote a comparatively small group.]

side or the other was to be compelled to abandon his claim or his objection by the damage inflicted on him and by the crippling of his strength. That purpose was most completely achieved if the victor's violence eliminated his opponent permanently, that is to say, killed him. This had two advantages: he could not renew his opposition and his fate deterred others from following his example. In addition to this, killing an enemy satisfied an instinctual inclination which I shall have to mention later. The intention to kill might be countered by a reflection that the enemy could be employed in performing useful services if he were left alive in an intimidated condition. In that case the victor's violence was content to subjugate him instead of killing him. This was a first beginning of the idea of sparing an enemy's life, but thereafter the victor had to reckon with his defeated opponent's lurking thirst for revenge and sacrificed some of his own security.

Such, then, was the original state of things: domination by whoever had the greater might—domination by brute violence or by violence supported by intellect. As we know, this régime was altered in the course of evolution. There was a path that led from violence to right or law. What was that path? It is my belief that there was only one: the path which led by way of the fact that the superior strength of a single individual could be rivalled by the union of several weak ones. 'L'union fait la force.' Violence could be broken by union, and the power of those who were united now represented law in contrast to the violence of the single individual. Thus we see that right is the might of a community. It is still violence, ready to be directed against any individual who resists it; it works by the same methods and follows the same purposes. The only real difference lies in the fact that what prevails is no longer the violence of an individual but that of a community. But in order that the transition from violence to this new right or justice may be effected, one psychological condition must be fulfilled. The union of the majority must be a stable and lasting one. If it were only brought about for the purpose of combating a single domineering individual and were dissolved after his defeat, nothing would have been accomplished. The next person who found himself superior in strength would once more seek to set up a dominion by violence and the game would be repeated *ad infinitum*. The community must be maintained permanently, must be organized, must draw up regulations to anticipate the risk of rebellion and must institute authorities to see that those regulations—the laws—are respected and to superintend the execution of legal acts of violence. The recognition of a community of interests such as these leads to the growth of emotional ties between the members of a united group of people—feelings of unity which are the true source of its strength.

Here, I believe, we already have all the essentials: violence overcome by the transference of power to a larger unity, which is held together by emotional ties between its members. What remains to be said is no more than an expansion and a repetition of this.

The situation is simple so long as the community consists only of a number of equally strong individuals. The laws of such an association will determine the extent to which, if the security of communal life is to be guaranteed, each individual must surrender his personal liberty to turn his strength to violent uses. But a state of rest of that kind is only theoretically conceivable. In actuality the position is complicated by the fact that from its very beginning the community comprises elements of unequal strength—men and women, parents and children—and soon, as a result of war and conquest, it also comes to include victors and vanquished, who turn into masters and slaves. The justice of the community then becomes an expression of the unequal degrees of power obtaining within it; the laws are made by and for the ruling members and find little room for the rights of those in subjection. From that time forward there are two factors at work in the community which are sources of unrest over matters of law but tend at the same time to a further growth of law. First, attempts are made by certain of the rulers to set themselves above the prohibitions which apply to everyone—they seek, that is, to go back from a dominion of law to a dominion of violence. Secondly, the oppressed members of the group make constant efforts to obtain more power and to have any changes that are brought about in that direction recognized in the laws—they press forward, that is, from unequal justice to equal justice for all. This second tendency becomes especially important if a real shift of power occurs within a community, as may happen as a result of a number of historical factors. In that case right may gradually adapt itself to the new distribution of power or, as is more frequent, the ruling class is unwilling to recognize the change, and rebellion and civil war follow, with a temporary suspension of law and new attempts at a solution by violence, ending in the establishment of a fresh rule of law. There is yet another source from which modifications of law may arise, and one of which the expression is invariably peaceful: it lies in the cultural transformation of the members of the community. This, however, belongs properly in another connection and must be considered later.

Thus we see that the violent solution of conflicts of interest is not avoided even inside a community. But the everyday necessities and common concerns that are inevitable where people live together in one place tend to bring such struggles to a swift conclusion and under such conditions there is an increasing probability that a peaceful solution will be found. But a glance at the history of the human race reveals an endless series of conflicts between one community and another or several others, between larger and smaller units—between cities, provinces, races, nations, empires—which have almost always been settled by force of arms. Wars of this kind end either in the spoliation or in the complete overthrow and conquest of one of the parties. It is impossible to make any sweeping judgement upon wars of conquest. Some, such as those waged by the Mongols and Turks, have brought nothing but evil. Others, on the contrary, have contributed to the transformation of violence into law by establishing larger units within which the use of violence was made impossible and in which a fresh system of law led to the solution of conflicts. In this way the conquests of the Romans gave the countries round the Mediterranean the priceless *pax Romana,* and the greed of the French kings to extend their dominions created a peacefully united and flourishing France. Paradoxical as it may sound, it must be admitted that war might be a far from inappropriate means of establishing the eagerly desired reign of 'everlasting' peace, since it is in a position to create the large units within which a powerful central government makes further wars impossible. Nevertheless it fails in this purpose, for the results of conquest are as a rule short-lived: the newly created units fall apart once again, usually owing to a lack of cohesion between the portions that have been united by violence. Hitherto, moreover, the unifications created by conquest, though of considerable extent, have only been *partial,* and the conflicts between these have cried out for violent solution. Thus the result of all these warlike efforts has only been that the human race has exchanged numerous, and indeed unending, minor wars for wars on a grand scale that are rare but all the more destructive.

If we turn to our own times, we arrive at the same conclusion which you have reached by a shorter path. Wars will only be prevented with certainty if mankind unites in setting up a central authority to which the right of giving judgement upon all conflicts of interest shall be handed over. There are clearly two separate requirements involved in this: the creation of a supreme authority and its endowment with the necessary power. One without the other would be useless. The League of

Nations is designed as an authority of this kind, but
the second condition has not been fulfilled: the League
of Nations has no power of its own and can only acquire
it if the members of the new union, the separate States,
are ready to resign it. And at the moment there seems
very little prospect of this. The institution of the
League of Nations would, however, be wholly unintelligible if one ignored the fact that here was a bold
attempt such as has seldom (perhaps, indeed, never on
such a scale) been made before. It is an attempt to base
upon an appeal to certain idealistic attitudes of mind
the authority (that is, the coercive influence) which
otherwise rests on the possession of power. We have
heard that a community is held together by two things:
the compelling force of violence and the emotional ties
(identifications is the technical name) between its
members. If one of the factors is absent, the community
may possibly be held together by the other. The ideas
that are appealed to can, of course, only have any
significance if they give expression to important concerns that are common to the members, and the question arises of how much strength they can exert.
History teaches us that they have been to some extent
effective. For instance, the Panhellenic idea, the sense
of being superior to the surrounding barbarians—an
idea which was so powerfully expressed in the Am-
phictyonies, the Oracles and the Games—was sufficiently strong to mitigate the customs of war among
Greeks, though evidently not sufficiently strong to
prevent warlike disputes between different sections of
the Greek nation or even to restrain a city or confedera-
tion of cities from allying itself with the Persian foe in
order to gain an advantage over a rival. In the same
way, the community of feeling among Christians,
powerful though it was, was equally unable at the time
of the Renaissance to deter Christian States, whether
large or small, from seeking the Sultan's aid in their
wars with one another. Nor does any idea exist to-day
which could be expected to exert a unifying authority

of the sort. Indeed it is all too clear that the national ideals by which nations are at present swayed operate in a contrary direction. Some people are inclined to prophesy that it will not be possible to make an end of war until Communist ways of thinking have found universal acceptance. But that aim is in any case a very remote one to-day, and perhaps it could only be reached after the most fearful civil wars. Thus the attempt to replace actual force by the force of ideas seems at present to be doomed to failure. We shall be making a false calculation if we disregard the fact that law was originally brute violence and that even to-day it cannot do without the support of violence.

I can now proceed to add a gloss to another of your remarks. You express astonishment at the fact that it is so easy to make men enthusiastic about a war and add your suspicion that there is something at work in them —an instinct for hatred and destruction—which goes halfway to meet the efforts of the warmongers. Once again, I can only express my entire agreement. We believe in the existence of an instinct of that kind and have in fact been occupied during the last few years in studying its manifestations. Will you allow me to take this opportunity of putting before you a portion of the theory of the instincts which, after much tentative groping and many fluctuations of opinion, has been reached by workers in the field of psycho-analysis?

According to our hypothesis human instincts are of only two kinds: those which seek to preserve and unite— which we call 'erotic', exactly in the sense in which Plato uses the word 'Eros' in his *Symposium,* or 'sexual', with a deliberate extension of the popular conception of 'sexuality'—and those which seek to destroy and kill and which we class together as the aggressive or destructive instinct. As you see, this is in fact no more than a theoretical clarification of the universally familiar opposition between Love and Hate which may perhaps have some fundamental relation to the polarity of attraction and repulsion that plays a part in your own field of knowledge. We must not be too hasty in introducing ethical judgements of good and evil. Neither of these instincts is any less essential than the other; the phenomena of life arise from the operation of both together, whether acting in concert or in opposition. It seems as though an instinct of the one sort can scarcely ever operate in isolation; it is always accompanied—or, as we say, alloyed—with an element from the other side, which modifies its aim or is, in some cases, what enables it to achieve that aim. Thus, for instance, the instinct of self-preservation is certainly of an erotic kind, but it must nevertheless have aggressiveness at its disposal if it is to fulfil its purpose. So, too, the instinct of love, when it is directed towards an object, stands in need of some contribution from the instinct of mastery if it is in any way to possess that object. The difficulty of isolating the two classes of instinct in their actual manifestations is indeed what has so long prevented us from recognizing them.

If you will follow me a little further, you will see that human actions are subject to another complication of a different kind. It is very rarely that an action is the work of a *single* instinctual impulse (which must in itself be compounded of Eros and destructiveness). In order to make an action possible there must be as a rule a *combination* of such compounded motives. This was perceived long ago by a specialist in your own subject, a Professor G. C. Lichtenberg who taught physics at Göttingen during our classical age—though perhaps he was even more remarkable as a psychologist than as a physicist. He invented a Compass of Motives, for he wrote: 'The motives that lead us to do anything might be arranged like the thirty-two winds and might be given names on the same pattern: for instance, "food-food-fame" or "fame-fame-food".' So that when human beings are incited to war they may have a whole number of motives for assenting—some noble and some base, some of which they speak openly and others on which they are silent. There is no need to enumerate them all. A lust for aggression and destruction is certainly among them: the countless cruelties in history and in our everyday lives vouch for its existence and its strength. The gratification of these destructive impulses is of course facilitated by their admixture with others of an erotic and idealistic kind. When we read of the atrocities of the past, it sometimes seems as though the idealistic motives served only as an excuse for the destructive appetites; and sometimes—in the case, for instance, of the cruelties of the Inquisition—it seems as though the idealistic motives had pushed themselves forward in consciousness, while the destructive ones lent them an unconscious reinforcement. Both may be true.

I fear I may be abusing your interest, which is after all concerned with the prevention of war and not with our theories. Nevertheless I should like to linger for a moment over our destructive instinct, whose popularity is by no means equal to its importance. As a result of a little speculation, we have come to suppose that this instinct is at work in every living being and is striving to bring it to ruin and to reduce life to its original condition of inanimate matter. Thus it quite seriously deserves to be called a death instinct, while the erotic instincts represent the effort to live. The death instinct turns into the destructive instinct if, with the help of special organs, it is directed outwards, on to objects. The living creature preserves its own life, so to say, by destroying an extraneous one. Some portion of the death instinct, however, remains operative *within* the living being, and we have sought to trace quite a number of normal and pathological phenomena to this internalization of the destructive instinct. We have even been guilty of the heresy of attributing the origin of conscience to this diversion inwards of aggressiveness. You will notice that it is by no means a trivial matter if this process is carried too far: it is positively unhealthy. On the other hand if these forces are turned to destruction in the external world, the living creature will be relieved and the effect must be beneficial. This would serve as a biological justification for all the ugly and dangerous impulses against which we are struggling. It must be admitted that they stand nearer to Nature than does our resistance to them, for which an explanation also needs to be found. It may perhaps seem to you as though our theories are a kind of mythology and, in the present case, not even an agreeable one. But does not every science come in the end to a kind of mythology like this? Cannot the same be said to-day of your own Physics?

For our immediate purpose then, this much follows from what has been said: there is no use in trying to get rid of men's aggressive inclinations. We are told that in certain happy regions of the earth, where nature provides in abundance everything that man requires, there are races whose life is passed in tranquillity and who know neither compulsion nor aggressiveness. I can scarcely believe it and I should be glad to hear more of these fortunate beings. The Russian Communists, too, hope to be able to cause human aggressiveness to disappear by guaranteeing the satisfaction of all material needs and by establishing equality in other respects among all the members of the community. That, in my opinion, is an illusion. They themselves are armed to-day with the most scrupulous care and not the least important of the methods by which they keep their supporters together is hatred of everyone beyond their frontiers. In any case, as you yourself have remarked, there is no question of getting rid entirely of human aggressive impulses; it is enough to try to divert them to such an extent that they need not find expression in war.

Our mythological theory of instincts makes it easy for us to find a formula for *indirect* methods of combating war. If willingness to engage in war is an effect of the destructive instinct, the most obvious plan will

be to bring Eros, its antagonist, into play against it.
Anything that encourages the growth of emotional ties
between men must operate against war. These ties may
be of two kinds. In the first place they may be relations
resembling those towards a loved object, though without having a sexual aim. There is no need for psycho-
analysis to be ashamed to speak of love in this connection, for religion itself uses the same words: 'Thou shalt
love thy neighbour as thyself.' This, however, is more
easily said than done. The second kind of emotional tie
is by means of identification. Whatever leads men to
share important interests produces this community of
feeling, these identifications. And the structure of
human society is to a large extent based on them.

A complaint which you make about the abuse of
authority brings me to another suggestion for the
indirect combating of the propensity to war. One
instance of the innate and ineradicable inequality of
men is their tendency to fall into the two classes of
leaders and followers. The latter constitute the vast
majority; they stand in need of an authority which will
make decisions for them and to which they for the most
part offer an unqualified submission. This suggests that
more care should be taken than hitherto to educate an
upper stratum of men with independent minds, not open
to intimidation and eager in the pursuit of truth, whose
business it would be to give direction to the dependent
masses. It goes without saying that the encroachments
made by the executive power of the State and the
prohibition laid by the Church upon freedom of thought
are far from propitious for the production of a class of
this kind. The ideal condition of things would of course
be a community of men who had subordinated their
instinctual life to the dictatorship of reason. Nothing
else could unite men so completely and so tenaciously,
even if there were no emotional ties between them. But
in all probability that is a Utopian expectation. No
doubt the other indirect methods of preventing war are
more practicable, though they promise no rapid success.

An unpleasant picture comes to one's mind of mills that grind so slowly that people may starve before they get their flour.

The result, as you see, is not very fruitful when an unworldly theoretician is called in to advise on an urgent practical problem. It is a better plan to devote oneself in every particular case to meeting the danger with whatever weapons lie to hand. I should like, however, to discuss one more question, which you do not mention in your letter but which specially interests me. Why do you and I and so many other people rebel so violently against war? Why do we not accept it as another of the many painful calamities of life? After all, it seems quite a natural thing, no doubt it has a good biological basis and in practice it is scarcely avoidable. There is no need to be shocked at my raising this question. For the purpose of an investigation such as this, one may perhaps be allowed to wear a mask of assumed detachment. The answer to my question will be that we react to war in this way because everyone has a right to his own life, because war puts an end to human lives that are full of hope, because it brings individual men into humiliating situations, because it compels them against their will to murder other men, and because it destroys precious material objects which have been produced by the labours of humanity. Other reasons besides might be given, such as that in its present-day form war is no longer an opportunity for achieving the old ideals of heroism and that owing to the perfection of instruments of destruction a future war might involve the exter- mination of one or perhaps both of the antagonists. All this is true, and so incontestably true that one can only feel astonished that the waging of war has not yet been unanimously repudiated. No doubt debate is possible upon one or two of these points. It may be questioned whether a community ought not to have a right to dispose of individual lives; every war is not open to condemnation to an equal degree; so long as there exist countries and nations that are prepared for the ruthless destruction of others, those others must be armed for war. But I will not linger over any of these issues; they are not what you want to discuss with me, and I have something different in mind. It is my opinion that the main reason why we rebel against war is that we cannot help doing so. We are pacifists because we are obliged to be for organic reasons. And we then find no difficulty in producing arguments to justify our attitude.

No doubt this requires some explanation. My belief is this. For incalculable ages mankind has been passing through a process of evolution of culture. (Some people, I know, prefer to use the term 'civilization'.) We owe to that process the best of what we have become, as well as a good part of what we suffer from. Though its causes and beginnings are obscure and its outcome uncertain, some of its characteristics are easy to perceive. It may perhaps be leading to the extinction of the human race, for in more than one way it impairs the sexual function; uncultivated races and backward strata of the population are already multiplying more rapidly than highly cultivated ones. The process is perhaps comparable to the domestication of certain species of animals and it is undoubtedly accompanied by physical alterations; but we are still unfamiliar with the notion that the evolution of culture is an organic process of this kind. The psychical modifications that go along with the cultural process are striking and unambiguous. They consist in a progressive displacement of instinctual aims and a restriction of instinctual impulses. Sensations which were pleasurable to our ancestors have become indifferent or even intolerable to ourselves; there are organic grounds for the changes in our ethical and aesthetic ideals. Of the psychological characteristics of culture two appear to be the most important: a strengthening of the intellect, which is beginning to govern instinctual life, and an internalization of the aggressive impulses, with all its consequent advantages and perils. Now war is in the crassest opposition to the psychical attitude imposed on us by the cultural process, and for that reason we are bound to rebel against it; we simply cannot any longer put up with it. This is not merely an intellectual and emotional repudiation; we pacifists have a constitutional intolerance of war, an idiosyncracy magnified, as it were, to the highest degree. It seems, indeed, as though the lowering of aesthetic standards in war plays a scarcely smaller part in our rebellion than do its cruelties.

And how long shall we have to wait before the rest of mankind become pacifists too? There is no telling. But it may not be Utopian to hope that these two factors, the cultural attitude and the justified dread of the consequences of a future war, may result within a measurable time in putting an end to the waging of war. By what paths or by what side-tracks this will come about we cannot guess. But one thing we *can* say: whatever fosters the growth of culture works at the same time against war.

I trust you will forgive me if what I have said has disappointed you, and I remain, with kindest regards,

Yours sincerely,

SIGM. FREUD

XXVI

THE ACQUISITION OF POWER OVER FIRE[1]

(1932)

IN a footnote on page 50 of my *Civilization and its Discontents* (1930) I mentioned—though only incidentally—the conjecture which might be drawn from psycho-analytical material on the subject of primitive man's acquisition of power over fire. I am led to resume this theme by Albrecht Schaeffer's opposition (1930), and by Erlenmeyer's (1932) striking citation of the Mongolian law against 'pissing upon ashes'.[2]

Now I conjecture that, in order to possess himself of fire, it was necessary for man to renounce the homosexually-tinged desire to extinguish it by a stream of urine. I think that this conjecture can be confirmed by the interpretation of the Greek myth of Prometheus, provided that we bear in mind the distortions to be expected in the transition from fact to the content of a myth. These are of the same nature as and no more strained than those which we recognize every day when we reconstruct from the dreams of our patients the repressed but extremely important experiences of their childhood. The mechanisms employed in such distortion are symbolic representation and the transformation of a given element into its opposite. I should not

[1] ['Zur Gewinnung des Feuers.' First published *Imago*, **18** (1932), 8; reprinted *Ges. Schr.*, **12**, 141, and *Ges. W.*, **16**. Translation, reprinted from *Int. J. Psycho-Anal.*, **13** (1932), 405, by Joan Riviere.]

[2] This refers no doubt to hot ashes from which fire can still be obtained, not to those in which it is wholly extinguished.—The criticism by Lorenz (1931, 462 f.) is based on the assumption that man's subjugation of fire only began at all when he discovered that he could produce it at will by some sort of manipulation. As against this, Dr. J. Hárnik refers me to some remarks by Dr. Richard Lasch (in Georg Buschan's compilation *Illustrierte Völkerkunde*, Stuttgart, 1922, **1**, 24): 'We may conjecture that the art of *conserving* fire was understood long before that of kindling it; we have evidence of this in the fact that, to-day, the pygmy-like aborigines of the Andamans, though they possess and conserve fire, have no indigenous method of producing it.'

venture to explain *all* the features of the myth in this
fashion; apart from the original facts, other and later
occurrences may well have contributed to its content.
At the same time the most striking and important
elements are those which can be interpreted analytically,
namely, the manner in which Prometheus carried off
the fire, the character of his act (an outrage, a robbery,
and a betrayal of the gods) and the meaning of his
punishment.

Prometheus the Titan, one of the heroes who are still
of the race of the gods,[1] perhaps even originally a demi-
urge and creator of man, brought to mankind the fire
which he stole from the gods hidden in a hollow rod, a
fennel-stalk. If we were interpreting a dream, we should
readily see in such an object a penis-symbol, though
the unusual stress laid on its hollowness might make
us hesitate. But what is the connection between this
penis-tube and the preservation of fire? There seems
little chance of finding one until we remember the procedure so common in dreams which often conceals their
meaning, the process of reversal, the transformation of
an element into its opposite, the inversion of the actual
relationships. It is not fire which man harbours in
his penis-tube; on the contrary, it is the means of
extinguishing fire, the water of his stream of urine. A
wealth of familiar analytical material links up at once
with this relation between fire and water.

Secondly, the acquisition of fire is a crime; it is
accomplished by robbery or theft. This is a constant
feature in all the legends about the acquisition of fire;
we find it amongst the most different and remotest
peoples, not merely in the Greek myth of Prometheus
the Fire-Bringer. Here then must be the essential core
of the distorted reminiscence of humanity. But why is
the acquisition of fire inseparably connected with the
idea of an outrage? Who is the victim of the injury and
betrayal? The Promethean myth in Hesiod gives us a
direct answer to this question; for, in another story not

[1] Heracles, thereafter, was a demigod, Theseus wholly human.

K

as such connected with fire, he tells how Prometheus so arranged the sacrifices as to trick Zeus out of his due share, in favour of men. The gods then are the victims of the fraud! We know that myths bestow upon them the gratification of all the lusts which mankind must renounce, as in the familiar case of incest. Speaking in analytical terms, we should say that the instinctual life, the id, is the god who is defrauded when the gratification of extinguishing fires is renounced: a human desire is transformed in the legend into a divine privilege. But the divinity in the story has nothing of the character of a super-ego: it is still the representative of the paramount instinctual life.

The most radical transformation of one element into its opposite is seen in a third feature of the legend, the punishment of the fire-bringer. Prometheus was chained to a rock and every day a vulture fed on his liver. In the fire-legends of other peoples also a bird plays a part; it must signify something in the story, but for the moment I will not attempt an interpretation. On the other hand, we feel on firm ground when we turn to the question why the liver is selected as the region of punishment. In ancient times the liver was regarded as the seat of all passions and desires; hence, such a punishment as that of Prometheus was the appropriate one for a criminal swayed by instinct, who had committed his offence at the prompting of evil lusts. But the exact opposite applies to the fire-bringer: he had renounced his instinctual desires and had shown how beneficent and at the same time how essential was such renunciation for the purposes of civilization. Why, indeed, should the legend treat at all as a crime worthy of punishment a deed so beneficial to culture? Well, if we are barely to recognize through all the distortions of the myth that the acquisition of fire necessitated a renunciation of instinct, there is, at any rate, no concealment of the resentment which the hero of civilization inevitably aroused in instinct-ridden humanity. And this is in accordance with what we know and expect. We are aware that the demand for renunciation of instinct, and its enforcement, call forth hostility and aggressive impulses, which only in a later phase of psychical development become transformed into a sense of guilt.

The obscurity of the Prometheus legend and of other fire-myths is increased by the fact that primitive man could not but regard fire as something analogous to the passion of love—or, as we should say, a symbol of the libido. The warmth radiated by fire evokes the same kind of glow as accompanies the state of sexual excitation, and the form and motion of the flame suggest the phallus in action. There can be no doubt about the mythological significance of flames as the phallus; we have further evidence of it in the story of the origin of the Roman king, Servius Tullius.[1] When we ourselves speak of the 'devouring fire' of passion or describe flames as 'licking' (comparing the flame with a tongue), we have not moved so very far from the thought of our primitive ancestors. Our account of the acquisition of fire presupposed, indeed, that to primal man the attempt to extinguish fire by means of his own water signified a pleasurable struggle with another phallus.

It may thus well be that by way of this symbolical assimilation other, purely phantastic elements have entered into the myth and become intertwined with the historical ones. It is difficult to resist the notion that, if the liver is the seat of passion, its symbolical significance is the same as that of fire itself, and that thus its daily consumption and renewal is an apt description of the behaviour of the appetite of love, which, though gratified daily, is daily renewed. The bird which sates itself by feeding on the liver would then signify the penis—a meaning which is in any case by no means foreign to it, as we see in legends, dreams, linguistic usage and the plastic representations of antiquity. A

---

[1] [His mother, Ocrisia, was a slave in the household of King Tarquin. One day she 'was offering as usual cakes and libations of wine on the royal hearth, when a flame in the shape of a male member shot out from the fire. . . . Ocrisia conceived by the god or spirit of the fire and in due time brought forth Servius Tullius.' (Frazer, 1911, **2,** 195.)]

short step further brings us to the phoenix, the bird which, as often as it is consumed by fire, emerges again rejuvenated. Probably the earliest significance of the phoenix was that of the revivified penis after its state of flaccidity, rather than that of the sun setting in the evening glow and then rising again.

One may raise the question whether it seems likely that our mythopoeic activities simply essay—as it were in play—to represent in a disguised form universally familiar, even if highly interesting, mental processes (with their own physical manifestations), for no other motive than the sheer pleasure of representation. We can assuredly give no certain answer to this question without a full grasp of the nature of myth, but in the two cases we are considering it is easy to recognize the same content, and in virtue of this, a definite trend. They describe the revival of the libidinal desires after they have been sated and extinguished. That is to say, they emphasize the imperishable nature of these desires, and this reassurance is particularly appropriate if the historical core of the myth deals with a defeat of the instinctual life, a renunciation of instinct which has become inevitable. It is, as it were, the second part of the understandable reaction of primitive man to the blow struck at his instinctual life; after the punishment of the criminal comes the assurance that, after all, he has done nothing irreparable.

We unexpectedly come across another instance of the reversal of an element into its opposite in a different myth which in appearance has very little to do with the fire-myth. The hydra of Lerna, with its innumerable darting serpent's heads (one of which is immortal), was according to its name, a water-snake. Heracles, the hero, combats it by cutting off its heads, but they always grow again, and only when he has burnt out the immortal head with fire can he master the monster. A water-serpent subdued by fire—surely that does not make sense. But, as in so many dreams, sense comes if we reverse the manifest content. In that case the hydra is a firebrand, the darting serpents' heads are the flames and, in proof of their libidinal nature, they, like Prometheus' liver, display the phenomenon of growing again, of renewal after attempted destruction. Now Heracles extinguishes this firebrand with—water. (The immortal head is no doubt the phallus itself and its destruction signifies castration.) But Heracles is also the deliverer of Prometheus, and slays the bird which devours his liver. Must we not divine a deeper connection between the two myths? It is as if the action of the one hero were set to rights by the other. Prometheus had forbidden the extinguishing of the fire (like the Mongolian law); Heracles permitted it in the case of the baleful firebrand. The second myth seems to correspond to the reaction of a later epoch of civilization to the circumstances in which power over fire was acquired. One has the impression that this approach might lead us quite a long way into the secrets of the myth, but, of course, we should not carry the feeling of certainty with us very far.

Besides the historical factor and the factor of symbolical phantasy contributing to the antithesis of fire and water, which dominates the entire sphere of these myths, we can point to yet a third, a physiological fact, described by the poet in the following lines:

> 'Was dem Menschen dient zum Seichen,
> Damit schafft er Seinesgleichen.'[1]

The male sexual organ has two functions, whose association is to many a man a source of annoyance. It is the channel for the evacuation of urine, and it performs the sexual act, which appeases the craving of the genital libido. Children still believe that they can combine these two functions; one of their ideas of the way babies are made is that the man urinates into the woman's body. But the adult knows that in reality the two acts are incompatible—as incompatible as fire and

[1] Heine. ['With that which serves a man to piss he creates his own kind.']

water. When the penis passes into that condition of excitation which has caused it to be compared with a bird and whilst those sensations are being experienced which suggest the heat of fire, urination is impossible. Conversely, when the penis is fulfilling its function of evacuating urine (the water of the body) all connection with its genital function appears to be extinguished. Having regard to the antithesis of these two functions, we might say that man quenches his own fire with his own water. And we may suppose that primitive man, who had to try to grasp the external world with the help of his own bodily sensations and states, did not fail to observe and apply the analogies presented to him by the behaviour of fire.

XXVII
MY CONTACT WITH
JOSEF POPPER-LYNKEUS[1]

(1932)

IT was in the winter of 1899 that my book on the *Interpretation of Dreams* (though its title-page was post-dated into the new century) at length lay before me. This work was the product of the labours of four or five years and its origin was unusual. Holding a lectureship in Nervous Diseases at the University, I had attempted to support myself and my rapidly increasing family by a medical practice among the so-called 'neurotics' of whom there were only too many in our society. But the task proved harder than I had expected. The ordinary methods of treatment clearly offered little or no help: other paths must be followed. And how was it remotely possible to give patients any help when one understood nothing of their illness, nothing of the causes of their sufferings or of the meaning of their complaints? So I eagerly sought direction and instruction from the great Charcot in Paris and from Bernheim at Nancy; finally, an observation made by my teacher and friend, Josef Breuer of Vienna, seemed to open a new prospect for understanding and therapeutic success.

For these new experiments made it a certainty that the patients whom we described as neurotic were in some sense suffering from *mental* disturbances and ought therefore to be treated by psychological methods. Our interest therefore necessarily turned to psychology. The psychology which ruled at that time in the academic schools of philosophy had very little to offer and

---

[1] ['Meine Berührung mit Josef Popper-Lynkeus' was first published on the occasion of the tenth anniversary of Popper's death in a memorial number of *Allgemeine Nährpflicht*, **15** (1932). Reprinted *Ges. Schr.*, **12**, 415, and *Ges. W.*, **16**. Translation, reprinted from *Int. J. Psycho-Anal.*, **23** (1942), 85, by James Strachey.]

nothing at all for our purposes: we had to discover afresh both our methods and the theoretical hypotheses behind them. So I worked in this direction, first in collaboration with Breuer and afterwards independently of him. Finally I hit upon the technical device of requiring my patients to tell me without criticism whatever occurred to their minds, even if they were ideas which did not seem to make sense or which it was distressing to report.

When they fell in with my instructions they told me their dreams, amongst other things, as though they were of the same kind as their other thoughts. This was a plain hint that I should assign as much importance to these dreams as to other, intelligible, phenomena. They, however, were *not* intelligible, but strange, confused, absurd: like dreams, in fact—which for that very reason, were condemned by science as random and senseless spasms of the organ of the mind. If my patients were right—and they seemed only to be repeating the ancient beliefs held by unscientific men for thousands of years—I was faced by the task of 'interpreting dreams' in a way that could stand up against scientific criticism.

To begin with, I naturally understood no more about my patients' dreams than the dreamers did themselves. But by applying to these dreams, and more particularly to my own dreams, the procedure which I had already used for the study of other abnormal psychological structures, I succeeded in answering most of the questions which could be raised by an interpretation of dreams. There were many such questions: What do we dream about? Why do we dream at all? What is the origin of all the strange characteristics which distinguish dreams from waking life?—and many more such questions besides. Some of the answers were easily given and turned out to confirm views that had already been put forward; but others involved completely new hypotheses with regard to the structure and functioning of the apparatus of the mind. People dream about the things that have engaged their minds during the waking day. People dream in order to allay impulses that seek to disturb sleep, and in order to be able to sleep on. But why should the dream seem so strange, so confusedly senseless, so obviously contrasted with the content of waking thought, in spite of being concerned with the same material? There could be no doubt that the dream was only a substitute for a rational process of thought and could be interpreted—that is to say, translated into a rational process. But what needed explaining was the fact of the distortion which the work of dreaming had carried out upon the rational and intelligible material.

Dream-distortion was the profoundest and most difficult problem of dream life. And in order to elucidate it I reached the conclusions that follow, which placed the dream in a class along with other psychopathological formations and revealed it, as it were, as the normal psychosis of mankind. Our mind, that precious instrument by whose means we maintain ourselves alive, is no peacefully self-contained unity. It is rather to be compared with a modern State in which a mob, eager for enjoyment and destruction, has to be held down forcibly by a prudent superior class. The whole flux of our mental life and everything that finds expression in our thoughts are derivations and representatives of the multifarious instincts that are innate in our physical constitution. But these instincts are not all equally susceptible to direction and education, or equally ready to fall in with the demands of the external world and of human society. Many of them have retained their primitive, ungovernable nature; if we let them have their way, they would infallibly bring us to ruin. Consequently, made wise by our sufferings, we have developed organizations in our mind which, in the form of inhibitions, set themselves up against the direct manifestations of the instincts. Every impulse in the nature of a wish that arises from the sources of instinctual energy must submit itself to examination by the highest agencies of our mind, and, if it is not approved, is rejected and restrained from exercising any influence upon our movements, that is, from coming into execution. Often enough, indeed, such wishes are even forbidden to enter consciousness, which is habitually unaware even of the existence of these dangerous instinctual sources. We describe such impulses as being *repressed* from the point of view of consciousness, and as surviving only in the unconscious. If what is repressed contrives somehow to force its way into consciousness or into movement or into both, we are no longer normal: at that point the whole range of neurotic and psychotic symptoms arise. The maintenance of the necessary inhibitions and repressions imposes upon our mind a great expenditure of energy, from which it is glad to be relieved. A good opportunity for this seems to be offered at night by the state of sleep, since sleep involves a cessation of our motor functions. The situation seems safe, and the severity of our internal police-force may therefore be relaxed. It is not entirely withdrawn, since one cannot be certain: may be the unconscious never sleeps at all. And now the reduction of pressure upon the repressed unconscious produces its effect. Wishes arise from it which during sleep might find the entrance to consciousness open. If we were to know them we should be appalled, alike by their subject-matter, their immense extent and indeed the mere possibility of their existence. This, however, occurs but seldom, and when it does we awake as speedily as may be, overcome by fear. But as a rule our consciousness does not experience the dream as it really was. It is true that the inhibitory forces (the dream censorship, as we may call them) are not completely awake, but neither are they wholly asleep. They have had an influence on the dream while it was struggling to find an expression in words and pictures, they have got rid of what was most objectionable, they have altered other parts of it till they are unrecognizable, they have severed real connections while introducing false ones, until the honest but brutal phantasy of a wish fulfilled which lay behind the dream has turned into the manifest dream as we remember it—more or less confused and almost always strange and incomprehensible. Thus the dream (or the distortion which characterizes it) is the expression of a compromise, the evidence of a conflict between the mutually incompatible impulses and strivings of our mental life. And do not let us forget that the same process, the same interplay of forces, which explains the dreams of a normal sleeper, gives us the key to understanding all the phenomena of neurosis and psychosis.

I must apologize if I have hitherto talked so much about myself and my work upon the problems of the dream; but it was a necessary preliminary to what follows. My explanation of dream-distortion seemed to me new: I had nowhere found anything like it. Years later (I can no longer remember when) I came across Josef Popper-Lynkeus' book *Phantasien eines Realisten*.[1] One of the stories contained in it bore the title of 'Träumen wie Wachen' ['Dreaming like Waking'], and it could not fail to arouse my deepest interest. There was a description in it of a man who could boast that he had never dreamt anything senseless. His dreams might be fantastic, like fairy tales, but they were not enough out of harmony with the waking world for it to be possible to say definitely that 'they were impossible or absurd in themselves'. Translated into my manner of speech this meant that in the case of this man no dream-distortion occurred; and the reason produced for its absence put one at the same time in possession of the reason for its occurrence.

[1] [Josef Popper (1838–1921) was a well-known Austrian writer chiefly upon sociological questions. *Phantasien eines Realisten*, a collection of short imaginative sketches, was first published, like Freud's *Traumdeutung*, in 1899, under the pseudonym of 'Lynkeus'. It has passed through many editions, the twenty-first having appeared in 1921. An account of Popper's schemes of social reform will be found in a book by Fritz Wittels which has been translated under the title *An End to Poverty* (London, 1925). This also contains a short biography of Popper himself by the translators, Eden and Cedar Paul.]

Popper allowed the man complete insight into the reasons for his peculiarity. He made him say: 'Order and harmony reign both in my thoughts and in my feelings, nor do the two struggle with each other. . . . I am one and undivided. Other people are divided and their two parts—waking and dreaming—are almost perpetually at war with each other.' And again, on the question of the interpretation of dreams: 'That is certainly no easy task; but with a little attention on the part of the dreamer himself it should no doubt always succeed.—You ask why it is that for the most part it does *not* succeed? In you other people there seems always to be something that lies concealed in your dreams, something unchaste in a curious way, a certain secret quality in your being which it is hard to express. And that is why your dreams so often seem to be without meaning or even to be nonsense. But in the deepest sense this is not in the least so; indeed, it cannot be so at all—for it is always the same man, whether he is awake or dreaming.'[1]

Now, if we leave psychological terminology out of account, this was the very same explanation of dream-distortion that I had arrived at from my study of dreams. Distortion was a compromise, something in its very nature disingenuous, the product of a conflict between thought and feeling, or, as I had put it, between what is conscious and what is repressed. Where a conflict of this kind was not present and repression was unnecessary, dreams could not be strange or senseless. The man who dreamed in a way no different from that in which he thought while awake was granted by Popper the very condition of internal harmony which, as a social reformer, he aimed at producing in the body politic. And if Science informs us that such a man, wholly without evil and falseness and devoid of all repressions, does not exist and could not survive, yet we may guess that, so far as an approximation to this

---

[1] [The passage is quoted more fully in *The Interpretation of Dreams* (Revised Translation, 1932), 295–6, footnote.]

ideal is possible, it had found its realization in the person of Popper himself.[1]

Overwhelmed by meeting with such wisdom, I began to read all his works—his books on Voltaire, on Religion, on War, on State Provision of Subsistence, etc.—till there was built up clearly before my eyes a picture of this simple-minded, great man, who was a thinker and a critic and at the same time a kindly humanitarian and reformer. I reflected much over the rights of the individual which he advocated and to which I should gladly have added my support had I not been restrained by the thought that neither the processes of Nature nor the aims of human society quite justified such claims. A special feeling of sympathy drew me to him, since he too had clearly had painful experience of the bitterness of the life of a Jew and of the hollowness of the ideals of present-day civilization. Yet I never saw him in the flesh. He knew of me through common acquaintances, and I once had occasion to answer a letter from him in which he asked for some piece of information. But I never sought him out. My innovations in psychology had estranged me from my contemporaries, and especially from the older among them: often enough when I approached some man whom I had honoured from a distance, I found myself repelled, as it were, by his lack of understanding for what had become my whole life to me. And after all Josef Popper had been a physicist: he had been a friend of Ernst Mach. I was anxious that the happy impression of our agreement upon the problem of dream-distortion should not be spoilt. So it came about that I put off calling upon him till it was too late and I could now only salute his bust in the gardens in front of our Rathaus.

[1] [Another short paper of Freud's on the same subject written some ten years earlier (1923c) ends with the words: 'I believe that what enabled *me* to discover the cause of dream-distortion was my moral courage. In the case of Popper it was the purity, love of truth and moral serenity of his nature'—the epithets which Popper himself applied to the man in his story.

XXVIII

A DISTURBANCE OF MEMORY
ON THE ACROPOLIS

AN OPEN LETTER TO ROMAIN ROLLAND ON THE OCCASION
OF HIS SEVENTIETH BIRTHDAY[1]

(1936)

MY DEAR FRIEND,

I have been urgently pressed to make some written contribution to the celebration of your seventieth birthday and I have made long efforts to find something that might in some sense be worthy of you and might give expression to my admiration for your love of the truth, for your courage in your beliefs and for your affection and devotion towards humanity; or, again, something that might bear witness to my gratitude towards you as a writer who has afforded me so many moments of exaltation and pleasure. But it was in vain. I am ten years older than you and my powers of production are at an end. All that I can find to offer you is the gift of an impoverished being, who has 'seen better days'.

You know that the aim of my scientific work was to throw light upon unusual, abnormal or pathological manifestations of the mind—that is to say, to trace them back to the psychological forces operating behind them and to indicate the mechanisms at work. I began by attempting this upon myself and then went on to apply it to other people and finally, by a bold extension, to the human race as a whole. During the last few years, a phenomenon of this sort, which I myself had experienced a generation ago, in 1904, and which I had never understood, has kept on recurring to my mind. I did not at first see why; but at last I determined to analyse

---

[1] ['Brief an Romain Rolland (Eine Erinnerungsstörung auf der Akropolis).' First published in the *Almanach der Psychoanalyse*, 1937, 9; reprinted *Ges. W.*, **16.** Translation, reprinted from *Int. J. Psycho-Anal.*, **22** (1941), 93, by James Strachey.]

the incident—and I now present you with the results of that inquiry. In the process, I shall have, of course, to ask you to give more attention to some events in my private life than they would otherwise deserve.

Every year, at that time, towards the end of August or the beginning of September, I used to set out with my younger brother on a holiday trip, which used to last for some weeks and used to take us to Rome or to some other region of Italy or to some part of the Mediterranean sea-board. My brother is ten years younger than I am, so he is the same age as you—a coincidence which has only now occurred to me. In that particular year my brother told me that his business affairs would not allow him to be away for long: a week would be the most that he could manage and we should have to shorten our trip. So we decided to travel by way of Trieste to the island of Corfu and there spend the few days of our holiday. At Trieste he called upon a business acquaintance who lived there, and I went with him. Our host inquired in a friendly way about our plans and, hearing that it was our intention to go to Corfu, advised us strongly against it: 'What makes you think of going there at this time of year? It would be too hot for you to do anything. You had far better go to Athens instead. The Lloyd boat sails this afternoon; it will give you three days there to see the town and will pick you up on its return voyage. That would be more agreeable and more worth while.'

As we walked away from this visit, we were both in remarkably depressed spirits. We discussed the plan that had been proposed, agreed that it was quite impracticable and saw nothing but difficulties in the way of carrying it out; we assumed, moreover, that we should not be allowed to land in Greece without passports. We spent the hours that elapsed before the Lloyd offices opened in wandering about the town in a discontented and irresolute frame of mind. But when the time came, we went up to the counter and booked our passages for Athens as though it were a matter of course, without bothering in the least about the supposed difficulties and indeed without having discussed with one another the reasons for our decision. Such behaviour, it must be confessed, was most strange. Later on we recognized that we had accepted the suggestion that we should go to Athens instead of Corfu instantly and most readily. But, if so, why had we spent the interval before the offices opened in such a gloomy state and foreseen nothing but obstacles and difficulties?

When, finally, on the afternoon after our arrival, I stood upon the Acropolis and cast my eyes around upon the landscape, a remarkable thought suddenly entered my mind: 'So all this really *does* exist, just as we learnt at school!' To describe the situation more accurately, the person who gave expression to the remark was divided, far more sharply than was usually observable, from another person who took cognizance of the remark; and both were astonished, though not by the same thing. The first behaved as though he were obliged, under the impact of an unequivocal observation, to believe in something the reality of which had hitherto seemed doubtful. If I may make a slight exaggeration, it was as if someone, walking beside Loch Ness, suddenly caught sight of the form of the famous Monster stranded upon the shore and found himself driven to the admission: 'So it really *does* exist—the sea-serpent we always disbelieved in!' The second person, on the other hand, was justifiably astonished, because he had been unaware that the real existence of Athens, the Acropolis, and the landscape around it had ever been objects of doubt. What he had been expecting was rather some expression of delight or admiration.

Now it would be easy to argue that this strange thought that occurred to me on the Acropolis only serves to emphasize the fact that seeing something with one's own eyes is after all quite a different thing from hearing or reading about it. But even so it would remain a most remarkable disguise for an uninteresting commonplace. Or it would be possible to maintain that it was true that when I was a schoolboy I had *thought* I was convinced of the historic reality of the city of Athens and its history, but that the occurrence of this idea on the Acropolis had precisely shown that in my unconscious I had *not* believed in it, and that I was only now acquiring a conviction that 'reached down to the unconscious'. An explanation of this sort sounds very profound, but it is easier to assert than to prove; moreover, it is very much open to attack upon theoretical grounds. No. I believe that the two phenomena, the depression at Trieste and the idea on the Acropolis, were intimately connected. And the first of these is more easily intelligible and may help us towards an explanation of the second.

The experience at Trieste was, it will be noticed, also no more than an expression of disbelief: 'We're going to see Athens? Out of the question!—it will be far too difficult!' The accompanying depression corresponded to a regret that it *was* out of the question: it would have been so lovely. And now we know where we are. It is one of those cases of 'too good to be true' that we come across so often. It is an example of the scepticism that arises so often when we are surprised by a piece of good news, when we hear we have won a prize, for instance, or drawn a winner, or when a girl learns that the man whom she has secretly loved has asked her parents for leave to pay his addresses to her.

When we have established the existence of a phenomenon, the next question is of course as to its cause. Disbelief of this kind is obviously an attempt to repudiate a piece of reality; but there is something strange about it. We should not be in the least astonished if an attempt of this kind were aimed at a piece of reality that threatened unpleasant consequences: the mechanism of our mind is, so to speak, planned to work along just such lines. But why should such disbelief arise in something which, on the contrary, promises to bring a high degree of pleasure? Truly paradoxical behaviour! But I recollect that on a previous occasion I dealt with the similar case of the people who, as I put it, are 'wrecked by success'.[1] As a rule people fall ill as a result of frustration, of the non-fulfilment of some vital necessity or desire. But with these people the opposite is the case; they fall ill, or even go entirely to pieces, because an overwhelmingly powerful wish of theirs has been fulfilled. But the contrast between the two situations is not so great as it seems at first. What happens in the paradoxical case is merely that the place of the external frustration is taken by an internal one. The sufferer does not permit himself happiness: the internal frustration commands him to cling to the external one. But why? Because—so runs the answer in a number of cases—one cannot expect fate to grant one anything so good. In fact, another instance of 'too good to be true', the expression of a pessimism of which a large portion seems to find a home in many of us. In another set of cases, just as in those who are wrecked by success, we find a sense of guilt or inferiority, which can be translated: 'I'm not worthy of such happiness, I don't deserve it.' But these two motives are essentially the same, for one is only a projection of the other. For, as has long been known, the fate which we expect to treat us so badly is a materialization of our conscience, of the severe super-ego within us, itself a residue of the punitive agency of our childhood.

This, I think, explains our behaviour in Trieste. We could not believe that we were to be given the joy of seeing Athens. The fact that the piece of reality that we were trying to repudiate was to begin with only a *possibility* determined the character of our immediate reactions. But when we were standing on the Acropolis the possibility had become an actuality, and the same disbelief found a different but far clearer expression. In an undistorted form this should have been: 'I could really not have imagined it possible that I should ever be granted the sight of Athens with my own eyes—as is

[1] ['Some Character-Types Met with in Psycho-Analytic Work' (1915c), *Collected Papers*, **4,** 323.]

now indubitably the case!' When I recall the passionate desire to travel and see the world by which I was dominated at school and later, and how long it was before that desire began to find its fulfilment, I am not surprised at its after-effect on the Acropolis; I was then forty-eight years old. I did not ask my younger brother whether he felt anything of the same sort. A certain amount of awkwardness surrounded the whole episode; and it was this which had already interfered with our exchanging thoughts at Trieste.

If I have rightly guessed the meaning of the thought that came to me on the Acropolis and if it did in fact express my joyful astonishment at finding myself at that spot, the further question now arises why this meaning should have been subjected in the thought itself to such a distorted and distorting disguise.

The essential subject-matter of the thought, to be sure, was retained even in the distortion—that is, incredulity: 'By the evidence of my senses I am now standing on the Acropolis, but I cannot believe it.' This incredulity, however, this doubt of a piece of reality was doubly displaced in its actual expression: first, it was shifted back into the past, and secondly it was transposed from my relation to the Acropolis on to the very existence of the Acropolis. And so something occurred which was equivalent to an assertion that at some time in the past I had doubted the real existence of the Acropolis—which, however, my memory rejected as being incorrect and, indeed, impossible.

The two distortions involve two independent problems. We can attempt to penetrate deeper into the process of transformation. Without for the moment particularizing as to how I have arrived at the idea, I will start from the presumption that the original factor must have been a sense of some feeling of the unbelievable and the unreal in the situation at the moment. The situation included myself, the Acropolis and my perception of it. I could not account for this doubt; I obviously could not attach the doubt to my sensory impressions of the Acropolis. But I remembered that in the past I had had a doubt about something which had to do with this precise locality, and I thus found the means for shifting the doubt into the past. In the process, however, the subject-matter of the doubt was changed. I did not simply recollect that in my early years I had doubted whether I myself would ever see the Acropolis, but I asserted that at that time I had altogether disbelieved in the reality of the Acropolis. It is precisely this effect of the displacement that leads me to think that the actual situation on the Acropolis contained an element of doubt of reality. I have certainly not yet succeeded in making the process clear; so I will conclude by saying briefly that the whole psychological situation, which seems so confused and is so difficult to describe, can be satisfactorily cleared up by assuming that at the time I had (or might have had) a momentary feeling: 'What I see here is not real.' Such a feeling is known as a 'feeling of derealization' ['*Entfremdungsgefühl*'].[1] I made an attempt to ward that feeling off, and I succeeded, at the cost of making a false pronouncement about the past.

These derealizations are remarkable phenomena which are still little understood. They are spoken of as 'sensations', but they are obviously complicated processes, attached to particular mental contents and bound up with decisions made about those contents. They arise very frequently in certain mental diseases, but they are not unknown among normal people, just as hallucinations occasionally occur in the healthy. Nevertheless they are certainly failures in functioning and, like dreams, which, in spite of their regular occurrence in healthy people, serve us as models of psychological disorder, they are abnormal structures. These phenomena are to be observed in two forms: the

---

[1] [The word has been rendered variously into English. Henderson and Gillespie, *Text-book of Psychiatry* (Fifth Edition, 1940), 102, use the term 'derealization', and make the same distinction as Freud between it and 'depersonalization'.]

subject feels either that a piece of reality or that a piece of his own self is strange to him. In the latter case we speak of 'depersonalizations'; derealizations and depersonalizations are intimately connected. There is another set of phenomena which may be regarded as their positive counterparts—what are known as *'fausse reconnaissance'*, *'déjà vu'*, *'déjà raconté'*, etc., illusions in which we seek to accept something as belonging to our ego, just as in the derealizations we are anxious to keep something out of us. A naïvely mystical and unpsychological attempt at explaining the phenomenon of *'déjà vu'* endeavours to find evidence in it of a former existence of our mental self. Depersonalization leads us on to the extraordinary condition of *'double conscience'*, which is more correctly described as 'split personality'. But all of this is so obscure and has been so little examined scientifically that I must refrain from talking about it any more to you.

It will be enough for my purposes if I return to two general characteristics of the phenomena of derealization. The first is that they all serve the purpose of defence; they aim at repudiating something, at keeping something away from the ego. Now, new elements, which may give occasion for defensive measures, approach the ego from two directions—from the real external world and from the internal world of thoughts and impulses that emerge in the ego. It is possible that this alternative coincides with the choice between derealizations proper and depersonalizations. There are an extraordinarily large number of methods (or mechanisms, as we say) used by our ego in the discharge of its defensive functions. An investigation is at this moment being carried on close at hand which is devoted to the study of these methods of defence: my daughter, the child analyst, is writing a book upon them.[1] The most primitive and thorough-going of these methods, 'repression', was the starting-point of the whole of our deeper understanding of psychopathology. Between

[1] [Anna Freud, *The Ego and the Mechanisms of Defence* (1936).]

repression and what may be termed the normal method of warding off what is painful or unbearable, by means of recognizing it, considering it, making a judgement upon it and taking appropriate action about it, there lie a whole series of more or less clearly pathological methods of behaviour on the part of the ego. May I stop for a moment to remind you of a marginal case of this kind of defence? You remember the famous lament of the Spanish Moors '*Ay de mi Alhama*' ['Alas for my Alhama'], which tells how King Boabdil received the news of the fall of his city of Alhama. He feels that this loss means the end of his rule. But he will not 'let it be true', he determines to treat the news as '*non arrivé*'. The verse runs:

> 'Cartas le fueron venidas
> que Alhama era ganada:
> las cartas echo en el fuego,
> y al mensajero matara.'[1]

It is easy to guess that a further determinant of this behaviour of the king was his need to combat a feeling of powerlessness. By burning the letters and having the messenger killed he was trying to show that his power was still at its full.

The second general characteristic of the derealizations—their dependence upon the past, upon the ego's store of memories and upon earlier painful experiences which have since perhaps fallen victim to repression—is not accepted without dispute. But precisely my own experience on the Acropolis, which actually culminated in a disturbance of memory and a falsification of the past helps us to demonstrate this connection. It is not true that in my school-days I ever doubted the real existence of Athens. I only doubted whether I should ever see Athens. It seemed to me beyond the realms of possibility that I should travel so far—that I should 'go such a long way'. This was linked up with the

---

[1] ['Letters had reached him telling that Alhama was taken. He threw the letters in the fire and killed the messenger.']

limitations and poverty of our conditions of life. My longing to travel was no doubt also the expression of a wish to escape from that pressure, like the force which drives so many adolescent children to run away from home. I had long seen clearly that a great part of the pleasure of travel lies in the fulfilment of these early wishes, that it is rooted, that is, in dissatisfaction with home and family. When first one catches sight of the sea, crosses the ocean and experiences as realities cities and lands which for so long had been distant, unattainable things of desire—one feels oneself like a hero who has performed deeds of improbable greatness. I might that day on the Acropolis have said to my brother: 'Do you still remember how, when we were young, we used day after day to walk along the same streets on our way to school, and how every Sunday we used to go to the Prater or on some excursion we knew so well? And now, here we are in Athens, and standing on the Acropolis! We really *have* gone a long way!' So too, if I may compare such a small event with a greater one, Napoleon, during his coronation as Emperor in Notre Dame, turned to one of his brothers—it must no doubt have been the eldest one, Joseph—and remarked: 'What would *Monsieur notre Père* have said to this, if he could have been here to-day?'

But here we come upon the solution of the little problem of why it was that already at Trieste we interfered with our enjoyment of the voyage to Athens. It must be that a sense of guilt was attached to the satisfaction in having got so far: there was something about it that was wrong, that was from earliest times forbidden. It was something to do with a child's criticism of his father, with the undervaluation which took the place of the overvaluation of earlier childhood. It seems as though the essence of success were to have got further than one's father, and as though to excel one's father were still something forbidden.

As an addition to this generally valid motive there was a special factor present in our particular case. The very theme of Athens and the Acropolis in itself contained evidence of the sons' superiority. Our father had been in business, he had had no secondary education, and Athens could not have meant much to him. Thus what interfered with our enjoyment of the journey to Athens was a feeling of *piety*. And now you will no longer wonder that the recollection of this incident on the Acropolis should have troubled me so often since I myself have grown old and stand in need of forbearance and can travel no more.

I am ever sincerely yours,

SIGM. FREUD

XXIX

THE SUBTLETIES OF A PARAPRAXIS[1]

(1936)

I WAS preparing a birthday present for a woman friend—a small engraved gem for insertion into a ring. It was fixed in the centre of a piece of stout cardboard and on this I wrote the following words: 'Order to Messrs. L., jewellers, for the supply of a gold ring . . . for the attached stone bearing an engraved ship with sail and oars.' But at the point at which I have here left a gap, between 'ring' and 'for' there stood a word which I was obliged to cross out since it was entirely irrelevant. This was the little word '*bis*' ['till']. Why should I have written it at all?

When I read the short inscription through, I was struck by the fact that it contained the word '*für*' ['for'] twice in rapid succession: '*for* the supply'—'*for* the attached stone'. That sounded ugly and should be avoided. It then occurred to me that '*bis*' had been substituted for '*für*' in an attempt to escape this stylistic awkwardness. No doubt that was so; but it was an attempt that made use of remarkably inadequate means. The preposition '*bis*' was quite out of place in this context and could not possibly be substituted for the necessary '*für*'. So why precisely '*bis*'?

But perhaps the word '*bis*' was not the preposition determining a time-limit. It may have been something totally different—the Latin '*bis*'—'for a second time', which has retained its meaning in French. '*Ne bis in idem*' is a maxim of Roman law. '*Bis! bis!*' cries a Frenchman if he wants a performance repeated. So that must be the explanation of my senseless slip of the pen. I was being warned against the second '*für*', against a repetition of the same word. Something else

¹ ['Die Feinheit einer Fehlhandlung.' First published in the *Almanach der Psychoanalyse* 1936; reprinted *Ges. W.*, **16.** Translation by James Strachey.]

must be put instead of it. The chance identity in sound between the foreign word '*bis*' which embodied the criticism of the original phraseology and the German preposition made it possible to insert '*bis*' instead of '*für*' as though by a slip of the pen. But this mistake gained its purpose not by being *made*, but only after it had been *corrected*. I had to cross out the '*bis*' and in so doing I had myself, so to speak, done away with the repetition which was disturbing me. A variant, not without interest, of the mechanism of a parapraxis!

I felt very much pleased with this solution. But in self-analysis the danger of incompleteness is particularly great. One is too easily satisfied with a part explanation, behind which resistance can easily keep back something that may perhaps be more important. I related this little analysis to my daughter, and she immediately saw how it went on:

'But you gave her a stone like that for a ring once before. *That's* probably the repetition you want to avoid. One can't always be making the same present.' It dawned on me that the objection was obviously to a repetition of the same *present*, not of the same *word*. There had been a displacement on to something trivial with the object of diverting attention from something more important: an aesthetic difficulty, perhaps, in place of an instinctual conflict.

For it was easy to discover the further sequel. I was looking for a motive for not making a present of the stone, and that motive was provided by the reflection that I had already made the same (or a very similar) present. Why should this objection have been concealed and disguised? Very soon I saw clearly why. I wanted not to give the stone away at all. I liked it very much myself.

The explanation of this parapraxis was found without raising any great difficulties. Indeed, a consoling thought soon occurred to me: regrets of this kind only enhance the value of a gift. What sort of gift would it be if one were not a little bit sorry to part with it?

Nevertheless it enables one to realize once more how complicated the most unobtrusive and apparently simplest mental processes may be. I made a slip in writing out an inscription—put in a *'bis'* where a *'für'* was needed—I noticed it and corrected it: a small mistake, or rather attempt at a mistake, and yet based upon this large number of premises and dynamic determinants! It is true that none of this could have occurred if the material had not been particularly favourable for the purpose.

XXX

ANALYSIS TERMINABLE AND INTERMINABLE[1]

(1937)

I

EXPERIENCE has taught us that psycho-analytic therapy—the liberation of a human being from his neurotic symptoms, inhibitions and abnormalities of character—is a lengthy business. Hence, from the very beginning, attempts have been made to shorten the course of analysis. Such endeavours required no justification: they could claim to be prompted by the strongest considerations alike of reason and expediency. But there probably lurked in them some trace of the impatient contempt with which the medical profession of an earlier day regarded the neuroses, seeing in them the unnecessary results of invisible lesions. If it had now become necessary to deal with them, they should at least be got rid of with the utmost despatch. Basing his procedure on the theory formulated in *Das Trauma der Geburt* (1924) Otto Rank made a particularly determined attempt to shorten analysis. He assumed that the cardinal source of neurosis was the experience of birth, on the ground of its involving a possibility that the infant's 'primal fixation' to the mother might not be surmounted but persist in the form of 'primal repression'. His hope was that, if this primal trauma were overcome by analysis, the whole neurosis would clear up, so that this one small piece of analytic work, for which a few months should suffice, would do away with the necessity for all the rest. Rank's argument was certainly bold and ingenious, but it did not stand the test of critical examination. Moreover, it was a child of its time, conceived under the stress of the contrast

---

[1] ['Die endliche und die unendliche Analyse.' First published *Int. Z. Psychoanal.*, **23** (1937), 209; reprinted *Ges. W.*, **16**. Translation, reprinted from *Int. J. Psycho-Anal.*, **18** (1937), 373, by Joan Riviere.]

between the post-war misery of Europe and the 'prosperity' of America, and designed to accelerate the tempo of analytic therapy to suit the rush of American life. We have heard little of the clinical results of Rank's plan. Probably it has not accomplished more than would be done if the men of a fire-brigade, summoned to deal with a house set on fire by an upset oil-lamp, merely removed the lamp from the room in which the conflagration had broken out. Much less time would certainly be spent in so doing than in extinguishing the whole fire. The theory and practice of Rank's experiment are now things of the past—no less than American 'prosperity' itself.

Before the war, I myself had already tried another way of speeding up analysis. I had undertaken to treat a young Russian, a rich man spoilt by riches, who had come to Vienna in a state of complete helplessness, accompanied by physician and attendant.[1] It was possible in the course of several years to restore to him a considerable measure of independence, and to awaken his interest in life, while his relations to the principal people in his life were adjusted. But then we came to a full stop. We made no progress in clearing up his childhood's neurosis, which was the basis of his later illness, and it was obvious that the patient found his present situation quite comfortable and did not intend to take any step which would bring him nearer to the end of his treatment. It was a case of the treatment obstructing itself: the analysis was in danger of failing as a result of its—partial—success. In this predicament I resorted to the heroic remedy of fixing a date for the conclusion of the analysis. At the beginning of a period of treatment I told the patient that the coming year was to be the last of his analysis, no matter what progress he made or failed to make in the time still left to him.

---

[1] Cf. my paper, published with the patient's consent, 'From the History of an Infantile Neurosis' (1918). It contains no detailed account of the young man's adult illness, which is touched on only when its connection with his infantile neurosis requires it.

At first he did not believe me, but, once he was convinced that I was in dead earnest, the change which I had hoped for began to take place. His resistances crumbled away, and in the last months of treatment he was able to produce all the memories and to discover the connecting links which were necessary for the understanding of his early neurosis and his recovery from the illness from which he was then suffering. When he took leave of me at mid-summer, 1914, unsuspecting as we all were, of what was so shortly to happen, I believed that his cure was complete and permanent.

In a postscript to this patient's case history (1923*d*) I have already reported that I was mistaken. When, towards the end of the war, he returned to Vienna, a refugee and destitute, I had to help him to master a part of the transference which had remained unresolved. Within a few months this was successfully accomplished and I was able to conclude my postscript with the statement that 'since then the patient has felt normal and has behaved unexceptionably, in spite of the war having robbed him of his home, his possessions, and all his family relationships'. Fifteen years have passed since then, but this verdict has not proved erroneous, though certain reservations have had to be made. The patient has remained in Vienna and has made good, although in a humble social position. Several times, however, during this period, his satisfactory state of health has broken down, and the attacks of neurotic illness from which he has suffered could be construed only as offshoots of his original neurosis. Thanks to the skill of one of my pupils, Dr. Ruth Mack Brunswick, a short course of treatment has sufficed on each occasion to clear up these attacks. I hope Dr. Mack Brunswick herself will report on this case before long.[1] Some of these relapses were caused by still unresolved residues of the transference; short-lived though the attacks were, they were distinctly paranoic in character. In other instances, however, the pathogenic material consisted

---

[1] [One such report had already appeared: Brunswick (1928*b*).]

of fragments from the history of the patient's childhood, which had not come to light while I was analysing
him and which now came away (the comparison is
obvious) like sutures after an operation or small pieces
of necrotic bone. I have found the history of this man's
recovery almost as interesting as that of his illness.

Since then I have employed the method of fixing a
date for the termination of analysis in other cases and I
have also inquired about the experience of other
analysts in this respect. There can be only one verdict
about the value of this blackmailing device. The
measure is effective, provided that one hits the right
time at which to employ it. But it cannot be held to
guarantee perfect accomplishment of the task of psycho-
analysis. On the contrary, we may be quite sure that,
while the force of the threat will have the effect of
bringing part of the material to light, another part will
be held back and become buried, as it were, and will be
lost to our therapeutic efforts. Once the date for dis-
continuing the treatment has been fixed we must not
extend the time; otherwise the patient will lose all his
faith in the analyst. The most obvious way out would
be to let him continue his treatment with another
analyst, although we know that a change of this sort
involves a fresh loss of time and the sacrifice of some of
the results of the work already done. Nor can any
general rule be laid down as to the right time for resort-
ing to this forcible technical method: the analyst must
use his own tact in the matter. A mistake, once made,
cannot be rectified. The saying that the lion springs
once and once only must hold good here.

II

The discussion of the technical problem of how to
accelerate the slow progress of an analysis suggests
another, more deeply interesting question: is there such
a thing as a natural end to an analysis or is it really
possible to conduct it to such an end? To judge by the

ordinary talk of analysts we should presume that it is, for we often hear them say, when deploring or excusing the admitted imperfection of some fellow-mortal: 'His analysis was not finished' or 'He was not completely analysed'.

Now we must first decide what is meant by the ambiguous term, 'the end of an analysis'. From the practical standpoint it is easily defined. An analysis is ended when analyst and patient cease to meet for the analytic session. This happens when two conditions have been approximately fulfilled. First, the patient must no longer be suffering from his former symptoms and must have overcome his various anxieties and inhibitions and, secondly, the analyst must have formed the opinion that so much repressed material has been brought into consciousness, so much that was inexplicable elucidated, and so much inner resistance overcome that no repetition of the patient's specific pathological processes is to be feared. If for external reasons one is prevented from reaching this goal, it is more correct to say that an analysis is imperfect than to say that it has not been completed.

The second definition of the 'end' of an analysis is much more ambitious. According to it we have to answer the question whether the effect upon the patient has been so profound that no further change would take place in him if his analysis were continued. The implication is that by means of analysis it is possible to attain to absolute psychical normality and to be sure that it will be maintained, the supposition being that all the patient's repressions have been lifted and every gap in his memory filled. Let us first consult our experience and see whether such things do in fact happen, and then examine our theory and learn whether there is any *possibility* of their happening.

Every analyst will have treated some cases with this gratifying outcome. He has succeeded in clearing up the patient's neurosis, there has been no relapse and no other nervous disturbance has succeeded it. We know

something of what determines these results. No noticeable modification had taken place in the patient's ego
and the causation of his illness was pre-eminently
traumatic. The aetiology of all neuroses is indeed a
mixed one; either the patient's instincts are excessively
strong and refuse to submit to the taming influence of
his ego or else he is suffering from the effects of premature traumas, by which I mean traumas which his
immature ego was unable to surmount. Generally there
is a combination of the two factors: the constitutional
and the accidental. The stronger the constitutional
factor the more readily will a trauma lead to fixation,
with its sequel in a disturbance of development; the
stronger the trauma the more certain is it that it will
have injurious effects even when the patient's instinctual life is normal. There can be no doubt that, when the
aetiology of the neurosis is traumatic, analysis has a far
better chance. Only when the traumatic factor predominates can we look for what psycho-analysis can
achieve in such a masterly fashion, namely, the replacement (owing to the strengthening of the ego) of the
inadequate decision made in infancy by a correct
solution. Only in such a case can one speak of a definitive end to an analysis. When such a result has been
attained analysis has done all that can be required of it
and need not be continued. If the patient who has made
such a good recovery never produces any more symptoms calling for analysis, it still, of course, remains an
open question how much of this immunity is due to a
benevolent fate which spares him too searching a test.

The factors which are prejudicial to analysis and
may cause it to be so long-drawn-out as to be really
interminable are a constitutional strength of instinct
and an unfavourable modification of the ego in the
defensive conflict, a modification comparable to a dis-
location or crippling. One is tempted to make the first
factor—the strength of the instincts—responsible for
the second—the modification of the ego—but it seems
that the latter has its own aetiology and indeed it must

L

322 COLLECTED PAPERS XXX

be admitted that our knowledge of these relations is as
yet imperfect. They are only just becoming the object
of analytic investigation. I think that here the interest
of analysts is quite wrongly orientated. Instead of
inquiring *how* analysis effects a cure (a point which in
my opinion has been sufficiently elucidated) we should
ask what are the obstacles which this cure encounters.

This brings me to two problems which arise directly
out of psycho-analytic practice, as I hope to show by the
following examples. A certain man, who had himself
been a most successful practitioner of analysis, came to
the conclusion that his relations with men as well as
with women—the men who were his rivals and the
woman whom he loved—were not free from neurotic
inhibitions, and he therefore had himself analysed by an
analyst whom he regarded as his superior. This critical
exploration of his own personality was entirely successful. He married the woman whom he loved and became
the friend and teacher of the men whom he had regarded
as rivals. Many years passed, during which his relation
to his former analyst remained unclouded. But then,
for no demonstrable external reason, trouble arose. The
man who had been analysed adopted an antagonistic
attitude to his analyst and reproached him for having
neglected to complete the analysis. The analyst, he said,
ought to have known and to have taken account of
the fact that a transference-relation could never be
merely positive; he ought to have considered the
possibilities of a negative transference. The analyst
justified himself by saying that, at the time of the
analysis, there was no sign of a negative transference.
But, even supposing that he had failed to observe some
slight indication of it, which was quite possible considering the limitations of analysis in those early days, it
was still doubtful, he thought, whether he would have
been able to activate a psychical theme or, as we say, a
'complex', by merely indicating it to the patient, so long
as it was not at that moment an actuality to him. Such
activation would certainly have necessitated real

unfriendly behaviour on the analyst's part. And, he added, every happy relation between an analyst and the subject of his analysis, during and after analysis, was not to be regarded as transference; there were friendly relations with a real basis, which were capable of persisting.

I now pass on to my second example, which raises the same problem. A girl who had left her childhood behind her had, since puberty, been cut off from life by an inability to walk, owing to acute pain in her legs. Her condition was obviously hysterical in character and it had resisted various kinds of treatment. After an analysis lasting nine months the trouble disappeared and the patient, whose character was truly sound and estimable, was able once more to take her place in life. In the years following her recovery she was consistently unfortunate: there were disasters in her family, they lost their money and, as she grew older, she saw every hope of happiness in love and marriage vanish. But this woman, who had formerly been an invalid, stood her ground valiantly and in difficult times was a support to her people. I cannot remember whether it was twelve or fourteen years after the end of her analysis that she had to undergo a gynaecological examination on account of profuse haemorrhages. A myoma was discovered which made a complete hysterectomy advisable. From the time that this operation took place she relapsed into neurosis. She fell in love with the surgeon and was overwhelmed by masochistic phantasies of the dreadful internal changes which had taken place in her —phantasies in which she disguised her romance. She proved inaccessible to a further attempt at analysis, and to the end of her life she remained abnormal. The successful analytic treatment took place so long ago that we could not expect too much from it; it was in the first years of my work as an analyst. It is no doubt possible that the patient's second neurosis sprang from the same root as the first, which had been successfully overcome, and that it was a different manifestation of repressed tendencies which the analysis had only partially resolved. But I am inclined to think that, but for the fresh trauma, there would have been no second outbreak of neurosis.

These two cases, purposely selected from a large number of similar ones, will suffice to set going a discussion of the problems we are considering. The sceptical, the optimistic and the ambitious will draw very different conclusions from them. Sceptics will say that they prove that even a successful analysis does not prevent the patient who is cured for the time being from subsequently developing another neurosis, or even a neurosis springing from the same instinctual root, that is to say, from a recurrence of his former trouble. The others will maintain that this is not proved. They will object that both the cases I have cited date from the early days of analysis, twenty and thirty years ago, respectively, and that since then we have acquired deeper insight and wider knowledge and, in adapting our technique to our new discoveries, we have modified it in many respects. To-day, they will argue, we may demand and expect that an analytic cure shall be permanent or, at least, that, if a patient falls ill again, his fresh neurosis shall not turn out to be a revival of his earlier instinctual disturbance, manifesting itself in a new guise. Our experience, they will say, is not such that we must limit so severely the demands which we may legitimately make upon psycho-analytic therapy.

Now, of course, my reason for selecting these particular cases as illustrations was precisely that they date so far back. It is obvious that the more recent the result of an analysis the less valuable is it for our theoretical discussion since we have no means of predicting what will happen later to a patient who has been cured. Clearly the expectations of the optimist presuppose a number of things which are not exactly a matter of course. In the first place he assumes that it is really possible to resolve an instinctual conflict (or, more accurately, a conflict between the ego and an instinct finally and for all time. Secondly, that when we are dealing with one such conflict in a patient, we can as it were, inoculate him against the possibility of any other instinctual conflicts in the future. And thirdly, that we have the power, for purposes of prophylaxis, to stir up a pathogenic conflict of this sort, when at the moment there is no indication of it, and that it is wise to do so. I merely suggest these questions: I do not propose to answer them now. In any case a definite answer is perhaps not possible at the present time.

Probably some light may be thrown on the subject from the theoretical standpoint. But already another point has become clear: if we wish to fulfil the more exacting demands which are now made upon therapeutic analysis, we shall not shorten its duration whether as a means or an end.

III

My analytic experience, extending now over several decades, and the change which has taken place in the nature and mode of my work encourage me to attempt an answer to the questions before us. In earlier days I dealt with a comparatively large number of patients, who, as was natural, wanted to be cured as quickly as possible. Of late years I have been mainly engaged in training-analyses and I have also had a relatively small number of patients suffering from severe neuroses, whose treatment has been carried on continuously, though with longer or shorter intermissions. In these cases the therapeutic aim is no longer the same as before. There is no question of shortening the treatment: the object has been completely to exhaust the possibilities of illness and to bring about a radical change in the personality.

Of the three factors which, as we have seen, determine the results of analysis—the effect of traumas, the constitutional strength of the instincts and the modification of the ego—we are at this point concerned with the second only: the strength of the instincts. Reflection immediately suggests a doubt as to whether it is necessary to use the qualifying adjective 'constitutional' (or 'congenital'). It is true that from the very beginning the constitutional factor is of crucial importance, but it is yet conceivable that the same effects might ensue from a reinforcement of instinctual energy at some later period in life. If this were so, we should have to modify our formula and say 'the strength of the instincts at a given moment' rather than 'the constitutional strength of the instincts'. Now the first of our questions was this: is it possible for analysis permanently and definitively to resolve a conflict between instinct and ego or to settle a pathogenic instinctual demand upon the ego? To avoid misunderstanding we must perhaps define more exactly what we mean by the phrase: 'a permanent settlement of an instinctual demand.' We certainly do not mean that we cause the demand to disappear, so that it never makes itself felt again. As a rule this is impossible and not even desirable. No, we mean something else, something which may be roughly described as the 'taming' of the instinct. That is to say, it is brought into harmony with the ego and becomes accessible to the influence of the other trends in the ego, no longer seeking for independent satisfaction. If we are asked how and by what means this result is achieved, we do not find it easy to answer. There is nothing for it but to 'summon help from the Witch'[1]—the Witch Metapsychology. Without metapsychological speculation and theorizing—I had almost said 'phantasy'—we shall not get a step further. Unfortunately, here as elsewhere, what our Witch reveals is neither very clear nor very exact. We have only a single clue to follow— but a clue the value of which cannot be exaggerated— namely, the antithesis between the primary and the secondary processes, and to this I must refer here.

Reverting to our first question, we find that our new approach to the problem makes a particular conclusion

[1] *'So muss denn doch die Hexe dran.'* [Goethe, *Faust*, Part I.]

inevitable. The question was as follows: is it possible permanently and definitively to resolve an instinctual conflict—that is to say, to 'tame' the instinctual demand? Formulated thus, the question contains no mention whatever of the strength of the instinct, but it is precisely this which determines the issue. Let us assume that what analysis achieves for neurotics is only what normal people accomplish for themselves without its help. But everyday experience teaches us that in a normal person any solution of an instinctual conflict holds good only for a particular strength of instinct, or rather, only where there is a particular relation between the strength of the instinct and the strength of the ego.[1] If the latter becomes enfeebled, whether through illness, exhaustion or for some similar cause, all the instincts which have so far been successfully tamed may renew their demands and strive in abnormal ways after substitutive satisfactions.[2] We have irrefutable proof of this statement in what takes place in dreams, when the reaction to the ego's condition in sleep is the awakening of instinctual demands.

The material relating to the strength of the instincts is equally unambiguous. Twice in the course of the development of the individual certain instincts are powerfully reinforced: at puberty and at the menopause in women. We are not in the least surprised if people who were normal before become neurotic at these times. When the instincts were not so strong these individuals succeeded in taming them, but they can no longer do so when the instincts acquire this new strength. The repressions behave like dams in time of flood. What occurs regularly at these two periods, when for physio-

[1] Or, to be perfectly accurate, where that relation falls within particular limits.

[2] Here we have a justification of the claim to aetiological importance of such unspecific factors as overwork, shock, etc. These have always been certain of general recognition and psycho-analysis has had to force them into the background. It is impossible to define health except in terms of metapsychology, *i.e.* of the dynamic relations between those agencies of the psychical apparatus, the existence of which psycho-analysis has discovered, or, if it is preferred, has deduced or conjectured.

logical reasons the instincts become stronger, may occur sporadically as the result of accidental influences at any other period in life. Factors contributing to the reinforcement of instinct are : fresh traumas, the infliction of frustration and collateral interaction between the various instincts. The result is always the same and it confirms the irresistible importance of the quantitative factor in the causation of illness.

I feel as if I ought to be ashamed of so much ponderous exposition, seeing that all I have said has long been familiar and self-evident. It is a fact that we have always behaved as if we knew these things, yet for the most part our theoretical concepts have failed to give the same importance to the economic as to the dynamic and topographical aspects of the case. So my excuse must be that I am drawing attention to this omission.

Before we decide on an answer to our question, however, we must listen to an objection the force of which lies in the fact that we are very likely predisposed in its favour. It will be contended that our arguments are all deduced from the spontaneous processes that take place between ego and instinct and that we are assuming that analytic therapy can accomplish nothing which does not occur spontaneously under favourable normal conditions. But is this really so? Is not the claim of our theory precisely that analysis produces a state which never does occur spontaneously within the ego and the creation of which constitutes the main difference between a person who has been analysed and a person who has not? Let us consider on what this claim is based. All repressions take place in early childhood; they are primitive defensive measures adopted by the immature, feeble ego. In later years there are no fresh repressions, but the old ones persist and are used by the ego for the purpose of further mastering instinct. New conflicts are resolved by what we call 'after-repression'. To these infantile repressions our general statement applies that they depend entirely on the relative strength of the various psychical forces and cannot withstand an increase in the strength of the instincts. But analysis enables the mature ego, which by this time has attained a greater strength, to review these old repressions, with the result that some are lifted, while others are accepted but reconstructed from more solid material. These new dams have a greater tenacity than the earlier ones; we may be confident that they will not so easily give way before the flood-tide of instinct. Thus the real achievement of analytic therapy would be the subsequent correction of the original process of repression, with the result that the supremacy of the quantitative factor is brought to an end.

So far our theory, to which we must adhere unless we are irresistibly compelled to abandon it. And what is the testimony of our *experience*? Perhaps it is not yet wide enough to enable us to come to a definite decision. Quite often it justifies our expectations, but not always. Our impression is that we must not be surprised if the difference between a person who has not and a person who has been analysed is, after all, not so radical as we endeavour to make it and expect and assert that it will be. Thus analysis does indeed sometimes succeed in counteracting the effect of increases in the strength of instinct, but it does not invariably do so. Sometimes its effect is simply to raise the power of the resistance put up by inhibitions, so that after analysis they are equal to a much heavier strain than before the analysis took place or if it had never taken place at all. I really cannot commit myself to a decision on this point nor do I know whether at the present time a decision is possible.

There is another angle from which we may approach this problem of the variability of the effect of analysis. We know that the first step towards the intellectual mastery of the world in which we live is the discovery of general principles, rules and laws which bring order into chaos. By such mental operations we simplify the world of phenomena, but we cannot avoid falsifying it

in so doing, especially when we are dealing with processes of development and change. We are trying to
discern a qualitative alteration and as a rule we neglect,
at any rate at first, the quantitative factor. In reality
transitional and intermediate stages are far more
common than sharply differentiated opposite states.
In studying various developments and changes we focus
our attention entirely on the result and we readily overlook the fact that such processes are usually more or
less incomplete, that is to say, the changes that take
place are really only partial. A shrewd satirist of the
old Austria, Johann Nestroy, once said: 'Every advance
is only half as great as it looks at first.' One is tempted
to think that this malicious dictum is universally valid.
There are almost always vestiges of what has been and a
partial arrest at a former stage. When an open-handed
Maecenas surprises us by some isolated trait of miserli-
ness or a person whose kind-heartedness has been excessive suddenly indulges in some unfriendly act, these
are 'vestiges' and are of priceless value for genetic
research. They show that these praiseworthy and
valuable qualities are based on compensation and over-
compensation which, as was only to be expected, have
not been absolutely and completely successful. Our
first account of libidinal development was that an
original oral phase was succeeded by a sadistic-anal, and
this in its turn by a phallic-genital phase. Later
investigation has not contradicted this view, but we
must now qualify our statement by saying that the one
phase does not succeed the other suddenly but gradually,
so that part of the earlier organization always persists
side by side with the later, and that even in normal
development the transformation is never complete, the
final structure often containing vestiges of earlier
libidinal fixations. We see the same thing in quite
different connections. There is not one of the erroneous
and superstitious beliefs of mankind that are supposed
to have been superseded but has left vestiges at the
present day in the lower strata of civilized peoples or

even in the highest strata of cultivated society. All that has once lived clings tenaciously to life. Sometimes one feels inclined to doubt whether the dragons of primaeval ages are really extinct.

Applying these remarks to our particular problem, I would say that the answer to the question how we explain the variable results or our analytic therapy might well be that our success in replacing insecure repressions by reliable and ego-syntonic controls is not always complete, *i.e.* is not radical enough. A change does occur but it is often only partial: parts of the old mechanisms remain untouched by analysis. It is difficult to prove that this is really so. We can only judge it by the result which it is supposed to explain. But the impressions we receive during our analytic work do not contradict this hypothesis—rather, they confirm it. We have to be careful not to imagine that the clarity of our own insight is a measure of the conviction we produce in the mind of the patient. This conviction may lack 'depth', so to speak; the point in question is always that quantitative factor which is so easily overlooked. If we now have the correct answer to our question, we may say that analysis is always right in theory in its claim to cure neurosis by ensuring control over instinct but that in practice its claim is not always justified. This is because it does not always succeed in laying sufficiently firm foundations for that control. The reason for this partial failure is easy to discover. The quantitative factor of instinctual strength in the past opposed the efforts of the patient's ego to defend itself, and now that analysis has been called in to help, that same factor sets a limit to the efficacy of this new attempt. If the instincts are excessively strong the ego fails in its task, although it is now mature and has the support of analysis, just as it failed in earlier days in its helpless state; its control over instinct is greater but not complete, because the change in the defensive mechanism is only partial. This is not surprising, for the power of analysis is not infinite; it is limited, and the final result always depends on the relative strength of the conflicting psychical agencies.

No doubt it is desirable to shorten analytic treatment, but we shall achieve our therapeutic purpose only when we can give a greater measure of analytic help to the patient's ego. At one time it seemed that hypnotic influence was a splendid way of achieving our end; the reasons why we had to abandon that method are well known. Hitherto no substitute for hypnosis has been discovered, but we can understand from this how such a master of analysis as Ferenczi came to devote his last years to therapeutic experiments which were, alas! in vain.

IV

The two further questions—whether, when dealing with one instinctual conflict, we can guard a patient against future conflicts and whether it is practicable and advisable to stir up for purposes of prophylaxis a conflict which is not at the moment manifest—must be treated together; for obviously the first task can be accomplished only if one performs the second, *i.e.* if one turns a possible future conflict into an actual one and then brings analytic influence to bear upon it. This new problem is really only an extension of the earlier one. In the first instance we were considering how to guard against the return of the *same* conflict: now we are considering the possible substitution of a second conflict for the first. This sounds a very ambitious proposal, but we are in fact only trying to make clear what limits are set to the efficacy of analytic therapy.

Tempting as it may be to our therapeutic ambition to propose such tasks for itself, experience bids us reject them out of hand. If an instinctual conflict is not an actual one and does not manifest itself in any way, it cannot be influenced by analysis. The warning that we should 'let sleeping dogs lie'—which we have so often heard in connection with our investigation of the psychical underworld—is peculiarly inapposite when applied to the conditions existing in mental life. For, if the instincts are causing disturbances it is a proof that the dogs are not sleeping and if they seem really to be sleeping, we have not the power to wake them. This last statement, however, does not seem entirely accurate and we must consider it in greater detail. Let us consider the means we have at our disposal for transforming a latent into an actual instinctual conflict. Clearly there are only two things we can do: either we can bring about situations in which the conflict becomes actual or we can content ourselves with discussing it in analysis and pointing out that it may possibly arise. The first of these two alternatives can be accomplished in two different ways, either in reality, or in the transference. In either case we expose the patient to a measure of real suffering through frustration and the damming-up of libido. Now it is true that in ordinary analytic practice we do make use of this technique. Otherwise, what would be the meaning of the rule that analysis must be carried through 'in a state of abstinence'? But we use it when we are dealing with a conflict which is already present. We try to bring this conflict to a head and to develop it in its most acute form in order to increase the instinctual energy available for its solution. Analytic experience has taught us that the better is always the enemy of the good and that in every phase of the patient's restoration we have to combat his inertia, which disposes him to be content with a partial solution of his conflicts.

If, however, our aim is the prophylactic treatment of instinctual conflicts which are not actual but merely possible, it is not enough to deal with the suffering which the patient is inevitably undergoing. We must make up our minds to conjure up fresh suffering— a thing which we have so far quite rightly left to fate. We should receive protests from all sides against the presumption of vying with fate in putting wretched human beings to such cruel experiments. And what sort of experiments would they be? Could we, for purposes of prophylaxis, take the responsibility of destroying a happy marriage or causing a patient to give up work upon which his livelihood depended? Fortunately there is no question of having to justify such interference with real life. We have not the plenary powers which such intervention would demand and most certainly the object of this therapeutic experiment would refuse to co-operate in it. In practice then, this method may be said to be excluded and there are, besides, theoretical objections to it, for the work of analysis progresses best when the patient's pathogenic experiences belong to the past so that the ego can stand at a distance from them. In conditions of acute crisis it is, to all intents and purposes, impossible to use analysis. In such states the whole interest of the ego is concentrated on the painful reality, and resists analysis, which seeks to penetrate below the surface and to discover the influences to which the patient has been exposed in the past. Thus to create a fresh conflict will only make the analysis longer and more difficult.

It may be objected that all this discussion is quite superfluous. Nobody imagines that a latent instinctual conflict can be treated by purposely conjuring up a fresh painful situation. As a prophylactic achievement this would not be much to boast of. Let us take an example: we know that when a patient recovers from scarlet fever he has become immune to a recurrence of that illness. But it never occurs to a physician on that account to infect a patient with scarlet fever in order to make him immune. It is not the business of prophylactic treatment to produce the same dangerous situation as that of the illness itself but only something much more mild, as in the case of vaccination and many similar procedures. Similarly, in the analytic prophylaxis of instinctual conflicts the only methods which we need really consider are the other two: the artificial production of new conflicts in the transference (conflicts which lack the character of reality) and the rousing of such conflicts in the imagination of the patient by talking to him about them and telling him that they may possibly arise.

I do not know if we can assert that the first of these two less drastic procedures is out of the question in analysis. No experiments have been made in this particular direction. But some difficulties at once suggest themselves which make the success of such an undertaking very problematic. In the first place the choice of such situations for the transference is very limited. The patient himself cannot embody all his conflicts in the transference, nor can the transference-situation be so employed by the analyst as to rouse all the instinctual conflicts in which the patient may possibly become engaged. We may incite him to jealousy or inflict upon him the pain of disappointed love, but no special technical design is necessary for that purpose. These things happen spontaneously in most analyses. But in the second place we must not overlook the fact that any such deliberate procedure would necessitate unkind behaviour on the part of the analyst towards the patient and this would have an injurious effect upon his affectionate attitude towards the analyst, *i.e.* upon the positive transference, which is the patient's strongest motive for co-operating in the work of analysis. So we shall not form any high expectation of the results of such a technique.

This leaves only the other method, which is probably the only one originally contemplated. The analyst will tell the patient about possible instinctual conflicts which may occur and will lead him to expect that they may occur in himself. This is done in the hope that the information and warning will have the effect of activating in the patient one of these conflicts in a moderate degree and yet sufficiently for it to be dealt with. But here experience speaks with no uncertain voice. The result hoped for is not achieved. The patient hears what we say but it rouses no response in his mind. He probably thinks to himself: 'That is very interesting, but I

see no sign of it in myself.' We have increased his knowledge but effected no other change in his mind. We
have much the same situation when people read psycho-
analytical writings. The reader is 'stimulated' only by
those passages which he feels apply to himself, *i.e.*
which refer to conflicts that are active in him. Everything else leaves him cold. I think we have a similar
experience when we enlighten children on matters of
sex. I am far from maintaining that this is a harmful
or unnecessary thing to do, but it is clear that the
prophylactic effect of this liberal measure has been
vastly over-estimated. After such enlightenment the
children know something that they did not know before
but they make no use of the new knowledge imparted to
them. We come to the conclusion that they are by no
means ready to sacrifice those sexual theories which
may be said to be a natural growth and which they have
constructed in harmony with and in dependence on
their undeveloped libidinal organization—theories about
the part played by the stork, about the nature of sexual
intercourse and about the way in which children are
born. For a long time after they have been enlightened
on these subjects they behave like primitive races who
have had Christianity thrust upon them and continue
in secret to worship their old idols.

V

Our starting-point was the question of how to
shorten the tediously long duration of an analysis and,
still pursuing the question of time, we went on to consider whether we can achieve permanent cure or prevent
illness in the future by prophylactic treatment. We saw
that the success of our therapeutic work depended on
the influence of traumatic factors in the aetiology of the
neurosis, on the relative strength of the instincts which
have to be controlled and on something which we called
modification of the ego. Only the second of these factors has been discussed in any detail and we have had

occasion in so doing to recognize the paramount importance of the quantitative factor and to stress the claim of the metapsychological standpoint to be taken into account in any attempt at explanation.

Of the third factor, the modification of the ego, we have as yet said nothing. The first impression received when we turn our attention to it is that there is much to ask and to answer, and that what we can say on the subject will prove very inadequate. This impression is confirmed when we go into the problem further. We know that the essence of the analytic situation is that the analyst enters into an alliance with the ego of the patient to subdue certain uncontrolled parts of his id, *i.e.* to include them in the synthesis of the ego. The fact that in the case of psychotics this co-operation is never successful brings us to our first definite conclusion. If we want to make a compact with the patient's ego, that ego must be normal. But such a normal ego is, like normality in general, an ideal fiction. The abnormal ego, which is of no use for our purpose, is unfortunately no fiction. Now every normal person is only approximately normal: his ego resembles that of the psychotic in one point or another, in a greater or lesser degree, and its distance from one end of the scale and proximity to the other may provisionally serve as a measure of what we have indefinitely spoken of as 'modification of the ego'.

If we ask what is the source of the great variety of kinds and degrees of ego-modification we cannot escape the first obvious alternative that such modifications are either congenital or acquired. The second case will be the easier to treat. If they are acquired it must certainly have been during the individual's development from the very beginning of his life. From the very outset the ego has to try to fulfil its task of acting as an intermediary between the id and the external world in the service of the pleasure principle, to protect the id from the dangers of the external world. If, while thus endeavouring, the ego learns to adopt a defensive attitude towards its own id and to treat the instinctual demands of the latter like external dangers, this is at any rate partly because it understands that satisfaction of instinct would lead to conflicts with the external world. Under the influence of its upbringing, the child's ego accustoms itself to shift the scene of the battle from outside to inside and to master the *inner* danger before it becomes *external*. Probably it is generally right in so doing. In this battle on two fronts—later there is a third front as well—the ego makes use of various methods of fulfilling its task, *i.e.*, to put it in general terms, of avoiding danger, anxiety and unpleasure. We call these devices *defensive mechanisms*. Our knowledge of them is as yet incomplete. Anna Freud's book (1936) has given us our first insight into their multiplicity and their manifold significance.

One of these mechanisms, that of repression, provided the starting-point for the study of neurotic processes in general. There was never any doubt that repression was not the only method which the ego could employ for its purposes. Nevertheless, repression is something quite peculiar, more sharply differentiated from the other mechanisms than these are from one another. I should like to make its relation to these other mechanisms clear by an analogy, but I know that analogies never carry us very far in such matters.

Let us imagine what might have happened to a book at the time when books were not printed in editions but written out separately by hand. We will imagine that such a book contained statements which at a later time were regarded as undesirable—as, for instance, according to Robert Eisler (1929), the writings of Flavius Josephus must have contained passages about Jesus Christ which were offensive to later Christendom. At the present day the only defedsive mechanism to which the official censorship would resort would be the confiscation and destruction of every copy of the whole edition. At that time other methods were employed to render the book innocuous. Either the offensive passages were heavily scored through, so that they were illegible, in which case they could not be transcribed and the next copyist of the book produced a text to which no exception could be taken but which had gaps in certain places, probably making the passages in question unintelligible. Or, not satisfied with this, the authorities tried to conceal any indication that the text had been mutilated. They therefore proceeded to tamper with the text. Single words here and there were left out or replaced by others and whole new sentences were interpolated; at best, the passage was completely erased and replaced by another in exactly the opposite sense. When the book was next transcribed the text aroused no suspicion, but had, in fact, been falsified. It no longer contained the author's statement and very probably the correction was not in the interests of truth.

Without pressing the analogy too closely we may say that repression is to the other methods of defence what the omission of words or passages is to the corruption of a text, and in the various forms of this falsification we can discover parallels to the manifold ways in which the ego may be modified. It may be objected that this analogy breaks down in an essential particular, for the corruption of a text is the work of a purposeful censorship to which we have no counterpart in the development of the ego. But this is not so, for this purpose is amply represented by the compelling force of the pleasure principle. The psychical apparatus is intolerant of unpleasure and strives to ward it off at all costs and, if the perception of reality involves unpleasure, that perception—*i.e.* the truth—must be sacrificed. For quite a long time flight and an avoidance of a dangerous situation serve as expedients in the face of external danger, until the individual is finally strong enough to remove the menace by actively modifying reality. But one cannot flee from oneself and no flight avails against danger from within; hence the ego's defensive mechanisms are condemned to falsify the inner perception, so that it transmits to us only an

imperfect and travestied picture of our id. In its relations with the id the ego is paralysed by its restrictions or blinded by its errors, and the result in the
sphere of psychical events may be compared to the
progress of a poor walker in a country which he does
not know.

The purpose of the defensive mechanisms is to avert
dangers. It cannot be disputed that they are successful;
it is doubtful whether the ego can altogether do without
them during its development, but it is also certain that
they themselves may become dangerous. Not infrequently it turns out that the ego has paid too high a
price for the services which these mechanisms render.
The expenditure of energy necessary to maintain them
and the ego-restrictions which they almost invariably
entail prove a heavy burden on the psychical economy.
Moreover these mechanisms are not relinquished after
they have helped the ego through the difficult years of
its development. Of course, no individual makes use of
all the possible mechanisms of defence: each person
merely selects certain of them, but these become fixated
in his ego, establishing themselves as regular modes of
reaction for that particular character, which are repeated throughout life whenever a situation occurs
similar to that which originally evoked them. They are,
in fact, infantilisms and share the fate of so many
institutions which struggle to maintain themselves
when they have outlived their usefulness. '*Vernunft
wird Unsinn, Wohltat Plage,*' [1] as the poet laments.
The adult ego with its greater strength continues to
defend itself against dangers which no longer exist in
reality and even finds itself impelled to seek out real
situations which may serve as a substitute for the
original danger, so as to be able to justify its clinging to
its habitual modes of reaction. Thus the defensive
mechanisms produce an ever-growing alienation from
the external world and a permanent enfeeblement of the

---

[1] ['Reason becomes unreason, kindness torment.' Goethe, *Faust*,
Part I.]

ego and we can easily understand how they pave the way for and precipitate the outbreak of neurosis.

For the moment, however, we are not concerned with the pathogenic role of the defensive mechanisms. Our purpose is to discover how our therapeutic work is affected by the ego-modification they produce. The material for the answer to this question is contained in Anna Freud's work, to which I have already referred. The main point is that the patient repeats these modes of reaction during analysis itself, exhibiting them, as it were, before our eyes; in fact, that is the only means we have of learning about them. This must not be taken to imply that they make analysis impossible. On the contrary, they constitute half of our analytic task. The other half, the first to be tackled by analysis in its early days, is the revelation of that which is hidden in the id. Our therapeutic work swings to and fro during the treatment like a pendulum, analysing now a fragment of the id and now a fragment of the ego. In the one case our aim is to bring a part of the id into consciousness and in the other to correct something in the ego. The crux of the matter is that the mechanisms of defence against former dangers recur in analysis in the shape of *resistances* to cure. It follows that the ego treats recovery itself as a new danger.

The therapeutic effect of analysis depends on the making conscious what is, in the widest sense, repressed within the id. We prepare the way for this operation by our interpretations and constructions, but so long as the ego clings to its former defences and refuses to abandon its resistances we have interpreted merely for ourselves and not for the patient. Now these resistances, although they belong to the ego, are nevertheless unconscious and, in a certain sense, they are segregated within the ego. The analyst recognizes them more easily than the hidden material in the id; one would suppose it would be enough to treat them as parts of the id and to bring them into relation with the rest of the ego by making them conscious. This would mean that half of our analytic task had been accomplished: we are hardly prepared for a resistance to the discovery of resistances. But what takes place is as follows. While we are analysing the resistances, the ego—more or less of set purpose—breaks the compact upon which the analytic situation is based. It ceases to support us in our efforts to reveal the id, it opposes those efforts, disobeys the fundamental rule of analysis and suffers no further derivatives of repressed material to emerge into consciousness. It is too much to expect that the patient should have a firm conviction of the curative power of analysis, but he may have come to the analyst with a certain amount of confidence and this, reinforced by the various factors in the positive transference which it is our business to evoke, makes him capable of doing his share. The effect of the unpleasurable impulses which he feels stirring in him when his defensive conflicts are once more roused may be that negative transferences gain the upper hand and break up the whole analytic situation. The patient now regards the analyst simply as an alien personality who makes disagreeable demands upon him and he behaves towards him exactly like a child who does not like a stranger and has no confidence in him. If the analyst tries to explain to the patient one of the distortions which his defence has produced and to correct it, he meets with a complete lack of comprehension and an imperviousness to valid arguments. We see then that there really *is* a resistance to the discovery of resistances and that the defensive mechanisms do deserve the name which we originally gave them before they had been more closely examined: they are resistances not only to the bringing of id-contents into consciousness but also to the whole process of analysis and so to cure.

The effect which the defensive activities produce within the ego is rightly described as 'modification of the ego', if by that we understand the deviation of the ego from an imaginary normal ego which would guarantee unswerving loyalty to the analytic compact.

We can well believe what our daily experience suggests, that the outcome of an analysis depends principally upon the strength and depth of the roots of the resistances constituting the ego-modification. Once more we realize the importance of the quantitative factor and once more we are reminded that analysis has only certain limited quantities of energy which it can employ to match against the hostile forces. And it does seem as if victory were really for the most part with the big battalions.

VI

Our next question will be whether all modification of the ego (in the sense in which we are using the term) is acquired during the defensive conflicts of early childhood. There can be no doubt about the answer. We have no reason to dispute the existence and importance of primary congenital variations in the ego. A single fact is decisive, namely, that every individual selects only *certain* of the possible defensive mechanisms and invariably employs those which he has selected. This suggests that each individual ego is endowed from the beginning with its own peculiar dispositions and tendencies, though it is true that we cannot predicate their nature and conditioning factors. Moreover, we know that we must not exaggerate the difference between inherited and acquired characteristics into an antithesis; what was acquired by our ancestors is certainly an important part of what we inherit. When we speak of our 'archaic heritage' we are generally thinking only of the id and we apparently assume that no ego is yet in existence at the beginning of the individual's life. But we must not overlook the fact that id and ego are originally one, and it does not imply a mystical over-valuation of heredity if we think it credible that, even before the ego exists, its subsequent lines of development, tendencies and reactions are already determined. The psychological peculiarities of families, races and nations, even in their attitude towards analysis, admit of no other explanation. Indeed, analytic experience convinces us that particular psychical contents, such as symbolism, have no other source than hereditary transmission, and research in various fields of social psychology seems to justify the assumption that there are other, no less specialized, deposits from primitive human development present in our archaic heritage.

When we recognize that the peculiarities of the ego which we detect in the form of resistances may be not only acquired in defensive conflicts but determined by heredity, the topographical differentiation between ego and id loses much of its value for our investigations. When we advance a step further in analytic experience we come upon resistances of another type, which we can no longer localize and which seem to be conditioned by certain fundamental characteristics of the mental apparatus. I can give only a few examples of the type of resistance to which I refer: this whole field of inquiry is still bewilderingly strange and has not been sufficiently explored. We come across people, for instance, of whom we should say that they display a peculiar 'adhesiveness of libido'. The processes which their analysis sets in motion are so much slower than in other people because they apparently cannot make up their minds to detach libidinal cathexes from one object and displace them to another, although we can find no particular reasons for this cathectic fidelity. Then we meet the opposite type, in which libido seems specially mobile: it readily enters upon the new cathexes suggested by the analysis, abandoning its former ones for these. The difference between the two types is comparable to that experienced by a sculptor according as he works in hard stone or soft clay. Unfortunately in the latter type the results of analysis often prove very evanescent; the new cathexes are soon abandoned and one feels not as if one had been working in clay but as if one had been writing on water. *'Wie gewonnen, so zerronnen,'* [1] as the proverb says.

In another group of patients we are surprised by an attitude which we can only put down to a loss of the plasticity we should expect, an exhaustion of the capacity for change and development. We are indeed prepared for a certain degree of psychical inertia in analysis; when new paths are pointed out for the instinctual impulses, we almost invariably see an obvious hesitation in entering upon them. We have described this attitude, though perhaps not quite rightly, as 'resistance from the id'. But in the cases which I have in mind all the mental processes, relations and distributions of energy are immutable, fixed and rigid. One finds the same state of affairs in very old people, when it is explained by what is described as force of habit, the exhaustion of receptivity through a kind of psychical entropy; but I am thinking of people who are still young. Our theoretical knowledge does not seem adequate to explain these types. Probably some element of a temporal nature is at work here, changes in some rhythm in the development of psychical life which we have not yet apprehended.

In yet another group of cases the patients' resistance to analysis and the obstacles in the way of therapeutic success are probably due to variations in the ego which spring from another and even deeper root. Here we come to the ultimate phenomena to which psychological research has penetrated—the behaviour of the two primal instincts, their distribution, fusion and defusion, things which we cannot imagine to be confined to a single province of the mental apparatus, whether it be id, ego or super-ego. Nothing impresses us more strongly in connection with the resistances encountered in analysis than the feeling that there is a force at work which is defending itself by all possible means against recovery and is clinging tenaciously to illness and suffering. We have recognized that part of this force is

[1] ['Light come, light go.']

the sense of guilt and the need for punishment, and that is undoubtedly correct; we have localized it in the ego's relation to the super-ego. But this is only one element in it, which may be described as psychically bound by the super-ego and which we thus perceive. We may suppose that other portions of the same force are at work, either bound or free, in some unspecified region of the mind. If we consider the whole picture made up of the phenomena of the masochism inherent in so many people, of the negative therapeutic reaction and of the neurotic's sense of guilt, we shall have to abandon the belief that mental processes are governed exclusively by a striving after pleasure. These phenomena are unmistakable indications of the existence of a power in mental life which, according to its aim, we call the aggressive or destructive instinct and which we derive from the primal death-instinct of animate matter. It is not a question of an optimistic as opposed to a pessimistic theory of life. Only by the concurrent or opposing action of the two primal instincts—Eros and the death-instinct—never by one or the other alone, can the motley variety of vital phenomena be explained.

How the elements of these two species of instinct combine to fulfil the various vital functions, under what conditions such combinations grow looser and break up, what disturbances correspond to these changes and what feelings they evoke in the perceptual scale of the pleasure principle—these are problems whose elucidation would be the most valuable achievement of psychological research. For the moment we must bow to those superior forces which foil our efforts. Even to exert a psychical influence upon a simple case of masochism is a severe tax on our powers.

In studying the phenomena which testify to the activity of the instinct of destruction we are not confined to the observation of pathological material. There are countless facts in normal mental life which require this explanation, and the keener the power of our discernment the greater the abundance in which they present themselves to our notice. The subject is too novel and too important to be treated as a side-issue in this discussion; I will content myself with selecting a few specimens of these phenomena.

Here is an example: It is well known that at all times there have been, as there still are, human beings who can take as their sexual objects persons of either sex without the one trend interfering with the other. We call these people bisexual and accept the fact of their existence without wondering much at it. But we have come to know that all human beings are bisexual in this sense and that their libido is distributed between objects of both sexes, either in a manifest or a latent form. But the following point strikes us. While in the individuals I first mentioned the libidinal impulses can take both directions without producing a clash, in the other and more frequent cases the result is an irreconcilable conflict. A man's heterosexuality will not tolerate homosexuality, and vice versa. If the former tendency is the stronger, it succeeds in keeping the latter in a state of latency and preventing its attaining satisfaction in actuality. On the other hand there is no greater danger for a man's heterosexual function than disturbance by latent homosexuality. We might explain these facts by saying that each individual has only a given quantity of libido at his disposal and that the two rival trends have to contend for it. But it is not clear why these rivals should not regularly divide between them the available quantity of libido, according to their relative strength, since that is what does in fact happen in some cases. We are forced to conclude that there is something peculiar in the tendency to conflict, something which introduces a new element into the situation, independently of the quantity of libido. It is difficult to account for this spontaneous tendency to conflict except as the intervention of an element of free aggressiveness.

If we recognize that the case which I have just described is a manifestation of the destructive or aggressive instinct we are at once confronted with the question whether this notion should not be extended to apply to other instances of conflict, or, indeed, whether we ought not to review all our knowledge of psychical conflict from this new angle. After all, we assume that, in the course of the development of human beings from their primitive state to civilization a considerable part of their aggressiveness is internalized or turned inwards; and, if this is so, internal conflicts would certainly be the correct equivalent of the external conflicts which have now ceased. I am well aware that the dualistic theory, according to which an instinct of death, destruction or aggression claims equal partnership with Eros as manifested in libido, has met with little general acceptance and has not really established itself even among psycho-analysts. My delight was proportionately great when I recently discovered that that theory was held by one of the great thinkers of ancient Greece. For the sake of this confirmation I am happy to sacrifice the prestige of originality, especially as I read so widely in earlier years that I can never be quite certain that what I thought was a creation of my own mind may not really have been an outcome of cryptomnesia.

Empedocles of Acragas (Girgenti),[1] born about 495 B.C., is one of the grandest and most remarkable figures in the history of Greek civilization. The interests of this many-sided personality took the most varied directions. He was a man of science and a thinker, a prophet and a magician, a politician, a philanthropist and a physician versed in natural science. He was said to have freed the town of Selinus from malaria, and his contemporaries worshipped him as a god. The sharpest contrasts seem to have co-existed in his mind; exact and sober in his researches in physics and physiology, he did not recoil from obscure mysticism and he indulged in cosmic speculations of astonishing imaginative boldness. Capelle compares him with Dr. Faust, to whom 'manch Geheimnis wurde kund'.[2] Born at a time when

[1] I have based what follows on a work by Wilhelm Capelle (1935).
[2] ['Many a secret was revealed.' Goethe, *Faust*, Part I.]

the realm of science was not yet divided into so many provinces, he held some theories which inevitably strike us as primitive. He explained the variety of things by the fusion of the four elements, earth, air, fire and water, and he held that all nature was animate and believed in the transmigration of souls. At the same time, however, he had such modern ideas as that of the gradual evolution of living beings, the survival of the fittest and the recognition of the part played by chance ($\tau\acute{\upsilon}\chi\eta$) in this development.

The theory of Empedocles which specially claims our attention is one which approximates so closely to the psycho-analytical theory of the instincts that we should be tempted to maintain that the two are identical, were it not for this difference: the Greek's theory is a cosmic phantasy, while our own confines its application to biology. At the same time, the fact that Empedocles ascribed to the whole universe the same animistic principle as is manifested in each individual organism makes this difference considerably less important.

The Greek philosopher taught that there were two principles governing events in the life of the universe as in that of the mind, and that these principles were eternally in conflict with each other. He called them $\phi\iota\lambda\acute{\iota}\alpha$ (love) and $\nu\epsilon\hat{\iota}\kappa\circ\varsigma$ (strife). Of these powers, which he really conceived of as 'natural forces working like instincts, and certainly not intelligences with a conscious purpose',[1] the one strives to unite the atoms of these four elements into a single unity, while the other seeks to dissolve these fusions and to separate the atoms of the elements. Empedocles conceives of the world-process as a continuous, never-ceasing alternation of periods in which the one or the other of the two fundamental forces triumphs, so that at one time love and, at another time, strife fulfils its purpose and governs the universe, after which the other, vanquished power asserts itself and in its turn prevails.

The two fundamental principles of Empedocles—

[1] Capelle (1935), 186.

φιλία and νεῖκος—are, both in name and in function, the same as our two primal instincts, *Eros* and *Destructiveness*, the former of which strives to combine existing phenomena into ever greater unities, while the latter seeks to dissolve these combinations and destroy the structures to which they have given rise. But we shall not be surprised to find that this theory has changed in certain respects on its re-emergence after two and a half millennia. Apart from our being necessarily restricted to the biopsychical field, we no longer take as our basic substance the four elements of Empedocles; animate matter is now sharply differentiated from inanimate and we no longer think of the mingling and separation of particles of matter but of the fusion and defusion of instinctual components. Moreover, we now have a certain biological basis for the principle of 'strife', since we have traced back the destructive instinct to the death instinct, the urge of animate matter to return to an inanimate state. We are not denying by this that an analogous instinct already existed earlier; nor are we asserting, of course, that such an instinct only came into existence with the emergence of life. Nor can anyone foresee in what guise the nucleus of truth contained in the theory of Empedocles will present itself to the vision of a later day.

VII

In 1927, Ferenczi read an instructive paper [published 1928] entitled 'Das Problem der Beendigung der Analysen'. He concluded it with the comforting assurance that 'analysis is by no means an interminable process. On the contrary, if the analyst has a thorough knowledge of his business and a sufficient fund of patience the treatment can be carried to a natural conclusion.' The paper as a whole, however, seems to me to convey a warning not to aim at the shortening but rather at the deepening of the analytic process. Ferenczi makes the further important point that success very largely depends upon the analyst's having profited by the lesson of his own 'errors and mistakes', and got the better of 'the weak points in his own personality'. This is an important contribution to our problem. Amongst the factors which influence the prospects of an analysis and add to its difficulties in the same manner as the resistances, we must reckon not only the structure of the *patient's* ego but the personal characteristics of the *analyst*.

It cannot be disputed that analysts do not in their own personalities wholly come up to the standard of psychical normality which they set for their patients. Opponents of analysis often point this out derisively and use it as an argument to prove the uselessness of the analytic method. We might seek to refute the criticism by asserting that it makes an unjustifiable demand upon analysts, who are individuals trained in the practice of a certain art and are presumably ordinary human beings. Nobody surely maintains that a physician is incapable of treating internal diseases because his own internal organs happen to be unsound. On the contrary, it may be argued that there is a certain advantage when a man who is himself threatened with tuberculosis specializes in the treatment of that disease. But the cases are not on all fours. So long as he is capable of practising at all, a physician suffering from lung or heart trouble is not handicapped in diagnosing or treating internal disease. The analyst, on the other hand, because of the peculiar conditions of his work, is really impeded by his own defects in his task of discerning his patient's situation correctly and reacting to it in a manner conducive to cure. So there is some reason in the demand for a comparatively high degree of psychical normality and correct adjustment in the analyst as one of his qualifications for his work. And there is another point: he must be in a superior position in some sense if he is to serve as a model for his patient in certain analytic situations and, in others, to act as his teacher. Finally, we must not forget that the relationship between analyst and patient is based on a love of truth, that is, on the acknowledgment of reality, and that it precludes any kind of sham or deception.

Here let us pause for a moment to assure the analyst that he has our sincere sympathy in the very exacting requirements he is expected to fulfil. It almost looks as if analysis were the third of those 'impossible' professions in which one can be quite sure of unsatisfying results. The other two, much older-established, are the bringing-up of children and the government of nations. Obviously we cannot demand that the prospective analyst should be a perfect human being before he takes up analysis, and that only persons of this rare and exalted perfection should enter the profession. But where and how is even the most inadequate of individuals to acquire the ideal qualifications for his work? The answer is: in his own analysis, with which he begins his preparation for his future activity. For practical reasons this analysis can be only short and incomplete: the main object of it is to enable the instructor to form an opinion whether the candidate should be accepted for further training. It has accomplished its purpose if it imparts to the learner a sincere conviction of the existence of the unconscious, enables him through the emergence of repressed material in his own mind to perceive in himself processes which otherwise he would have regarded as incredible and gives him a first sample of the technique which has proved to be the only correct method in conducting analyses. This in itself would not constitute adequate instruction, but we hope and believe that the stimuli received in the learner's own analysis will not cease to act upon him when that analysis ends, that the processes of ego-transformation will go on of their own accord and that he will bring his new insight to bear upon all his subsequent experience. This does indeed happen and, in so far as it happens, it qualifies the learner who has been analysed to become an analyst.

Unfortunately something else happens as well. One

can only give one's impressions in describing this second result. Hostility on the one hand and partisanship on the other create an atmosphere unfavourable to objective investigation. It looks as if a number of analysts learn to make use of defensive mechanisms which enable them to evade the conclusions and requirements of analysis themselves, probably by applying them to others. They themselves remain as they are and escape the critical and corrective influence of analysis. This seems to confirm the dictum of a writer who warns us that it is hard for a mortal who acquires power not to misuse it.[1] Sometimes when we try to understand this attitude in analysts, we are irresistibly and disagreeably reminded of the effect of X-rays on those who use them without due precaution. It would scarcely be surprising if constant pre-occupation with all the repressed impulses which struggle for freedom in the human mind should sometimes cause all the instinctual demands which have hitherto been restrained to be violently awakened in the analyst himself. These are 'dangers of analysis', threatening not the passive but the active partner in the analytic situation, and it is our duty to face them. There can be no doubt how they must be encountered. Every analyst ought periodically himself to enter analysis once more, at intervals of, say, five years, and without any feeling of shame in so doing. So not only the patient's analysis but that of the analyst himself has ceased to be a terminable and become an interminable task.

At this point we must guard against a misconception. It is not my intention to assert that analysis in general is an endless business. Whatever our theoretical view may be, I believe that in practice analyses do come to an end. Every analyst of experience will be able to think of a number of cases in which he has taken permanent leave of the patient *rebus bene gestis*. There is a far smaller discrepancy between theory and practice in cases of so-called character-analysis. Here it is

[1] Anatole France, *La révolte des anges*.

M

not easy to predict a natural end to the process, even if we do not look for impossibilities or ask too much of analysis. Our object will be not to rub off all the corners of the human character so as to produce 'normality' according to schedule, nor yet to demand that the person who has been 'thoroughly analysed' shall never again feel the stirrings of passions in himself or become involved in any internal conflict. The business of analysis is to secure the best possible psychological conditions for the functioning of the ego; when this has been done, analysis has accomplished its task.

VIII

Both in therapeutic and character-analyses we are struck by the prominence of two themes which give the analyst an extraordinary amount of trouble. It soon becomes clear that some general principle is at work here. These two themes are connected with the difference between the sexes: one is characteristic of men and the other equally characteristic of women. In spite of the difference in their content there is an obvious correspondence between the two. Some factor common to both sexes is forced, by the difference between them, to express itself differently in the one and in the other.

The two corresponding themes are, in women, envy for the penis—the striving after the possession of a male genital—and, in men, the struggle against their passive or feminine attitude towards other men. What is common to these two themes was singled out by early psycho-analytic nomenclature as an attitude to the castration complex. Subsequently Alfred Adler brought the term 'masculine protest' into current use. It fits the case of men perfectly; but I think that, from the first, 'repudiation of femininity' would have been the correct description of this remarkable feature in the psychical life of mankind.

Supposing that we now try to introduce this notion into the structure of psycho-analytical theory we shall find that, by its very nature, this factor cannot occupy the same place in the case of both sexes. In males the masculine striving is from the beginning and throughout entirely ego-syntonic; the passive attitude, since it implies an acceptance of castration, is energetically repressed, and often the only indications of its existence are exaggerated over-compensations. In females also the striving after masculinity is ego-syntonic at a certain period, namely, in the phallic phase, before development in the direction of femininity has set in. But later it succumbs to that momentous process of repression, the outcome of which (as has often been pointed out) determines the fortunes of the woman's femininity. A great deal depends upon whether a sufficient amount of her masculinity-complex escapes repression and exercises a lasting influence on her character. Normally, large portions of that complex undergo transformation and contribute to the development of femininity: the unsatisfied wish for a penis should be converted into a wish for a child and for a man, who possesses a penis. Very often indeed, however, we find that the wish for masculinity persists in the unconscious and, in its repressed state, exercises a disturbing influence.

As is plain from what has just been said, in both cases it is the attitude belonging to the sex opposite to the subject's own which succumbs to repression. I have stated elsewhere[1] that it was Wilhelm Fliess who called my attention to this point. Fliess was inclined to regard the difference between the sexes as the true cause and original motive of repression. I can only repeat that I do not accept this view: I do not think we are justified in sexualizing repression in this way—that is to say, in explaining it on a biological instead of a purely psychological basis.

The paramount importance of these two themes— the wish for a penis in women and, in men, the struggle against passivity—did not escape the notice of Ferenczi.

[1] ' "A Child is being Beaten" ' (1919), *Collected Papers*, **2,** 172.

In the paper that he read in 1927 he laid it down as a principle that in every successful analysis these two complexes must have been resolved.[1] From my own experience I would observe that in this I think Ferenczi was asking a very great deal. At no point in one's analytic work does one suffer more from the oppressive feeling that all one's efforts have been in vain and from the suspicion that one is 'talking to the winds' than when one is trying to persuade a female patient to abandon her wish for a penis on the ground of its being unrealizable, or to convince a male patient that a passive attitude towards another man does not always signify castration and that in many relations in life it is indispensable. The rebellious over-compensation of the male produces one of the strongest transference-resistances. A man will not be subject to a father-substitute or owe him anything and he therefore refuses to accept his cure from the physician. There is no analogous form of transference which can arise from the feminine wish for a penis, but it is the source of attacks of acute depression, because women patients feel an inner conviction that the analysis will avail them nothing and that they will be none the better for it. We can only agree with them when we discover that their strongest motive in coming for treatment was the hope that they might somehow still obtain a male organ, the lack of which is so painful to them.

All this shows that the form of the resistance is immaterial: it does not matter whether it appears as a transference or not. The vital point is that it prevents any change from taking place—everything remains as it was. We often feel that, when we have reached the wish for a penis and the masculine protest, we have penetrated all the psychological strata and reached

[1] '. . . in every male patient the sign that his castration-anxiety has been mastered must be forthcoming, and this sign is a sense of equality of rights with the analyst; and every female patient, if her cure is to rank as complete and permanent, must have finally conquered her masculinity-complex and become able to submit without bitterness to thinking in terms of her feminine role.' (Ferenczi, 1928,8.)

'bedrock' and that our task is accomplished. And this is probably correct, for in the psychical field the biological factor is really the rock-bottom. The repudiation of femininity must surely be a biological fact, part of the great riddle of sex.[1] Whether and when we have succeeded in mastering this factor in an analysis is hard to determine. We must console ourselves with the certainty that everything possible has been done to encourage the patient to examine and to change his attitude to the question.

[1] We must not be misled by the term 'masculine protest' into supposing that what the man repudiates is the *attitude* of passivity, or, as we may say, the social aspect of femininity. Such a notion is speedily contradicted by the observation that the attitude such men display towards women is often masochistic or actually slavish. What they reject is not passivity in general but passivity in relation to *men*. That is to say, the 'masculine protest' is in fact nothing other than fear of castration.

XXXI

CONSTRUCTIONS IN ANALYSIS[1]

(1937)

I

IT has always seemed to me to be greatly to the credit of a certain well-known man of science that he treated psycho-analysis fairly at a time when most other people felt themselves under no such obligation. On one occasion, nevertheless, he gave expression to an opinion upon analytic technique which was at once derogatory and unjust. He said that in giving interpretations to a patient we treat him upon the famous principle of 'Heads I win, tails you lose'. That is to say, if the patient agrees with us, then the interpretation is right; but if he contradicts us, that is only a sign of his resistance, which again shows that we are right. In this way we are always in the right against the poor helpless wretch whom we are analysing, no matter how he may respond to what we put forward. Now, since it is in fact true that a 'No' from one of our patients is not as a rule enough to make us abandon an interpretation as incorrect, a revelation such as this of the nature of our technique has been most welcome to the opponents of analysis. It is therefore worth while to give a detailed account of how we are accustomed to arrive at an assessment of the 'Yes' or 'No' of our patients during analytic treatment—of their expression of agreement or of denial. The practising analyst will naturally learn nothing in the course of this apologia that he does not already know.

It is familiar ground that the work of analysis aims at inducing the patient to give up the repressions (using the word in the widest sense) belonging to his early life and to replace them by reactions of a sort that would

[1] ['Konstruktionen in der Analyse.' First published *Int. Z. Psychoanal.*, **23** (1937), 459; reprinted *Ges. W.*, **16**. Translation, reprinted from *Int. J. Psycho-Anal.*, **19** (1938), 377, by James Strachey.]

correspond better to a psychically mature condition. It is with this purpose in view that he must be got to recollect certain experiences and the emotions called up by them which he has at the moment forgotten. We know that his present symptoms and inhibitions are the consequences of repressions of this kind: that is, that they are a substitute for these things that he has forgotten. What sort of material does he put at our disposal which we can make use of to put him on the way to recovering the lost memories? All kinds of things. He gives us fragments of these memories in his dreams, invaluable in themselves but seriously distorted as a rule by all the factors concerned in the formation of dreams. Again, he produces ideas, if he gives himself up to 'free association', in which we can discover allusions to the repressed experiences and derivatives of the suppressed emotions as well as of the reactions against them. And, finally, there are hints of repetitions of the affects belonging to the repressed material to be found in actions performed by the patient, some important, some trivial, both inside and outside the analytic situation. Our experience has shown that the relation of transference, which becomes established towards the analyst, is particularly calculated to favour the reproduction of these emotional connections. It is out of such raw material—if we may so describe it—that we have to put together what we are in search of.

What we are in search of is a picture of the patient's forgotten years that shall be alike trustworthy and in all essential respects complete. But at this point we are reminded that the work of analysis consists of two quite different portions, that it is carried on in two separate localities, that it involves two people, to each of whom a distinct task is assigned. It may for a moment seem strange that such a fundamental fact should not have been pointed out long ago; but it will immediately be perceived that there was nothing being kept back in this, that it is a fact which is universally known and even self-evident and is merely being brought into relief here and separately examined for a particular purpose. We all know that the person who is being analysed has to be induced to remember something that has been experienced by him and repressed; and the dynamic determinants of this process are so interesting that the other portion of the work, the task performed by the analyst, has been pushed into the background. The analyst has neither experienced nor repressed any of the material under consideration; his task cannot be to remember anything. What then *is* his task? His task is to make out what has been forgotten from the traces which it has left behind or, more correctly, to *construct* it. The time and manner in which he conveys his constructions to the person who is being analysed, as well as the explanations with which he accompanies them, constitute the link between the two portions of the work of analysis, between his own part and that of the patient.

His work of construction, or, if it is preferred, of reconstruction, resembles to a great extent an archaeologist's excavation of some dwelling-place that has been destroyed and buried or of some ancient edifice. The two processes are in fact identical, except that the analyst works under better conditions and has more material at his command to assist him, since what he is dealing with is not something destroyed but something that is still alive—and perhaps for another reason as well. But just as the archaeologist builds up the walls of the building from the foundations that have remained standing, determines the number and position of the columns from depressions in the floor and reconstructs the mural decorations and paintings from the remains found in the débris, so does the analyst proceed when he draws his inferences from the fragments of memories, from the associations and from the behaviour of the subject of the analysis. Both of them have an undisputed right to reconstruct by means of supplementing and combining the surviving remains. Both of them, moreover, are subject to many of the same difficulties and sources of error. One of the most ticklish problems that confronts the archaeologist is notoriously the determination of the relative age of his finds; and if an object makes its appearance in some particular level, it often remains to be decided whether it belongs to that level or whether it was carried down to that level owing to some subsequent disturbance. It is easy to imagine the corresponding doubts that arise in the case of analytic constructions.

The analyst, as we have said, works under more favourable conditions than the archaeologist since he has at his disposal material which can have no counterpart in excavations, such as the repetitions of reactions dating from infancy and all that emerges in connection with these repetitions through the transference. But in addition to this it must be borne in mind that the excavator is dealing with destroyed objects of which large and important portions have quite certainly been lost, by mechanical violence, by fire and by plundering. No amount of effort can result in their discovery and lead to their being united with the surviving fragments. The one and only course left open is that of reconstruction, which for this very reason can often reach only a certain degree of probability. But it is different with the psychical object whose early history the analyst is seeking to recover. Here we are regularly met by a situation which in archaeology occurs only in such rare circumstances as those of Pompeii or of the tomb of Tutankhamen. All of the essentials are preserved, even things that seem completely forgotten are present somehow and somewhere, and have merely been buried and made inaccessible to the subject. Indeed, it may, as we know, be doubted whether any psychical structure can really be the victim of total destruction. It depends only upon analytic technique whether we shall succeed in bringing what is concealed completely to light. There are only two other facts that weigh against the extraordinary advantage which is thus enjoyed by the work of analysis: namely, that psychical objects are incomparably more complicated than the excavator's material ones and that

M 2

we have insufficient knowledge of what we may expect to find, since their finer structure contains so much that is still mysterious. But our comparison between the two forms of work can go no further than this; for the main difference between them lies in the fact that for the archaeologist the reconstruction is the aim and end of his endeavours while for analysis the construction is only a preliminary labour.

II

It is not, however, a preliminary labour in the sense that the whole of it must be completed before the next piece of work can be begun, as, for instance, is the case with house-building, where all the walls must be erected and all the windows inserted before the internal decoration of the rooms can be taken in hand. Every analyst knows that things happen differently in an analytic treatment and that there both kinds of work are carried on side by side, the one kind being always a little ahead and the other following upon it. The analyst finishes a piece of construction and communicates it to the subject of the analysis so that it may work upon him; he then constructs a further piece out of the fresh material pouring in upon him, deals with it in the same way and proceeds in this alternating fashion until the end. If, in accounts of analytic technique, so little is said about 'constructions', that is because 'interpretations' and their effects are spoken of instead. But I think that 'construction' is by far the more appropriate description. 'Interpretation' applies to something that one does to some single element of the material, such as an association or a parapraxis. But it is a 'construction' when one lays before the subject of the analysis a piece of his early history that he has forgotten, in some such way as this: 'Up to your nth year you regarded yourself as the sole and unlimited possessor of your mother; then came another baby and brought you grave disillusionment. Your mother left you for some time, and even after her reappearance she was never again devoted to you exclusively. Your feelings towards your mother became ambivalent, your father gained a new importance for you,'. . . and so on.

In the present paper our attention will be turned exclusively to this preliminary labour performed by constructions. And here, at the very start, the question arises of what guarantee we have while we are working on these constructions that we are not making mistakes and risking the success of the treatment by putting forward some construction that is incorrect. It may seem that no general reply can in any event be given to this question; but even before discussing it we may lend our ear to some comforting information that is afforded by analytic experience. For we learn from it that no damage is done if, for once in a way, we make a mistake and offer the patient a wrong construction as the probable historic truth. A waste of time is, of course, involved, and anyone who does nothing but present the patient with false combinations will neither create a very good impression on him nor carry the treatment very far; but a single mistake of the sort can do no harm. What in fact occurs in such an event is rather that the patient remains as though he were untouched by what has been said and reacts to it with neither a 'Yes' nor a 'No'. This may possibly mean no more than that his reaction is postponed; but if nothing further develops we may conclude that we have made a mistake and we shall admit as much to the patient at some suitable opportunity without sacrificing any of our authority. Such an opportunity will arise when some new material has come to light which allows us to make a better construction and at the same time to correct our error. In this way the false construction drops out, as if it had never been made; and, indeed, we often get an impression as though, to borrow the words of Polonius, our bait of falsehood had taken a carp of truth. The danger of our leading a patient astray by suggestion, by persuading him to accept things which we ourselves believe but which he ought not to, has certainly been enormously exaggerated. An analyst would have had to behave very incorrectly before such a misfortune could overtake him; above all, he would have to blame himself with not allowing his patients to have their say. I can assert without boasting that such an abuse of 'suggestion' has never occurred in my practice.

It already follows from what has been said that we are not at all inclined to neglect the indications that can be inferred from the patient's reaction when we have offered him one of our constructions. The point must be gone into in detail. It is true that we do not accept the 'No' of a person under analysis at its face value; but neither do we allow his 'Yes' to pass. There is no justification for accusing us of invariably twisting his remarks into an assent. In reality things are not so simple and we do not make it so easy for ourselves to come to a conclusion.

A plain 'Yes' from a patient is by no means unambiguous. It can indeed signify that he recognizes the correctness of the construction that has been presented to him; but it can also be meaningless, or can even deserve to be described as 'hypocritical', since it may be convenient for his resistance to make use of an assent in such circumstances in order to prolong the concealment of a truth that has not been discovered. The 'Yes' has no value unless it is followed by indirect confirmations, unless the patient, immediately after his 'Yes', produces new memories which complete and extend the construction. Only in such an event do we consider that the 'Yes' has dealt completely with the subject under discussion.

A 'No' from a person in analysis is no more unambiguous than a 'Yes', and is indeed of even less value. In some rare cases it turns out to be the expression of a legitimate dissent. Far more frequently it expresses a resistance which may have been evoked by the subject-matter of the construction that has been put forward but which may just as easily have arisen from some other factor in the complex analytic situation. Thus, a patient's 'No' is no evidence of the correctness of a construction, though it is perfectly compatible with it. Since every such construction is an incomplete one, since it covers only a small fragment of the forgotten events, we are free to suppose that the patient is not in fact disputing what has been said to him but is basing his contradiction upon the part that has not yet been discovered. As a rule he will not give his assent until he has learnt the whole truth—which often covers a very great deal of ground. So that the only safe interpretation of his 'No' is that it points to incompleteness; there can be no doubt that the construction has not told him everything.

It appears, therefore, that the direct utterances of the patient after he has been offered a construction afford very little evidence upon the question whether we have been right or wrong. It is of all the greater interest that there are indirect forms of confirmation which are in every respect trustworthy. One of these is a form of words that is used (almost as though there were a conspiracy) with very little variation by the most different people: 'I've never thought (or, I should never have thought) that (or, of that).' This can be translated without any hesitation into: 'Yes, you're right this time —about my *unconscious*.' Unfortunately this formula which is so welcome to the analyst, reaches his ears more often after single interpretations than after he has produced an extensive construction. An equally valuable confirmation is implied (expressed this time positively) when the patient answers with an association which contains something similar or analogous to the subject-matter of the construction. Instead of taking an example of this from an analysis (which would be easy to find but lengthy to describe) I prefer to give an account of a small extra-analytical experience which presents a similar situation so strikingly that it produces an almost comic effect. It concerned one of my colleagues who—it was long ago—had chosen me as a consultant in his medical practice. One day, however, he brought his young wife to see me, as she was causing him trouble. She refused on all sorts of pretexts to have sexual relations with him, and what he expected of me was evidently that I should lay before her the consequences of her ill-advised behaviour. I went into the matter and explained to her that her refusal would probably have unfortunate results for her husband's health or would lay him open to temptations that might lead to a break-up of their marriage. At this point he suddenly interrupted me with the remark: 'The Englishman you diagnosed as suffering from a cerebral tumour has died too.' At first the remark seemed incomprehensible; the 'too' in his sentence was a mystery, for we had not been speaking of anyone else who had died. But a short time afterwards I understood. The man was evidently intending to confirm what I had been saying; he was meaning to say: 'Yes, you're certainly quite right. Your diagnosis was confirmed in the case of the other patient too.' It was an exact parallel to the indirect confirmations that we obtain in analysis from associations. I will not attempt to deny that there were other thoughts as well, put on one side by my colleague, which had a share in determining his remark.

Indirect confirmation from associations that fit in with the content of a construction—that give us a 'too' like the one in my story—provide a valuable basis for judging whether the construction is likely to be confirmed in the course of the analysis. It is particularly striking when a confirmation of this kind slips into a direct denial by means of a parapraxis. I once published elsewhere a nice example of this.[1] The name 'Jauner' (a familiar one in Vienna) came up repeatedly in one of my patient's dreams without a sufficient explanation appearing in his associations. I finally put forward the interpretation that when he said 'Jauner' he probably meant 'Gauner' [swindler], whereupon he

---

[1] [In Chapter V of *Zur Psychopathologie des Alltagslebens* (1904) (not included in the English translation of 1914).]

promptly replied: 'That seems to me too "jewagt" [instead of "gewagt" (far-fetched)].' Or there was the other instance, in which, when I suggested to a patient that he considered a particular fee too high, he meant to deny the suggestion with the words 'Ten dollars mean nothing to me' but instead of dollars put in a coin of lower denomination and said 'ten shillings'.

If an analysis is dominated by powerful factors that impose a negative therapeutic reaction, such as a sense of guilt, a masochistic need for suffering or a striving against receiving help from the analyst, the patient's behaviour after he has been offered a construction often makes it very easy for us to arrive at the decision that we are in search of. If the construction is wrong, there is no change in the patient; but if it is right or gives an approximation to the truth, he reacts to it with an unmistakable aggravation of his symptoms and of his general condition.

We may sum the matter up by asserting that there is no justification for the reproach that we neglect or underestimate the importance of the attitude taken up by those under analysis towards our constructions. We pay attention to them and often derive valuable information from them. But these reactions on the part of the patient are rarely unambiguous and give no opportunity for a final judgement. Only the further course of the analysis enables us to decide upon the correctness of uselessness of our constructions. We do not pretend that an individual construction is anything more than a conjecture which awaits examination, confirmation or rejection. We claim no authority for it, we require no direct agreement from the patient, nor do we argue with him if at first he denies it. In short, we conduct ourselves upon the model of a familiar figure in one of Nestroy's farces—the man-servant who has a single answer on his lips to every question or objection: 'All will become clear in the course of future developments.

III

It is hardly worth while describing how this occurs in the process of the analysis—the way in which our conjecture is transformed into the patient's conviction. All of this is familiar to every analyst from his daily experience and is intelligible without difficulty. Only one point requires investigation and explanation. The path that starts from the analyst's construction ought to end in the patient's recollection; but it does not always lead so far. Quite often we do not succeed in bringing the patient to recollect what has been repressed. Instead of that, if the analysis is carried out correctly, we produce in him an assured conviction of the truth of the construction which achieves the same therapeutic result as a recaptured memory. The problem of what the circumstances are in which this occurs and of how it is possible that what appears to be an incomplete substitute should nevertheless produce a complete result—all of this is material for a later enquiry.

I shall conclude this brief paper with a few remarks which open up a wider perspective. I have been struck by the manner in which, in certain analyses, the communication of an obviously apt construction has evoked in the patients a surprising and at first incomprehensible phenomenon. They have had lively recollections called up in them—which they themselves have described as 'unnaturally distinct'—but what they have recollected has not been the event that was the subject of the construction but details relating to that subject. For instance, they have recollected with abnormal sharpness the faces of the people involved in the construction or the rooms in which something of the sort might have happened, or, a step further away, the furniture in such rooms—on the subject of which the construction had naturally no possibility of any knowledge. This has occurred both in dreams immediately after the construction had been put forward and in waking states in the nature of a day-dream. These recollections have themselves led to nothing further and it has seemed plausible to regard them as the product of a compromise. The 'upward drive' of the repressed, stirred into activity by the putting forward of the construction, has striven to carry the important memory-traces into consciousness; but a resistance has succeeded—not, it is true, in *stopping* that movement—but in *displacing* it on to adjacent objects of minor significance.

These recollections might have been described as hallucinations if a belief in their actual presence had been added to their clearness. The importance of this analogy seemed greater when I noticed that true hallucinations occasionally occurred in the case of other patients who were certainly not psychotic. My line of thought proceeded as follows. Perhaps it may be a general characteristic of hallucinations to which sufficient attention has not hitherto been paid that in them something that has been experienced in infancy and then forgotten re-emerges—something that the child has seen or heard at a time when he could still hardly speak and that now forces its way into consciousness, probably distorted and displaced owing to the operation of forces that are opposed to this re-emergence. And, in view of the close relation between hallucinations and particular forms of psychosis, our line of thought may be carried still further. It may be that the delusions into which these hallucinations are so constantly incorporated may themselves be less independent of the upward drive of the unconscious and the return of the repressed than we usually assume. In the mechanism of a delusion we stress as a rule only two factors: the turning away from the real world and its forces on the one hand and the influence exercised by wish-fulfilment upon the subject-matter of the delusion on the other. But may it not be that the dynamic process is rather that the turning away from reality is exploited by the upward drive of the repressed in order to force its subject-matter into consciousness, while the resistances stirred up by this process and the impulse to wish-fulfilment share the responsibility for the distortion and displacement of what is recollected? This is after all the familiar mechanism of dreams, which intuition has equated with madness from time immemorial.

This view of delusions is not, I think, entirely new, but it nevertheless emphasizes a point of view which is not usually brought into the foreground. The essence of it is that there is not only *method* in madness, as the poet has already perceived, but also a fragment of historic truth; and it is plausible to suppose that the compulsive belief attaching to delusions derives its strength precisely from infantile sources of this kind. All that I can produce to-day in support of this theory are reminiscences, not fresh impressions. It would probably be worth while to make an attempt to study cases of the disorder in question on the basis of the hypotheses that have been here put forward and also to carry out their treatment upon the same lines. The vain effort would be abandoned of convincing the patient of the error of his delusion and of its contradiction of reality; and, on the contrary, the recognition of its kernel of truth would afford common ground upon which the therapeutic process could develop. That process would consist in liberating the fragment of historic truth from its distortions and its attachments to the actual present day and in leading it back to the point in the past to which it belongs. The transposing of material from a forgotten past on to the present or on to an expectation of the future is indeed a habitual occurrence in neurotics no less than in psychotics. Often enough, when a neurotic is led by an anxiety-state to expect the occurrence of some terrible event, he is in fact merely under the influence of a repressed memory (which is seeking to enter consciousness but cannot become conscious) that something which was at that time terrifying did really happen. I believe that we should gain a great deal of valuable knowledge from work of this kind upon psychotics even if it led to no therapeutic success.

I am aware that it is of small service to handle so

important a subject in the cursory fashion that I have here employed. But none the less I have not been able to resist the seduction of an analogy. The delusions of patients appear to me to be the equivalents of the constructions which we build up in the course of an analytic treatment—attempts at explanation and cure, though it is true that these, under the conditions of a psychosis, can do no more than replace the fragment of reality that is being repudiated in the present by another fragment that had already been repudiated in the remote past. It will be the task of each individual investigation to reveal the intimate connections between the material of the present repudiation and that of the original repression. Just as our construction is only effective because it recovers a fragment of lost experience, so the delusion owes its convincing power to the element of historic truth which it inserts in the place of the rejected reality. In this way a proposition which I originally asserted only of hysteria would apply also to delusions—namely, that those who are subject to them are suffering from their own recollections. I never intended by this short formula to dispute the complexity of the causation of the illness or to exclude the operation of many other factors.

If we consider mankind as a whole and substitute it for the single human individual, we discover that it too has developed delusions which are inaccessible to logical criticism and which contradict reality. If, in spite of this, they are able to exert an extraordinary power over men, investigation leads us to the same explanation as in the case of the single individual. They owe their power to the element of historic truth which they have brought up from the repression of the forgotten and primaeval past.

XXXII
SPLITTING OF THE EGO IN THE DEFENSIVE PROCESS[1]

(1938)

I FIND myself for a moment in the interesting position of not knowing whether what I have to say should be regarded as something long familiar and obvious or as something entirely new and puzzling. But I am inclined to think the latter.

I have at last been struck by the fact that the ego of a person whom we know as a patient in analysis must, dozens of years earlier, when it was young, have behaved in a remarkable manner in certain particular situations of pressure. We can assign in general and somewhat vague terms the conditions under which this comes about by saying that it occurs under the influence of a psychical trauma. I prefer to select a single sharply defined special case, though it certainly does not cover all the possible modes of causation.

Let us suppose, then, that a child's ego is under the sway of a powerful instinctual demand which it is accustomed to satisfy and that it is suddenly frightened by an experience which teaches it that the continuance of this satisfaction will result in an almost intolerable danger. It must now decide either to recognize the real danger, give way to it and do without the instinctual satisfaction, or to repudiate reality and persuade itself that there is no reason for fear, so that it may be able to retain the satisfaction. Thus there is a conflict between the demand of the instinct and the command of reality. But in fact the child takes neither course, or rather he

---

[1] [Unfinished fragment, 'Die Ichspaltung im Abwehrvorgang'. First published posthumously *Int. Z. Psychoanal. Imago*, **25** (1940), 241; reprinted *Ges. W.*, **17**, 59. It takes up a subject already touched upon in Freud, 1927, page 198 above, and further dealt with in Freud, 1938b, 73 ff. The manuscript is dated January 2, 1938. Translation, reprinted from *Int. J. Psycho-Anal.*, **22** (1941), 65, by James Strachey.]

takes both simultaneously, which comes to the same
thing. He replies to the conflict with two contrary reactions, both of which are valid and effective. On the one
hand, with the help of certain mechanisms he rejects
reality and refuses to accept any prohibition; on the
other hand, in the same breath he recognizes the danger
of reality, takes over the fear of that danger as a symptom and tries subsequently to divest himself of the fear.
It must be confessed that this is a very ingenious solution of the difficulty. Both of the parties to the dispute
obtain their share: the instinct is allowed to retain its
satisfaction and proper respect is shown to reality. But
everything has to be paid for in one way or another, and
this success is achieved at the price of a rift in the ego
which never heals but which increases as time goes on.
The two contrary reactions to the conflict persist as the
centre-point of a split in the ego. The whole process
seems so strange to us because we take for granted the
synthetic nature of the workings of the ego. But we are
clearly at fault in this. The synthetic function of the
ego, though it is of such extraordinary importance, is
subject to particular conditions and is liable to a whole
series of disturbances.

It will assist if I interpolate an individual case
history into this schematic disquisition. A little boy,
while he was between three and four years of age, had
become acquainted with the female genitals through
being seduced by an older girl. After these relations
had been broken off, he carried on the sexual stimulation
which had been set going in this way by zealously practising manual masturbation; but he was soon caught at it
by his energetic nurse and was threatened with castration, the carrying out of which was, as usual, ascribed to
his father. There were thus present in this case conditions calculated to produce a tremendous effect of
fright. A threat of castration by itself need not produce
a great impression. The child will refuse to believe in it,
for he cannot easily imagine the possibility of losing
such a highly prized part of his body. A sight of the

female genitals, on the other hand, might convince him of that possibility. But he would draw no conclusion from this alone, since his disinclination to doing so would be too great and there would be no motive present which could compel him to. On the contrary, whatever uneasiness he might feel would be calmed by the reflection that what was missing would yet make its appearance: she would grow one (a penis) later. Anyone who has observed enough small boys will be able to recollect having come across some such remark at the sight of a baby sister's genitals. But it is different if both factors are present together. In that case the threat revives the memory of the perception which had hitherto been regarded as harmless and finds in that memory a dreaded confirmation. The little boy now thinks he understands why the girl's genitals showed no sign of a penis and no longer ventures to doubt that his own genitals may meet with the same fate. Thenceforward he cannot help believing in the reality of the danger of castration.

The usual result of the fright of castration, the result that passes as the normal one, is that, either immediately or after some considerable struggle, the boy gives way to the threat and obeys the prohibition either wholly or at least in part (that is, by no longer touching his genitals with his hand). In other words, he gives up, in whole or in part, the satisfaction of the instinct. We are prepared to hear, however, that our present patient found another way out. He created a substitute for the penis which he missed in women, that is to say, a fetish. In so doing, it is true that he had given the lie to reality, but he had saved his own penis. So long as he was not obliged to acknowledge that women have lost their penis, there was no need for him to believe the threat that had been made against him: he need have no fears for his own penis, so he could proceed with his masturbation undisturbed. This behaviour on the part of our patient strikes us forcibly as being a turning away from reality—a procedure which we should prefer to reserve for psychotics. And it is in fact not very different. Yet we must suspend our judgement, for upon closer inspection we shall discover a not unimportant distinction. The boy did not simply contradict his perceptions and hallucinate a penis where there is none to be seen; he effected no more than a displacement of value—he transferred the importance of the penis to another part of the body, a procedure in which he was assisted by the mechanism of regression (in a manner which need not here be explained). This displacement, it is true, related only to the female body; as regards his own penis nothing was changed.

This way of dealing with reality, which almost deserves to be described as artful, was decisive as regards the boy's practical behaviour. He continued with his masturbation as though it implied no danger to his penis; but at the same time, in complete contradiction to his apparent boldness or indifference, he developed a symptom which showed that he nevertheless did recognize the danger. He had been threatened with being castrated by his father, and immediately afterwards, simultaneously with the creation of his fetish, he developed an intense fear of his father punishing him, which it required the whole force of his masculinity to master and overcompensate. This fear of his father, too, was silent on the subject of castration: by the help of regression to an oral phase, it assumed the form of a fear of being eaten by his father. At this point it is impossible to forget a primitive fragment of Greek mythology which tells how Kronos, the old Father God, swallowed his children and sought to swallow his youngest son Zeus like the rest, and how Zeus was saved by the craft of his mother and later on castrated his father. But we must return to our case history and add that the boy produced yet another symptom, though it was a slight one, which he has retained to this day. This was an anxious susceptibility against either of his little toes being touched, as though, in all the to and fro between denial and acknowledgement, it was nevertheless castration that was finding the clearer expression. . . .

XXXIII
SOME ELEMENTARY LESSONS IN PSYCHO-ANALYSIS[1]
(1938)

AN author who sets out to introduce some branch of knowledge—or, to put it more modestly, some branch of research—to the lay public must clearly make his choice between two methods or techniques.

It is possible to start off from what everyone knows (or thinks he knows) and regards as self-evident, without in the first instance contradicting the learner. An opportunity will soon occur for drawing his attention to facts in the same field, which, though they are known to him, he has so far neglected or insufficiently appreciated. Beginning from these, one can introduce further facts to him of which he has *no* knowledge and so prepare him for the necessity of going beyond his earlier judgements, of seeking new points of view and of taking new hypotheses into consideration. In this way one can get him to take a part in building up a new theory about the subject and one can deal with his objections to it during the actual course of the work. A method of this kind might well be called *genetic*. It follows the path along which the investigator himself has already travelled. In spite of all its advantages, it has the defect of not making a sufficiently striking effect upon the learner. He will not be nearly so much impressed by something which he has watched coming into existence and passing through a slow and difficult period of growth as he

[1] ['Some Elementary Lessons in Psycho-Analysis'—the original title is in English—was written in London during the second half of 1938 and left unfinished. It appears to be the beginning of a fresh version of the *Outline of Psycho-Analysis* (1938*b*). It was first published in *Schriften aus dem Nachlass* (London, 1941), p. 141; identical with *Ges. W.*, **17**, 141. Some portions of it had previously been printed *Int. Z. Psychoanal.*, *Imago*, **25** (1940), 21; translated *Int. J. Psycho-Anal.*, **21** (1940), 83. Translation by James Strachey.]

would be by something that is presented to him ready-made as an apparently self-consistent whole.

It is precisely this last effect which is produced by the alternative method of presentation. This other method, the *dogmatic* one, begins straight away by stating its conclusions. Its premises make demands upon the audience's attention and faith and very little is adduced in support of them. And there is then a danger that a critical hearer may shake his head and say: 'All this sounds most peculiar: where does the fellow get it from?'

In what follows I shall not rely exclusively upon either of the two methods of presentation: I shall make use now of one and now of the other. I am under no delusion about the difficulty of my task. Psycho-analysis has little prospect of becoming popular. It is not merely that much of what it has to say offends people's feelings. Almost as much difficulty is created by the fact that our science involves a number of hypo-theses—it is hard to say whether they should be regarded as postulates or as products of our researches—which are bound to seem very strange to ordinary modes of thought and which fundamentally contradict current views. But there is no help for it. We must begin our brief study with two of these hazardous hypotheses.

THE NATURE OF THE MENTAL

Psycho-analysis is a part of the mental science of psychology. It is also described as 'depth psychology'—we shall later discover why. If someone asks what 'the mental' really means, it is easy to reply by enumerating its constituents: our perceptions, ideas, memories, feelings and acts of volition—all these form part of what is mental. But if the questioner goes further and asks whether there is not some common quality possessed by all these processes which makes it possible to get nearer to the *nature*, or, as people sometimes say, the *essence* of the mental, then it is harder to give an answer.

If an analogous question had been put to a physicist (as to the nature of electricity, for instance), his reply, until quite recently, would have been: 'For the purpose of explaining certain phenomena, we assume the existence of electrical forces which are present in things and which emanate from them. We study these phenomena, discover the laws that govern them and even put them to practical use. This satisfies us provisionally. We do not know the *nature* of electricity. Perhaps we may discover it later, as our work goes on. It must be admitted that what we are ignorant of is precisely the most important and interesting part of the whole business, but for the moment that does not worry us. It is simply how things happen in the natural sciences.'

Psychology, too, is a natural science. What else can it be? But its case is different. Not everyone is bold enough to make judgements about physical matters; but everyone—the philosopher and the man in the street alike—has his opinion on psychological questions and behaves as if he were at least an *amateur* psychologist. And now comes the remarkable thing. Everyone—or almost everyone—was agreed that what is mental really *has* a common quality in which its essence is expressed: namely the quality of *being conscious*—unique, indescribable, but needing no description. All that is conscious, they said, is mental, and conversely all that is mental is conscious: that is self-evident and to contradict it is nonsense. It cannot be said that this decision threw much light upon the nature of the mental; for consciousness is one of the fundamental facts of our life and our researches come up against it like a blank wall and can find no path beyond it. Moreover the equation of what is mental with what is conscious had the unwelcome result of divorcing mental processes from the general context of events in the universe and of setting them in complete contrast to all others. But this would not do, since the fact could not long be overlooked that mental phenomena are to a large extent dependent upon somatic influences and on their side have the most powerful effects upon somatic processes. If ever human thought found itself in an *impasse* it was here. To find a way out, the philosophers at least were obliged to assume that there were organic processes parallel to the conscious mental ones, related to them in a manner that was hard to explain, which acted as intermediaries in the reciprocal relations between 'body and mind', and which served to re-insert the mental into the texture of life. But this solution remained unsatisfactory.

Psycho-analysis escaped such difficulties as these by energetically denying the equation between what is mental and what is conscious. No; being conscious cannot be the essence of what is mental. It is only a *quality* of what is mental, and an unstable quality at that—one that is far oftener absent than present. The mental, whatever its nature may be, is in itself unconscious and probably similar in kind to all the other natural processes of which we have obtained knowledge.

Psycho-analysis bases this assertion on a number of facts, of which I shall now proceed to give a selection.

We know what is meant by ideas 'occurring' to one —thoughts that suddenly come into consciousness without one's being aware of the steps that led up to them, though they, too, must have been mental acts. It can even happen that one arrives in this way at the solution of some difficult intellectual problem which has previously baffled one's efforts. All the complicated processes of selection, rejection and decision which occupied the interval were withdrawn from consciousness. We shall not be putting forward any new theory in saying that they were unconscious and perhaps remained so.

In the second place, I shall pick a single instance to represent an immensely large class of phenomena.[1] The President of a public body (the Lower House of the Austrian Parliament) on one occasion opened a sitting with the following words: 'I take notice that a full quorum of members is present and herewith declare the sitting closed.' It was a slip of the tongue—for there can

[1] Cf. *The Psychopathology of Everyday Life* (1904), Chap. V.

be no doubt that what the President intended to say was 'opened'. Why, then, did he say the opposite? We shall expect to be told it was an accidental mistake, a failure in carrying out an intention such as may easily happen for various reasons: it had no meaning—and in any case contraries are particularly easily substituted for each other. If, however, we bear in mind the situation in which the slip of the tongue occurred, we shall be inclined to prefer another explanation. Many of the previous sittings of the House had been disagreeably stormy and had accomplished nothing, so that it would be only too natural for the President to think at the moment of making his opening statement: 'If only the sitting that's just beginning were finished! I would much rather be closing than opening it!' When he began to speak he was probably not aware of this wish—not conscious of it—but it was certainly present and it succeeded in making itself effective, against the speaker's will, in his apparent mistake. A single instance can scarcely enable us to decide between two such different explanations. But what if every other instance of a slip of the tongue could be explained in the same way, and similarly every slip of the pen, every case of mis-reading or mis-hearing, and every faulty action? What if in all those instances (one might actually say, without a single exception) it was possible to demonstrate the presence of a mental act—a thought, a wish or an intention—which would account for the apparent mistake and which was unconscious at the moment at which it became effective, even though it may have been conscious previously? If that were so, it would really no longer be possible to dispute the fact that mental acts which are unconscious do exist and that they are even sometimes active while they are unconscious and that they can even sometimes get the better of conscious intentions. The person concerned in a mistake of this kind can react to it in various ways. He may overlook it completely or he may notice it himself and become embarrassed and ashamed. He cannot as a rule find the explanation of it himself without outside help; and he often refuses to accept the solution when it is put before him—for a time, at all events.

In the third place, finally, it is possible in the case of persons in a state of hypnosis to prove experimentally that there are such things as unconscious mental acts and that consciousness is not an indispensable condition of [mental] activity. Anyone who has witnessed such an experiment will receive an unforgettable impression and a conviction that can never be shaken. Here is more or less what happens. The doctor enters the hospital ward, puts his umbrella in the corner, hypnotizes one of the patients and says to him: 'I'm going out now. When I come in again, you will come to meet me with my umbrella open and hold it over my head.' The doctor and his assistants then leave the ward. As soon as they come back, the patient, who is no longer under hypnosis, carries out exactly the instructions that were given him while he was hypnotized. The doctor questions him: 'What's this you're doing? What's the meaning of all this?' The patient is clearly embarrassed. He makes some lame remark such as: 'I only thought, doctor, as it's raining outside you'd open your umbrella in the room before you went out.' The explanation is obviously quite inadequate and made up on the spur of the moment to offer some sort of motive for his senseless behaviour. It is clear to the spectators that he is in ignorance of his real motive. We, however, know what it is, for we were present when the suggestion was made to him which he is now carrying out, while he himself knows nothing of the fact that it is at work in him.[1]

The question of the relation of the conscious to the mental may now be regarded as settled: consciousness is only a *quality* or attribute of what is mental and moreover an unstable one. But there is one further objection

[1] I am describing experiments made by Bernheim at Nancy in 1889 at which I myself assisted. In these days there is no need for me to discuss any doubts as to the genuineness of hypnotic phenomena of this kind.

with which we have to deal. We are told that, in spite of the facts that have been mentioned, there is no necessity to abandon the identity between what is conscious and what is mental: the so-called unconscious mental processes are the organic processes which have long been recognized as running parallel to the mental ones. This, of course, would reduce our problem to an apparently indifferent matter of definition. Our reply is that it would be unjustifiable and inexpedient to make a breach in the unity of mental life for the sake of propping up a definition, since it is clear in any case that consciousness can only offer us an incomplete and broken chain of phenomena. And it can scarcely be a matter of chance that it was not until the change had been made in the definition of the mental that it became possible to construct a comprehensive and coherent theory of mental life. . . .

Nor need it be supposed that this alternative view of the mental is an innovation due to psycho-analysis. A German philosopher, Theodor Lipps, asserted with the greatest explicitness that the mental is in itself unconscious and that the unconscious is the truly mental. The concept of the unconscious has long been knocking at the gates of psychology and asking to be let in. Philosophy and literature have often toyed with it, but science could find no use for it. Psycho-analysis has seized upon the concept, has taken it seriously and has given it a fresh content. By its researches it has led to a knowledge of characteristics of the unconscious mental which have hitherto been unsuspected, and it has discovered some of the laws which govern it. But none of this implies that the quality of being conscious has lost its importance for us. It remains the one light which illuminates our path and leads us through the darkness of mental life. In consequence of the special character of our discoveries, our scientific work in psychology will consist in translating unconscious processes into conscious ones, and thus filling in the gaps in conscious perception. . . .

LIST OF WORKS REFERRED TO
IN THE TEXT

₊ Titles of books and periodicals are in italics; titles of papers are in inverted commas. Abbreviations are in accordance with the *World List of Scientific Periodicals*, Oxford, 1934. Numerals in thick type refer to volumes; ordinary numerals refer to pages. The word '*Trans.*' before an entry indicates that the reference is not to the original but to an English translation.

ABRAHAM, K. (1921). (*Trans.*) 'Manifestations of the Female Castration Complex', *Selected Papers*, London, 1927, Chap. XXII.
   (1924). (*Trans.*) 'A Short Study of the Development of the Libido', *Selected Papers*, London, 1927, Chap. XXVI.
AICHHORN, A. (1925). (*Trans.*) *Wayward Youth*, New York, 1935, and London, 1936.
BERNFELD, S. (1944). 'Freud's Earliest Theories and the School of Helmholtz', *Psychoanal. Quart.*, **13**, 341.
BERNHEIM, H. (1886). *De la suggestion et de ses applications à la thérapeutique*, Paris.
BOURKE, J. G. (1891). *Scatalogic Rites of all Nations*, Washington.
BREUER, J. and FREUD, S. (1893). (*Trans.*) 'On the Psychical Mechanism of Hysterical Phenomena', in FREUD, S., *Coll. Papers*, **1**, 24.
   (1895). (*Trans.*) *Studies in Hysteria*, New York, 1936.
BRUNSWICK, R. MACK (1928a). 'The Analysis of a Case of Paranoia', *J. Nerv. Ment. Dis.*, **70** (1929), 177.
   (1928b). 'A Supplement to Freud's "History of an Infantile Neurosis" ', *Int. J. Psycho-Anal.*, **9**, 439.
CAPELLE, W. (1935). *Die Vorsokratiker*, Leipzig.
DEUTSCH, H. (1925). *Psychoanalyse der weiblichen Sexualfunktionen*, Vienna.
   (1930). (*Trans.*) 'The Significance of Masochism in the Mental Life of Women', *Int. J. Psycho-Anal.*, **11** (1930), 48.
DOSTOYEVSKY, A. (1921). *Fyodor Dostoyevsky*, London.
EISLER, R. (1929). *Jesus Basileus*, Heidelberg.
ELLIS, HAVELOCK (1919). *The Philosophy of Conflict and other Essays in Wartime*, London.
ERLENMEYER, E. H. (1932). (*Trans.*) 'Note on Freud's Hypothesis Regarding the Taming of Fire', *Int. J. Psycho-Anal.*, **13** (1932), 411.
FENICHEL, O. (1930). (*Trans.*) 'The Pregenital Antecedents of the Oedipus Complex', *Int. J. Psycho-Anal.*, **12** (1931), 141.

FERENCZI, S. (1923). (*Trans.*) 'On the Symbolism of the Head of Medusa', *Further Contributions*, London, 1926, 360.

—— (1928). 'Das Problem der Beendigung der Analysen', *Int. Z. Psychoanal.*, **14**, 1.

FLUGEL, J. C. (1924). 'Polyphallic Symbolism and the Castration Complex', *Int. J. Psycho-Anal.*, **5**, 155.

FRAZER, J. G. (1911). *The Magic Art* (*The Golden Bough*, 3rd. ed., Part I), 2 vols., London.

FREUD, A. (1936). (*Trans.*) *The Ego and the Mechanisms of Defence*, London, 1937.

FREUD, S. (1893). (*Trans.*) 'Some Points in a Comparative Study of Organic and Hysterical Paralyses', *Coll. Papers*, **1**, 42.

—— (1896a). (*Trans.*) 'Further Remarks on the Defence Neuro-Psychoses', *Coll. Papers*, **1**, 155.

—— (1896b). (*Trans.*) 'The Aetiology of Hysteria', *Coll. Papers*, **1**, 183.

—— (1900). (*Trans.*) *The Interpretation of Dreams*, London, Revised Ed., 1932.

—— (1904). (*Trans.*) *The Psychopathology of Everyday Life*, New York, 1914.

—— (1905a). (*Trans.*) *Wit and its Relation to the Unconscious*, New York, 1917.

—— (1905b). (*Trans.*) *Three Essays on the Theory of Sexuality*, London, 1949.

—— (1905c). (*Trans.*) 'Fragment of an Analysis of a Case of Hysteria', *Coll. Papers*, **3**, 13.

—— (1908). (*Trans.*) 'Hysterical Phantasies and their Relation to Bisexuality', *Coll. Papers*, **2**, 51.

—— (1910). (*Trans.*) *Leonardo da Vinci*, London, 1922.

—— (1911a). (*Trans.*) 'Formulations Regarding the Two Principles in Mental Functioning', *Coll. Papers*, **4**, 13.

—— (1911b). (*Trans.*) 'Psycho-Analytic Notes upon an Auto-biographical Account of a Case of Paranoia (Dementia Para-noides)', *Coll. Papers*, **3**, 387.

—— (1912–13). (*Trans.*) *Totem and Taboo*, London, 1919.

—— (1914). (*Trans.*) 'On the History of the Psycho-Analytic Movement', *Coll. Papers*, **1**, 287.

—— (1915a). (*Trans.*) 'Instincts and their Vicissitudes', *Coll. Papers*, **4**, 60.

—— (1915b). (*Trans.*) 'Repression', *Coll. Papers*, **4**, 84.

—— (1915c). (*Trans.*) 'Some Character-Types Met with in Psycho-Analytic Work', *Coll. Papers*, **4**, 318.

—— (1916–17). (*Trans.*) *Introductory Lectures on Psycho-Analysis*, London, Revised Ed., 1929.

—— (1917) (*Trans.*) 'One of the Difficulties of Psycho-Analysis', *Coll. Papers*, **4**, 347.

(1918). (*Trans.*) 'From the History of an Infantile Neurosis', *Coll. Papers*, **3,** 473.

(1919). (*Trans.*) ' "A Child is Being Beaten" ', *Coll. Papers*, **2,** 172.

(1920). (*Trans.*) *Beyond the Pleasure Principle*, 1922 and 1950.

(1921). 'Psychoanalyse und Telepathie', *Ges. Werke*, **17,** 27.

(1922). (*Trans.*) 'Dreams and Telepathy', *Coll. Papers*, **4,** 408.

(1923*a*). (*Trans.*) 'The Infantile Genital Organization of the Libido', *Coll. Papers*, **2,** 244.

(1923*b*). (*Trans.*) *The Ego and the Id*, London, 1927.

(1923*c*). 'Josef Popper-Lynkeus und die Theorie des Traumes', *Ges. Schriften*, **11,** 295, and *Ges. Werke*, **13,** 357.

(1923*d*). (*Trans.*) Postscript to 'From the History of an Infantile Neurosis', *Coll. Papers*, **3,** 605.

(1924*a*). (*Trans.*) 'Neurosis and Psychosis', *Coll. Papers*, **2,** 250.

(1924*b*). (*Trans.*) 'The Passing of the Oedipus Complex', *Coll. Papers*, **2,** 269.

(1924*c*). (*Trans.*) 'The Loss of Reality in Neurosis and Psychosis', *Coll. Papers*, **2,** 277.

(1925*a*). (*Trans.*) *An Autobiographical Study*, London, Revised Ed., 1935.

(1925*b*). (*Trans.*) 'Some Psychological Consequences of the Anatomical Distinction between the Sexes', *Coll. Papers*, **5,** 186.

(1926). (*Trans.*) *The Question of Lay Analysis*, London, 1948.

(1927). (*Trans.*) 'Fetishism', *Coll. Papers*, 5, 198.

(1930). (*Trans.*) *Civilization and its Discontents*, London, 1930.

(1931). (*Trans.*) 'Female Sexuality', *Coll. Papers*, **5,** 252.

(1932). (*Trans.*) *New Introductory Lectures on Psycho-Analysis*, London, 1933.

(1938*a*) (*Trans*) 'Splitting of the Ego in the Defensive Process', *Coll. Papers*, 5, 372.

(1938*b*). (*Trans.*) *An Outline of Psycho-Analysis*, London, 1949.

FÜLÖP-MILLER, R. (1924). 'Dostojewskis Heilige Krankheit', *Wissen und Leben*, Zurich, Heft 19–20.

FÜLÖP-MILLER, R. and ECKSTEIN, F. (Ed.) (1925). *Dostojewski am Roulette*, Munich.

(Ed.) (1926). *Der unbekannte Dostojewski*, Munich.

(Ed.) (1928). *Die Urgestalt der Brüder Karamasoff*, Munich.

HENRI, V. and C. (1897). 'Enquête sur les premiers souvenirs de l'enfance', *L'année psychologique*, **3,** 184.

HORNEY, K. (1923). (*Trans.*) 'On the Genesis of the Castration Complex in Women', *Int. J. Psycho-Anal.*, **5** (1924), 50.

(1926). (*Trans.*) 'The Flight from Womanhood', *Int. J. Psycho-Anal.*, **7** (1926), 324.

HÜCKEL, A. (1888). *Die Rolle der Suggestion bei gewissen Erscheinungen der Hysterie und des Hypnotismus*, Jena.

386 COLLECTED PAPERS

JONES, E. (1927). 'The Early Development of Female Sexuality', *Int. J. Psycho-Anal.*, **8,** 459.

KAAN, H. (1893). *Der neurasthenische Angstaffect bei Zwangsvorstellungen*, etc., Vienna.

KLEIN, M. (1928). (*Trans.*) 'Early Stages of the Oedipus Conflict', *Int. J. Psycho-Anal.*, **9** (1928), 167.

LAFORGUE, R. (1926). 'Verdrängung und Skotomisation', *Int. Z. Psychoanal.*, **12,** 54.

LAMPL - DE GROOT, J. (1927). (*Trans.*) 'The Evolution of the Oedipus Complex in Women', *Int. J. Psycho-Anal.*, **9** (1928), 332.

LINDNER, S. (1879). 'Das Saugen an den Fingern, Lippen, etc., bei den Kindern (Ludeln)', *Jb. Kinderheilk.*, N.F., **14,** 68.

LORENZ, E. (1931). 'Chaos und Ritus', *Imago*, **17,** 433.

MILLER, O. (1882). 'Zur Lebensgeschichte Dostojewskis', in DOSTOJEWSKI, F. M., *Autobiographische Schriften*, Munich, 1921.

MOLL, A. (1898). *Untersuchungen über die Libido sexualis*, Berlin.

NEUFELD, J. (1923). *Dostojewski: Skizze zu seiner Psychoanalyse*, Vienna.

RANK, O. (1909). (*Trans.*) *The Myth of the Birth of the Hero*, New York, 1914.

(1912). *Das Inzestmotiv in Dichtung und Sage*, Vienna.

(1924). (*Trans.*) *The Trauma of Birth*, London, 1929.

RANK, O. and SACHS, H. (1913). (*Trans.*) *The Significance of Psycho-Analysis for the Mental Sciences*, New York, 1915.

REIK, T. (1919). (*Trans.*) *Ritual*, London, 1931.

SANCTIS, S. DE (1924). *La conversione religiosa*, Bologna.

SCHAEFFER, A. (1930). 'Der Mensch und das Feuer', *Psychoanal. Bewegung*, **2,** 201.

VARIOUS (1919). (*Trans.*) *Psycho-Analysis and the War Neuroses*, London, 1921.

ZWEIG, S. (1920). (*Trans.*) *Three Masters*, New York and London, 1938.

(1927). (*Trans.*) *Conflicts*, New York and London, 1939.

INDEX

Displacement, 52–3, 90, 114, 121, 375
  of cathexes, 26, 195–6, 219, 343–5
  on to triviality, 52, 314, 369
  See Distortion

Dissociation, 25–32, 39–46, 109, 202
  See Amnesia *and* Repression

Distortion, 72, 114–16, 139, 144–6, 151–4, 168, 288, 296–301, 306
  See Displacement

Dostoevsky, F. M., 222–42, 258 *n*

Dostoyevsky, A., 227 *n*

Dreams, 70–3, 136–62, 296–301
  ambivalence in, 140
  and compulsion to repeat, 144–6
  and hysteria, 26, 31
  and myths, 288, 291–3
  and sexuality, 127–8
  anxiety in, 155, 157
  censorship in, 72, 115, 139, 147, 154–6
  confirmatory and compliant, 141–4
  displacement and distortion in, 72, 114–15, 121, 139, 144–8, 151
  effects of resistance on, 137, 151, 154–7, 288, 296–301, 358–370
  ego in, 148–9, 155–7
  experimental, 141
  general theory of, 114–15, 296–8
  in psycho-analytic treatment, 136–153
  interpretation of, 93, 114, 136–7, 146, 150–4, 296, 300
  moral responsibility for, 154–7
  occult significance of, 158–62
  of recovery, 138–40
  premonitory, 70–3, 159
  punishment, 147, 156
  suggestion and, 140–5
  super-ego in, 149
  symbolism in, 78, 116, 137, 288–90
  telepathic, 158–62
  wish-fulfilment and, 114–15, 137, 147, 156, 296–300, 369

Dubowitz, H., 103

Eaten, fear of being, 254, 266

Eckstein, F., 222 *n*, 224 *n*, 227 *n*, 228, 237, 238 *n*

Ecstasy, 217

Education, psycho-analysis and, 98–100

Ego—
  and derealization, 309
  and id, 337–8, 340, 344–5
  and narcissism, 82, 86, 123–5, 133, 216–17, 248–9
  and psycho-analytic treatment, *see* Psycho-analytic treatment, ego in
  and sexual impulses, conflict between, 93, 121, 131–3
  and super-ego, 196, 218–21, 231–2, 248–9, 345–6
  conflict in, in war neuroses, 84–7
  defence, *see* Defence *and* Defensive mechanisms
  immature, 321, 329, 340
  in dreams, 148–9, 155–7
  in humour, 215–21
  in neurosis and psychosis, 202, 224–5
  in traumatic neuroses, 87, 321
  instincts, 131
  modification, 321, 325–7, 336–43, 352
  pleasure- and reality-, 183
  splitting of, in defensive process, 201, 225, 372–5
  strengthening of, in psycho-analysis, 126, 325–7
  synthetic function of, 225, 373

Einstein, A., 273

Eisler, R., 338

Eitingon, M., 123

Ellis, Havelock, 101–2

' Electra complex ', 256

Empedocles, 347–51

Enuresis and masturbation, 189

Epilepsy, 224–38

Epileptiform attacks, 27, 225–8

Erection as reassurance, 105–6

Erlenmeyer, E. H., 288

Eros—
  and death instinct, 135, 169, 251, 280–1, 283–4, 346–50
  and war, 284

Erotic libidinal type, 248–5

392   INDEX

Libido (*contd.*)—
  fixation of, 119, 121
  narcissistic, 81, 86, 124, 133–4
  object, 82, 119, 120, 124, 132, 134
  theory, 86, 131–5, 247–51
  See Sexuality
Lichtenberg, G. C., 281
Lindner, S., 190
Lipps, T., 382
Livy, 139
Lorenz, E., 288
Lott, 35
Ludwig, O., 53

Mach, Ernst, 301
Mania, 219
Marcuse, M., 107 *n*
Marriage, 134, 258, 263
Masculine protest, 123, 192 *n*, 354,
  357 *n*
Masculinity, 191–7, 230, 255–7,
  259, 267, 271, 355–7, 375
Masochism, 224, 232, 346, 357 *n*,
  367
Masturbation, 66
  and bed-wetting, 189
  and castration threat, 188–9,
    241, 260–1, 270, 373–5
  and Oedipus complex, 189, 190,
    242
  clitoridal, 193–4, 255, 257, 260–
    1, 267
  gambling and, 237–42
Medicine and psycho-analysis, 92,
  166–8, 207–14
Medusa's head, 105–6
Melancholia and depression, 39,
  79–82, 124, 219, 305
Memories, screen, 47–69
Memory—
  a disturbance of, 302–12
  and consciousness, 176
  apparatus of, 175–80
  childhood, 47–69, 92, 103–4, 308
  recovery of, in psycho-analysis,
    51, 111, 320, 359, 369
  under hypnosis, 110
  See Amnesia *and* Dissociation
Menopause, 328
Mental—
  essential nature of, the, 167, 297,
    376–82

Mental (*contd.*)—
  events, determination of, 111
  functioning in infancy, 47
  See Unconscious mind
Metapsychology, 156, 325–7, 337
Miller, Orest, 227
Moll, A., 131
Mother—
  as prostitute, 241
  genitals of, dreaded, 105
  See Oedipus complex
Mourning, 79–81, 233
Myths, 54, 75, 95, 105–6, 116, 129,
  235, 288–94

Nancy school of hypnotism, 11–23
Nansen, Fridtjof, 273
Napoleon, 311
Narcissism, 81, 86, 124, 133–4
  and coprophilia, 90
  and crime, 250
  and cure, 144
  and ego, 82, 86, 123–5, 133,
    216–17, 248–9
  and feminine sexuality, 192–4
  and humour, 217
  and penis, 196
  and psycho-analysis, 173
  and sympathy, 237
Narcissistic libidinal type, 247–51
Negation, 181–5
  in psycho-analytic treatment,
    181, 185, 358–9, 363–5
  See Denial
Negativism, 185
Nervousness, common, 39, 117
Nestroy, J., 330, 367
Neufeld, J., 242 *n*
Neurasthenia, 34, 39
Neuroses—
  antithetic ideas in, 38–46
  narcissistic, 86, 124
  transference, 86–7, 124, 131,
    133
  See Traumatic neuroses *and* War
    neuroses
Neurosis—
  aetiological factors, 86, 120–2,
    196, 250, 253, 316, 321, 327
  and libidinal types, 250
  and psychosis, 202
  ego in, 202, 224–5